# THE GREAT UFO HOAX

# THE GREAT UFO HOAX

*The Final Solution to the UFO Mystery*

Gregory M. Kanon

1997
Galde Press, Inc.
Lakeville, Minnesota

FIRST EDITION
First Printing, 1997


Cover by Christopher Wells



Library of Congress Cataloging-in-Publication Data

Kanon, Gregory M., 1949–
    The great UFO hoax : the final solution to the UFO mystery /
Gregory M. Kanon. — 1st ed.
        p.    cm.
    Includes index.
    ISBN 1–880090–41–4 (pbk.)
    1. Unidentified flying objects.    2. Imposters and imposture.
I. Title.
TL789.K355    1996
001.942 — dc21                                                    96–44407
                                                                              CIP




Galde Press, Inc.
PO Box 460
Lakeville, Minnesota 55044

To Truth-Seekers everywhere.
*You know who you are.*

# Contents

# Acknowledgments

Writing is not fun. It is hard work. It is, as someone, referring to the rigors of the creative process, put it: "one-tenth inspiration, nine-tenths perspiration."

*Amen.*

The burden of birthing this particular opus was eased considerably by the loving support and deft editorial suggestions of my wife, Elizabeth, or "Eli," as she prefers to be called these days. Special thanks, too, to my parents, John and Terry, for not making truth and empiricism dirty words when I was growing up.

I am also indebted to Lisa Jenio, David Kadosh, Debbie Kalvee, Joan Grandy, and Margaret Rice.

And, of course, much love and thanks to Cody—our always lovable, rarely obedient yellow lab—for keeping my feet warm during the long nights of writing.

# Foreword

There have been some great hoaxes in history.

Clifford Irving. Anastasia. *The Hitler Diaries.* And, I suppose, you could include those writers who tried to convince us that Elvis is still alive.

But the greatest hoax of all is taking place now. It is real. It is devious. It is *scary.*

To illustrate what I mean, I want you to conduct an experiment. I want you to try it on the very next person you're with. It can be anybody — a friend, a stranger, the Avon Lady; it doesn't matter.

What you do is this: bring up the subject of UFOs — I know it sounds strange, but just do it — and then say something to the effect that you believe that the whole UFO thing is a joke, and next — this is the fun part — firmly state that you believe UFOs are actually secret U.S. military aircraft. What do you think will happen? Will your remark be met with (A) curiosity, (B) rational acceptance, or (C) something else?

The answer is C. Nine times out of ten, you'll receive an odd, even suspicious glance. Then — again, nine times out of ten — you'll be hit with some real razorback resistance. Even hostility.

To the point, most everyone believes that UFOs are from outer space and *they're not afraid to tell you so,* particularly when confronted with "heresy." UFOs are real, they'll assert. Real — and piloted by small aliens with big eyes. You know, like the one on the covers of those Whitley Strieber books — *ugly bug-eyed monsters from outer space who do nasty things to motorists on darkened roads.*

Why are such notions so thoroughly entrenched in the American psyche? Why do most Americans prefer an extraterrestrial explanation of UFOs? Why do they, by and large, reject more prosaic and rational solutions to the mystery? It's not as if a UFO has landed on the White House lawn, after all.

Since the close of World War II, the American public has been led — brainwashed, some might say — to believe that UFOs are craft from another world. The ruse began in early July 1947 when something reportedly crashed in the New Mexico desert, near Roswell Army Air Field, the home of the 509th, America's legendary atomic bomb group. Shortly thereafter, a public affairs officer assigned to the base issued a press release stating that a "flying saucer" had been retrieved at the crash site.[1]

The officer was *ordered* to announce to the world that the United States Air Force had captured a craft from another world. He was ordered to do so by the base's commanding officer. And the commander, it was later revealed, had received *his* orders from the Pentagon.[2]

The Air Force subsequently retracted the Roswell statement, claiming that the nearly mile-long stretch of debris was attributable to a downed weather balloon.[3] In years to come, the "true believers" would point to this back-pedaling as proof of a government cover-up.

A seed was planted in the American psyche in those early years of the Cold War. This seed took root like kudzu in Tennessee soil. A new belief sprouted in the minds of Americans. *UFOs are real and the government knows what they are.*

Since then, military intelligence and counterintelligence officers have come forth claiming to have seen official documents providing proof of alien visitation; some say they've actually seen crashed UFOs and dead—even *live*—aliens. Take Robert O. Dean, for example.

Dean, a retired U.S. Army command sergeant major, was formerly assigned to the war room of NATO's Supreme Headquarters Operations Center (SHOC) in Europe. According to Dean, he saw something there that forever changed his life. He claims he was "shown" a top-secret report asserting that Earth is being visited by *several* advanced extraterrestrial civilizations. The report, Dean claims, provided details of UFO crashes and the retrieval of aliens. In 1961 one such alien craft purportedly fell from the sky onto a tiny village near the German-Russian border. Troops later discovered twelve small alien bodies.[4] Whitley Strieber's *little grays.*

Then there's the case of film producers Robert Emenegger and Allan Sandler. In 1973, Emenegger and Sandler were offered a deal they couldn't refuse. They were invited to Norton Air Force Base, San Bernardino, California, where they met with the head of the Air Force's Office of Special Investigations (OSI) and Paul Shartle, requirements chief of Norton's audiovisual program, who offered to provide them with photographs and film footage of a "UFO landing" at Holloman Air Force Base in Alamogordo, New Mexico.

But the filmmakers were stiffed. Without explanation, they were later denied the promised materials, further feeding the notion that *UFOs are real and the government knows what they are.*[5]

Filmmaker Linda Moulton Howe also fell victim to the military's dangling-carrot ploy. She, too, was offered film and photographs of the Holloman landing. Again, the offer never materialized.[6]

So, you might ask, do these military officers really possess proof of alien craft visiting Earth? Have these highly trained officers risked everything to tell their fellow Americans the truth? Are they the ultimate whistle-blowers?

Let's recall some recent history. Remember the Rosenbergs? They were wrenched away from their children and cruelly put to death for passing A-bomb secrets to the Soviets. And then there's Aldrich Ames. Remember him? The FBI pounced on him like leopards on an antelope carcass.

So why have the individuals who've divulged "the secret of the ages" not been similarly treated?

Curiously, none of the military personnel—there have been many—who have revealed this state secret have received so much as a slap on the wrist. Those still on active duty have suffered no repercussions. Those who are retired continue to receive fat military pensions.

In the United States, it is against the law for government agencies to spread disinformation. In other words, they're not supposed to lie. They can only tell the truth.

At least that's the way it's supposed to work. But we all know better. The assassination of John F. Kennedy—and later, Vietnam and Watergate—destroyed within us any idealistic notions of a government that exists only to serve the people.

This cynicism has proven invaluable to the perpetrators of the greatest hoax in history: the public distrusts government, and they believe the government knows more than it is telling. Ergo: the government is lying about UFOs; it knows UFOs are real and from *out there.*

In the chapters that follow, you will learn the truth about *The Great UFO Hoax.* You will learn how the government has purposefully guided

American public opinion regarding UFOs through the years. You will also discover *why* the government has been so anxious to have you believe in alien visitations.

The real truth about UFOs is far more bizarre — and disturbing — than any invasion from outer space. *The Great UFO Hoax* is a story of deception, intrigue, and danger. It is the story of *Oz* and the people who fail to see the "man behind the curtain." It is a story you cannot afford to ignore....

# 1

# Where Are They?

*Man can will nothing unless he has first understood that he must count on no one but himself; that he is alone, abandoned on earth in the midst of his infinite responsibilities, without help, with no other aim than the one he sets himself, with no other destiny than the one he forges for himself on this earth.* —Jean Paul Sartre

Carl Sagan was a real sourpuss.

Just ask *Beavis and Butt-Head*. Or, specifically, Apple Computer.

You may recall that the cosmology guru brought legal action against the computer manufacturer for code-naming one of its prototype computer systems "Carl Sagan" — or BHA, as some employees preferred to call it. BHA, it turned out, stood for "Butt-Head Astronomer," a moniker derived from MTV's megahit animated series *Beavis and Butt-Head*. The irreverent cartoon has lampooned just about everybody on the face of the planet, from Alice Cooper to Bill Clinton, and Apple seems to have been spreading a little in-house good cheer. Apparently Sagan didn't get the joke.[1]

The nineties were not kind to Sagan. During the 1970s and '80s, he authored numerous books promoting the idea that the universe is teeming with intelligent life. He became a celebrity, a frequent guest on talk shows, and a highflying jet-setter. His theories, however, have fallen on hard times lately.

To the point: if there are other intelligent life forms in the universe, *where are they?* This question was posed back in 1943 by Enrico Fermi, the Nobel prize-winning physicist who helped develop the atomic bomb.[2] It is a question, fifty years later, that Sagan and his cohorts have been unable to answer, despite extensive research efforts that have proved costly to the American taxpayer.

In October 1993, Congress pulled the plug on the Search for Extraterrestrial Intelligence (SETI), a massive program that for decades scoured the heavens with a vast array of radio telescopes in search of talkative aliens. Specifically, these giant electronic ears sought to detect evidence of microwave signals beamed at us from the cosmos. Hundreds of star systems, presumed to be the most likely to harbor life, were targeted for study during the life of the project.

SETI was a colossal bust. No squawks, bleeps, or intergalactic mathematical theorems were ever received. *Nothing.**

Sagan, a radio astronomy pioneer, was a boisterous SETI supporter, despite the program's no-show results. Not surprising. Radio astronomers — whose funding has depended upon the supposition that extraterrestrial life exists — have always been far more favorable in their assessments of the likelihood of galactic neighbors than mainstream astronomers and other scientists, who have taken a decidedly pessimistic view of the whole affair.

Michael H. Hart, of the National Center for Atmospheric Research in Colorado, is convinced we are alone in the universe. He believes that if civilizations capable of interstellar flight exist, they would have visited us by now.[3]

Tulane University physicist Frank J. Tipler agrees. Says Tipler: "I based my claim that we are alone in our galaxy on the idea that interstellar travel would be simple and cheap for a civilization only slightly in advance of our own. Thus if a civilization approximately at our level has ever existed in the galaxy, their spaceships would already be here. Since they are not, they do not exist."[4]

---

*Radio astronomers heading Operation Phoenix, a privately funded research effort carried out in the wake of federal SETI funding cuts, claimed they detected radio signals from space "several times" during the group's five-month search of 209 designated stars, chosen for their similarity to our own sun. The announcement was made the day before Operation Phoenix, conducted at New South Wales' radio telescope facility at Parkes, was shut down, according to the *Melbourne Herald Sun* (June 26, 1995). Dr. Bobbie Vaile conceded, however, that when the signals were rechecked "they weren't there," adding that the group had been unable to prove the existence of alien radio emanations. In the end, Phoenix researchers were left with meaningless data — signals that could have just as likely come from satellites or terrestrial radio sources, as so often occurred with earlier SETI efforts.

Equally skeptical is University of Virginia physics professor James S. Trefil. Trefil states that the impossibility of extraterrestrial life can best be understood in terms of the "galactic year." In this scheme, the lifetime of the universe is compressed into a single year, a billion years roughly equal to one month. The tortuously slow evolution of the cosmos now passes in the blink of an eye.

In the "galactic year," the Big Bang occurs at midnight on January 1, and the galaxies form before the end of the day. Stars are born, burn up, and explode, creating new stars through much of the winter, spring, and summer. In September, within a half-hour, our sun and planets are formed. By October, primitive algae appears on earth and, on Christmas Eve, the first living creatures scurry from the sea onto land. Around noon on December 29, dinosaurs emerge; they last but twenty-four hours, becoming extinct by noon the following day. Warm-blooded mammals now appear and, just before midnight on New Year's Eve, Neanderthal man arrives on the scene. The entire history of Man, up to the present, lasts all of three minutes.[5]

"The principal argument for a large number of advanced civilizations," says Trefil, "is that all through this great expanse of time, civilizations have been coming into existence and that a large number of them last for a billion years.... If any civilization had reached our present level at any time prior to New Year's Eve, they would have spread throughout the galaxy before *Homo sapiens* ever appeared on the scene."[6]

Trefil calculates that, assuming an intelligent civilization in the galaxy would appear, expand, and disappear in approximately sixty million years, there has been ample opportunity, during the past ten billion years, for about 150 different races to have completely explored our relatively tiny portion of the universe.[7] *So where are they?*

Much of the optimistic views of extraterrestrial life have stemmed from the so-called Green Bank Equation, formulated by radio astronomer Frank Drake in 1961. More a subjective statement than a true scientific equality, the Green Bank Equation attempts to express the number of advanced intelligent civilizations possessing the technology to communicate with us across the vast distances of space. Variables considered in the equation include estimates of the number of stars in the galaxy, the number of stars that have planets, the number of stars capable of supporting life on a nearby planet, and the number of planets that could stave off self-destruction long enough to communicate with us.[8]

Using his equation, Drake concluded that our own galaxy has many advanced civilizations. But other scientists, not so married to the SETI concept, have concluded otherwise.

The Green Bank Equation is weighted heavily in favor of the ET hypothesis. Even using conservative estimates for the equation's variables, Trefil arrived at the conclusion that there should now be no fewer than eighteen colonizing civilizations in the galaxy.[9] He doubts this is so and, furthermore, states that the odds are 100,000 to 1 against the emergence of any future civilizations capable of galactic exploration.[10]

Then there is the matter of planets. Or the apparent lack of them beyond our own solar system.

UCLA scientist Andrea Ghez has conducted research indicating that three-quarters of young stars are born with one or more companion stars. If so, the chances of planets forming elsewhere is bleak indeed. These companion stars, Ghez explains, would sweep through and deplete orbiting material that might otherwise form a planet. Says Ghez: "Solar systems may be the exception, not the rule, in our galaxy."[11]

Even if there are planets elsewhere in the universe, the chances that they would contain life is slim. Some would say, nil.*

Biologist George Gaylord has stated that there is virtually no chance that intelligent beings have evolved on another planet. He

---

*According to the Associated Press, in October 1995 several astronomers discovered a planet half the size of Jupiter orbiting a star named 51 Pegasus, about forty light-years from earth. But other astrogazers, including George Gatewood of the University of Pittsburgh, aren't ready to jump on the planetary bandwagon. These critics note that even if the "slight wobble" observed in the star's movement, *suggesting* the tug of a planet, is for real, the planet would be too close to the fiery star to harbor life. Early the following year, the Observer News Service reported that astronomers discovered indications of another object orbiting Virginis 70, in the constellation Virgo. A privately funded SETI project, Serendip 3, then reviewed its records for data retrieved from the vicinity of the star and —*voilá*— they found a previously unnoticed pattern of radio signals. But many remain skeptical. Says Gatewood: "The byways are littered with the corpses of [alleged] planetary systems."

doubts that the events that led to intelligence here could ever happen again elsewhere.[12]

Intelligent, sentient beings don't spring up like carrots. They take more than water and fertile soil.

Let's speculate for a moment. Let's say that out there, somewhere in the universe, there's a planet *exactly* like earth with a sun *exactly* like ours. We'll even say that conditions there are the same as on earth when the first signs of life appeared. What do you think the chances are, given this ideal scenario, that intelligent life — *Man* — could evolve on this hypothetical planet?

If you like long shots, you might want to place a bet. Otherwise, you'd be wise to hold onto your money.

Mankind is, in many ways, a fluke, the result of chemical and biological processes that were neither smooth nor uniform. Before higher life forms could even evolve here, an amazing chain of events took place. Small organic molecules somehow formed from the earth's original material. These "impossible" molecules combined into long chains capable of reproducing, and then cells and multicellular organisms emerged, eventually evolving into various species of plants and animals.

Without a hospitable environment, these processes would never had taken place. Any closer to the sun, the earth might have been too hot to promote life; further away, it might have been too cold. If the earth had followed a more elongated, rather than circular, orbit around the sun, it most likely would have done so forever devoid of life. The spin of the earth, providing a delicate balance between night and day, also contributed to the evolution of life. A planet that spins too quickly will experience strong winds and violent weather; a planet spinning too slowly, extremes in temperature.

When the earth first formed, its atmosphere contained an abundance of hydrogen, ammonia, methane, and water, but little oxygen. As lower animals evolved, an oxygen-carbon dioxide exchange occurred, creating an oxygen-rich atmosphere for the evolution of animals and Man. This is why most scientists believe that an oxygen atmosphere points strongly toward the existence of life. So far, though, the earth appears to be the only planet with such an atmosphere.

"The evidence we have at present clearly favors the conclusion that we are alone," says Trefil. "From the formation of the sun as a single

G star to the evolution of the earth's atmosphere to the conditions of the earth's recent climate, everything points to the same conclusion — we are special."[13]

Psychiatrist Carl Jung, Freud's rebellious student, likened UFOs — flying saucers — to the mandala, the mythical round shape, often found in modern art, that represents wholeness and universal Oneness.[14] "Like God," Anthony Mansueto observes, "the UFO divides our society into believers and nonbelievers, cautious hopefuls and equally cautious agnostics. But whether or not we believe, the UFO has a lot to tell us about ourselves."[15]

Transpersonal psychologists might argue that UFOs represent our collective despair — our fear of losing identity in a world which seems to have less and less need for the individual. The more we consume, the less happy and more isolated we seem to become. Feelings of isolation can become fertile soil for irrational, wishful thinking. Is Man, subconsciously, awaiting the arrival of a celestial cavalry to save him? Do we secretly yearn for salvation from afar, rather than facing our true selves? Have UFOs become a psychic placebo?

Fanciful thinking — myth and the like — was encouraged by the architects of the Third Reich. The public was encouraged to believe mad myths. Reason — and the seeking of truth — became tantamount to treason. Those who questioned were exterminated. Those who believed in the sanctity and nobility of the individual were crushed. The State — and those who created it — became all-powerful. Hitler's vision of a *New World Order* became the German people's placebo.

Placebos are dangerous. As in pharmaceutical testing, those who receive medication — truth, if you will — live; those receiving placebos often die.

Jacques Vallee, an astrophysicist and computer scientist, has no use for placebos. He has dedicated his life to discovering the truth about UFOs. He is a maverick, a freethinker, unburdened by conformity and misguided mainstream thought.

Vallee feels that UFOs might be just about anything — *except extraterrestrial craft.* In June 1989, speaking before the Eighth Annual Conference of the Society for Scientific Exploration, Vallee noted: "Scientific opinion has generally followed public opinion in the belief that unidentified flying objects either do not exist...or, if they do, must represent evidence of a visitation by some advanced race of space travelers.... Research on UFOs need not be restricted to these two alternatives. On the contrary, the accumulated data base exhibits several patterns tending to indicate that UFOs are real...and that the facts do not support the common concept of 'space visitors.' "[16]

Vallee observes that there have been many reports—as many as 5,000 according to some researchers—of so-called close encounters. Says Vallee: "It is difficult to claim that space explorers would need to land 5,000 times on the surface of a planet to analyze its soil, take samples of the flora and fauna, and produce a complete map."[17]

He states that the true number of close encounters may, in fact, be much higher. Only one in ten such cases may actually be reported. If so, the actual figure may be closer to 50,000.

The majority of close encounters have reportedly taken place in sparsely populated areas. A preponderance of reports have emanated from North America, Europe, and Australia. Assuming that the phenomenon is global and that there have been few witnesses to the events in remote locales, the CE figure must be even higher, perhaps as high as one million, contends Vallee.

But even this estimate may be too low. Vallee notes that frequency distribution studies indicate that close encounters have most often occurred in the early evening and predawn hours, and rarely during daylight. The data corresponds with people's work and sleep habits, indicating that there are far more UFO landings than reported. Vallee's computations, based upon the sighting report curve, suggest that as many as *fourteen million* landings may have actually taken place on earth—far too many to support the extraterrestrial hypothesis.[18]

Then there's the physiology of "aliens" so often reported during close encounters. Most witnesses have reported seeing creatures with distinctly *humanoid* features, which puzzles Vallee. Aliens from other worlds, he states, would not likely resemble earthlings.*

---

*Certainly not the two types of "aliens" most frequently reported in UFO close-encounter cases. The short, large-eyed "grays" and the tall, blond "Nordics" seem like cartoon versions of America's World War II adversaries—the Japanese and Germans. These similarities, too striking to be dismissed as coincidence, raise disturbing questions about the true nature of the close-encounter/abduction phenomenon.

Planets are unique. Each of the planets in our own solar system has a different chemical composition, atmosphere, and gravity. Even on our own world, the physiology of living creatures varies dramatically.

"How, then," asks Vallee, "can we expect that extraterrestrial visitors from a completely different planetary environment would not only resemble us, but breathe our air and walk normally on the earth?"[19]

Furthermore, Vallee feels that reports of UFO abductions, popularized by Strieber and others, do not support the extraterrestrial hypothesis. These cases have often involved frightening medical examinations at the hands of "aliens." UFO abductees have described abuse that reminds one more of the excesses of the Inquisition than any medical procedure. Says Vallee: "Whatever the supposed aliens are doing if they actually perform what appear to be shockingly crude and cruel simulacra of biological experiments on the bodies of their abductees is unlikely to represent a scientific mission relevant to the goals of extraterrestrial visitors. *The answers may have to be sought in other directions* [emphasis added]."[20]

If UFOs are not extraterrestrial, then what are they? What is their purpose? Is *A Modern Myth of Things Seen in the Skies* — Jung's description of UFOs — being forged into the psyche of Man?

For the answers, we need to go back to the early years following World War II. It was then that *The Great UFO Hoax* began.

# 2

# "Ignore That Man Behind the Curtain"

*This life's dim windows of the soul*
*Distorts the heavens from pole to pole*
*And leads you to believe a lie*
*When you see with, not through, the eye.*

— William Blake

On June 24, 1947 — only days before the Roswell "UFO crash" — a Boise businessman named Kenneth Arnold, a licensed air-rescue pilot, was flying his private plane near Mt. Rainier, Washington, searching for a downed aircraft, when he spotted nine unknown objects zipping across the sky in an undulating motion like "a saucer skipping over water." An experienced observer, Arnold estimated that the objects were traveling in excess of 1,700 miles per hour, a speed unattainable by *any known aircraft* in that postwar year.

Arnold later drew a picture of the objects he had sighted. Although the press widely reported that he had seen "saucer-shaped" objects, Arnold's drawing revealed what appeared to be a futuristic aircraft with sweptback wings.[1] Of course, the public could not have known at the time, but the drawing was a dead ringer for today's advanced stealth aircraft.

On July 8 — the same day the Air Force announced it had captured a "flying saucer" — Army Air Forces General Nathan F. Twining, commander of the Air Materiel Command (AMC), flatly denied that the saucers were U.S. experimental aircraft. "Neither the AAF nor any other component of the armed forces had any plane, guided missile or other aerial device under development which could possibly be mistaken for a saucer or formation of flying discs," General Twining told reporters by telephone from Kirtland Army Air Base in Albuquerque.[2]

But Twining privately expressed different views to AAF Brigadier General George Schulgen. In a secret report, Twining wrote that *"due consideration must be given [to]…the possibility that these objects are of domestic origin — the product of some high security project not known to [Army Air Forces Command] or [AMC]."* He added that *"[It] is possible within the present U.S. knowledge…to construct a piloted aircraft which has the general description of the [reported flying disks]."* No doubt referring to the Roswell incident, he concluded that reports of flying disks, or "flying saucers," were *unsupported* by "physical evidence in the shape of crash recovered exhibits [emphasis added]."³

In March 1993, amid a flurry of publicity about Roswell, Representative Steven H. Schiff, R-New Mexico, asked the Air Force to declassify and supply him with all material relating to the incident. The military claimed they had no information on Roswell and referred him instead to the National Archives which, he soon discovered, had no information. The Congressman was miffed, and promptly asked the General Accounting Office, the government watchdog agency, to find out if the Air Force was giving him the runaround.

With the GAO on its heels, the Air Force was suddenly able to produce documents from its own files. It issued a short report, concluding that the Roswell wreckage was part of Project Mogul, a top-secret project aimed at detecting Soviet nuclear tests by monitoring sound waves in the upper atmosphere with balloon-transported sensing devices.⁴ "From the rather benign description of the 'event' and the recovery of some material as described in the original newspaper accounts," wrote Colonel Richard Weaver, author of the report, "the 'Roswell Incident' has since grown to mythical (if not mystical) proportions…"⁵ He concluded: "The Air Force research did not locate or develop any information that the 'Roswell Incident' was a UFO event."⁶

The Air Force claimed to have left no stone unturned. Investigators submitted original negatives of newspaper photos, purportedly showing pieces of wreckage, to a "national level organization" — most likely, the CIA's National Photographic Interpretation Center — for digital analysis. The center, capable of enhancing orbiting spy satellite photographs enough to make out the whiskers on Castro's face, reported that the Roswell photos — taken by a professional news photographer — were of "insufficient quality" to produce substantive results.⁷

The Air Force had run the gamut of "solutions." First it had asserted that the Roswell debris was a flying saucer; then, a weather balloon. Now, nearly fifty years later, it was claiming Moguls.*

The General Accounting Office isn't satisfied with the Air Force's explanations, either. "But we do believe that something did happen at Roswell," a GAO official said. *"Something big.* We don't know if it was a plane that crashed with a nuclear device on it…or if it was some other *experimental situation.* But everything we've seen so far points to an attempt on the part of the Air Force *to lead anybody that looks at this down another track* [emphasis added]."***8

Shortly after the release of the Air Force report, a story surfaced, alleging that film producer Steven Spielberg was shown an actual film of the Roswell crash site taken by a "military officer" and that he plans to release a big-budget film exposing the government's "cover-up" of the incident. Kris Kelley, a spokesman for Spielberg's Amblin Productions, denied the report. However, some believe that such a film, fake or not, has been dangled before the filmmaker. Says public relations consultant Michael Luckman: "My inclination is that there is something to all of it."9

---

*The Mogul "solution" has problems. According to the Air Force report, the material recovered near Roswell was probably from Mogul Flight 4. However, the original Mogul flight log, attached to the AF report, lists no such flight. There is no evidence that Flight 4 ever existed. Furthermore, a Project Mogul engineer confirmed that remains of the high-altitude balloons, made of neoprene, were susceptible to sunlight and would "look like dark gray or black flakes or ashes" — hardly the description of the material found near Roswell.

**Most Roswell residents, around at the time of the crash, were unswayed by lurid accounts of "flying saucers." They were cognizant of top-secret government research in the area, and had few doubts about the true nature of the debris. One Roswellian told the *Roswell Daily Record*: "I have come to the conclusion that there are some disks flying around, and I think it is an experiment of some tactical branch of our armed forces." Another area resident: "I think the United States government is trying out something new. These disks may be radio-controlled instruments of some kind. In fact, I would make a guess that it is some military division of the government trying out radio-controlled objects flying through the air, possibly at [supersonic] speeds." The Roswell "flying saucer" story died a quick death and was only recently revived by the UFO community.

This same carrot was dangled before Ray Santilli, a British documentary filmmaker. No sooner had the Spielberg rumors died down then Roswell film footage, also allegedly taken by a military cameraman back in 1947, again surfaced. Early on, Philip Mantle, director of investigations for the British UFO Research Association (BUFORA), declared the film, which Santilli acquired, to be the "Holy Shroud of the UFO movement," adding, "It is the closest we have yet come to proving not only that UFOs are plying our skies but also that aliens have landed on earth."[10]

The 16mm film — fourteen canisters of it — shows, among other things, a grainy black-and-white scene of men in radiation suits dissecting an alien creature, presumably recovered from the crash site.[11] This would seem to confirm sketchy, secondhand reports of "little bodies" discovered among the wreckage in 1947.[12] Or so we would be led to believe.

There's one problem — the decrepit film footage is an outlandish hoax. Even die-hard ufologists who were among the first to see the film were unimpressed. Those attending the Third International Symposium on UFOs and Related Phenomena in San Marino, Italy, in May 1995, raised troubling questions regarding the film footage and blurry slides of individual film frames they were shown. Paolo Fiorino, a professional nurse, voiced concern over a series of slides showing the "alien autopsy"; according to Fiorino, the alien showed no signs of rigor mortis, and the table used for the autopsy lacked drainage ports, so necessary for an autopsy. Even BUFORA's Mantle, originally aglow over the film, grew glum.[13]

The Roswell incident raises disturbing questions. Why the obfuscation? Why are films promoting an extraterrestrial explanation for the Roswell incident only now coming to light? Why are military higher-ups continuing to put the wraps on a case that is ancient history? If an experimental craft did indeed go down in the New Mexico desert back in 1947, surely this technology would hardly be secret today. *Or would it?**

---

*We may never know what crashed at Roswell. According to GAO findings, reported in the July 30, 1995, issue of the *Roswell Daily Record*, all outgoing messages from Roswell Army Air Field from October 1946 to December 1949 were destroyed without proper authorization.

In the late 1980s, copies of a document supplying startling information about the Roswell "UFO crash" were sent anonymously to various UFO investigators. The document, stamped Top Secret, purports to be a briefing paper prepared in 1952 for President Eisenhower by the so-called Majestic-12 committee, headed by former CIA director Vice Admiral Roscoe Hillenkoetter. The document confirms that four dead, badly decomposed alien bodies were retrieved at the site. It goes on to note that civilian and military witnesses were debriefed and that news reporters were given the "cover story" that the object was a weather balloon.[14]

British author Timothy Good says he now regards a copy of the document he received from a U.S. intelligence source in 1987 to be a fake. He argues that President Truman's signature on an attached memo, allegedly sent to Secretary of Defense James Forrestal authorizing the MJ-12 committee, is almost certainly a forgery.[15]

Jacques Vallee agrees. He states that the MJ-12 document is a "contrived hoax."[16]

Another obvious hoax, touting the Roswell alien scenario, is the KRILL papers, a lengthy and ludicrous document supposedly authored by a spaceman of the same name. The document purports, among other things, that:

- Craft from another world have crashed on earth.

- The government has conducted autopsies on alien cadavers.

- Early U.S. government efforts at acquiring alien technology were successful.

- The U.S. government has had a working relationship with alien forces for some time, with the express purpose of gaining technology in gravitational propulsion, beam weaponry, and mind control.

- Our civilization is one of many that has existed in the last billion years.

The KRILL papers assert that MJ-12 is genuine, and goes on to describe the various beings visiting earth. Like MJ-12, the document surfaced anonymously, suddenly appearing in UFO researchers' mailboxes and on various computer bulletin boards.*[17]

Then there's the Maury Island tragedy. The place: off the coast of Tacoma, Washington. The date: June 21, 1947, around the time of the Arnold sighting and Roswell crash.

Reportedly, a marine salvager named Harold A. Dahl was on his boat just off Maury Island, near Tacoma, with his fifteen-year-old son, two crewmen, and the boy's dog when a group of doughnut-shaped UFOs appeared overhead. One of the unknown craft, fluttering as if disabled, showered a stream of metallic flakes and hot slaglike material onto the boat. The dog was killed, and the young boy was injured. Then the UFOs departed.

Dahl reported the encounter to his boss, fellow salvager Fred L. Crisman, who later discovered the materials described by Dahl strewn along the shoreline. Air Force intelligence officers were summoned to the scene and collected some of the slaglike material. Later the officers boarded their B-25 aircraft for the return flight to Hamilton Air Force Base.

Soon after takeoff, one of the plane's engines burst into flames. Two enlisted men aboard parachuted to safety, but the intelligence officers perished when the plane crashed.[18]

The following day a sensational headline appeared in the *Tacoma Times*—"SABOTAGE HINTED IN CRASH OF ARMY BOMBER." In the accompanying story, reporter Paul Lance claimed that a mysterious telephone informant had called his office, indicating that the plane had been "sabotaged or shot down to prevent shipment of [the] flying disc fragments" to Hamilton Field. "Lending substance to the caller's story," Lance's account continued, "is the fact that 12 hours before the Army released official identification, he correctly identified the dead in the crash as Captain William Davidson, pilot, and First Lieutenant Frank M. Brown." An intelligence officer at McChord Field confirmed the mystery caller's claim that the aircraft was carrying "classified material."[19]

Later, Dahl and Crisman claimed the whole affair was a hoax. Strangely, neither of the men was ever prosecuted, despite the resultant

---

*There is a series of books, *What-Do-I-Do-Now* (Tor), written for young people. The title of the first book is *Zork: The Forces of KRILL.*

tragedy. Dahl disappeared after the incident, and Crisman was reportedly recalled into military service, subsequently transferred to Alaska, then Greenland.

Twenty years later, Crisman's name popped up again in connection with another unsavory event—the assassination of John F. Kennedy. District Attorney Jim Garrison of New Orleans purportedly subpoenaed Crisman to testify before the grand jury hearing Garrison's evidence against Clay Shaw and others accused of conspiring to kill Kennedy. It was rumored that Crisman was a CIA operative.[20]

Interestingly, the CIA has long been involved with UFOs. In the opening days of 1953, a secret top-level panel convened by the Central Intelligence Agency met in Washington, D.C. A report of the proceedings was not completely declassified until twenty-two years later. The subject of the meeting was UFOs. Present were CIA officials Dr. H. Marshall Chadwell, Ralph L. Clark, and Philip G. Strong, as well as top-level scientists including physicist and weapons system expert H. P. Robertson (chairman), Einstein associate Samuel A. Goudsmit, high-energy physicist Thornton Page, and Lloyd Berkner, a physicist who had accompanied Admiral Byrd on the 1928–30 Antarctic expedition.

Ostensibly, the so-called Robertson Panel was set up to scientifically analyze recent reports of unidentified flying objects, but it soon became apparent that the CIA had a hidden agenda. The agency's real focus turned out not to be UFOs per se, but rather *the effects of UFO reports upon the general public.*

The CIA focused on the potential of such reports for use in "psychological warfare." The panel's final report emphasized the public's "current gullibility…and consequently their susceptibility to clever hostile propaganda." The agency ordered that private UFO investigation groups be placed under surveillance. Furthermore, it was suggested that Walt Disney Studios might be approached to aid in the agency's "educational program."[21] Final copies of the report were distributed to key personnel in the Pentagon, including Air Force intelligence chief Major General Charles Cabell,[22] who years later, as CIA deputy director, was fired by President Kennedy for bungling the Bay of Pigs invasion.

In the early 1960s, the CIA, in fact, utilized some "hostile propaganda" of its own involving UFOs. CIA agent Desmond Fitzgerald, a

Kennedy detractor involved in early Mafia-CIA assassination attempts against Castro, used bogus UFO reports against China to spread disinformation. Years later, CIA intelligence officer Miles Copeland revealed that the UFO exercise was "just to keep the Chinese off-balance and make them think we were doing things we weren't." He added: "The project got the desired results, as I remember..."[23]

The CIA also appears to have made good on its promise of spying on UFO groups, in gross violation of its original charter prohibiting domestic operations. A special target may have been the Aerial Phenomena Research Organization (APRO), located in Tucson. "Salesmen" frequently visited the home of Jim and Coral Lorenzen, the group's founders, and engaged them in probing conversations with no regard to promoting business. On at least one occasion, the couple was monitored by the local Air Force Office of Special Investigations (AFOSI).

In 1974, astronomer J. Allen Hynek visited APRO headquarters requesting a list of the organization's field investigators, including addresses and telephone numbers. Although not a formal member of the Robertson Panel, he was able to sit in on sessions without restrictions.

"I do not know if Dr. Hynek was actually employed as a CIA consultant subsequent to the Robertson Panel," writes Timothy Good, "but it seems evident that he was in the best position to perform such a function, with worldwide contacts at official and unofficial levels. Many fellow researchers in a number of countries agree with me that while Hynek was always interested in gathering information, he seemed reluctant to give out much in return."[24]

The National Investigations Committee on Aerial Phenomena (NICAP) was another target of the CIA. NICAP was one of the nation's most influential UFO groups during the 1950s and '60s but, by the '70s, was all but dead. The organization had been a vitriolic opponent of government secrecy and had pushed relentlessly for Congressional hearings on UFOs.

Major Donald Keyhoe, an early NICAP director, was ousted from the organization in 1969 when he began to focus criticism on the CIA. What was not generally known at the time was that NICAP was teeming with "former" high-ranking CIA officials, many of whom were on the board of directors which removed Keyhoe. Board members included Colonel Joseph Bryan, former chief of the CIA's

Psychological Warfare Staff. Other prominent NICAP officials were Vice Admiral Roscoe Hillenkoetter, the first director of the CIA; CIA Psychological Warfare Staff member Nicholas de Rochefort; and Bernard J. O. Carvalho, a CIA contract agent.

Following Keyhoe's dismissal, John Acuff, who was head of an agency with close ties to the CIA and Defense Department intelligence agencies, was made director of NICAP. Alan Hall, NICAP's next director, was a "retired" CIA employee. A principal supporter of Hall was Senator Barry Goldwater aide Charles Lombard, previously a CIA covert operative.

Clearly, NICAP, once a thorn in the side of the government, was gutted by the CIA. NICAP finally became so ineffective that it was shut down, and the organization's files were transferred to the Center for UFO Studies, founded by Hynek.[25]

And what of the CIA's plans involving Disney? Recently Walt Disney World in Orlando revamped Tomorrowland and constructed a $100 million attraction, the ExtraTERRORestrial Alien Encounter. Disney has even produced a film on UFOs and the "government cover-up," while promoting its latest addition to Tomorrowland.

In the film's opening sequence, a UFO races across the sky as actor Robert Urich intones: "This is not swamp gas. It is not a flock of birds. This is an actual spacecraft piloted by alien intelligence—one sighting from tens of thousands made over the last fifty years on virtually every continent on the globe. Intelligent life from distant galaxies is now attempting to make open contact with the human race and tonight we'll show you the evidence."

The next scene features classic Disney animation—as the Robertson Panel had recommended—followed by the appearance of Disney CEO Michael Eisner. Then Urich returns, explaining that aliens were attracted to earth by the atomic-bomb explosion in 1945.[26]

Astrophysicist Vallee states that the UFO scene represents a "control system" of some kind. He asks: "Would there be a need to conduct covert experiments, to monitor civilian research groups, even to finance through devious channels the investigative efforts of certain ufologists, if the Air Force did have flying saucers sitting helplessly in its hangars and little aliens under the scalpel of its surgeons?" The expectation of visitors from space, he adds, is being fostered by "various groups for their own purposes."[27]

It is apparent that the government — specifically, the military and CIA — has been playing good-cop/bad-cop with the American public. With one hand, it "leaks" disinformation asserting that UFOs are extraterrestrial and then, with the other, publicly debunks the UFO phenomenon.

The orchestrators of *The Great UFO Hoax* are a cold-veined lot, for sure. On January 7, 1948, Kentucky National Guard pilot Captain Thomas Mantell, flying from Marietta, Georgia, to Standiford Field, Kentucky, crashed while pursuing a "metallic object" that was "tremendous in size." Soon thereafter, General Cabell, who years later would figure prominently in Kennedy assassination conspiracy theories, pushed hard for fighter interceptor missions being kept on alert to challenge UFOs, despite General Twining's earlier assessment that the craft were, most likely, our own.[28]

Was Cabell, as Air Force intelligence chief, following a secret agenda? Was he purposely promoting aerial confrontations — war games — between unwitting military pilots and advanced, still-secret, military aerodynes, otherwise known as UFOs? Was he privy to top-secret, off-the-books military operations, of which Twining was unaware?

The story of Mel Noel (pseudonym) dramatically illustrates that the military was anything but baffled by the nature of UFOs. In 1976, Noel, a former Air Force pilot, told author Good that back in the 1950s he had been assigned to a reserve squadron at Lowry Air Force Base, Colorado. The squadron had an unusual assignment: to film UFOs.

Prior to missions, Noel said he and the other pilots were provided briefings by a Colonel Peterson from Washington, D.C. Peterson revealed an extraordinary knowledge of "UFOs." He instructed pilots on specific maneuvers that would be necessary in the event of a UFO encounter. They were warned about electromagnetic effects — radio static and instrument malfunctions — that could befall them during a UFO pursuit. They were told unequivocally, however, that there would be no adverse effect on their F-86A Sabre jets' engines or hydraulic systems, as long as they didn't cross the path of the objects which, they were warned, had resulted in *damage to or loss of aircraft.*

Naturally, the pilots doubted they would ever see any UFOs, and wondered privately if the military brass were playing a joke on them. Their skepticism turned to awe in December 1953 when they spotted a large cluster of unknown craft flying in formation over the Rockies in Idaho. Noel counted sixteen saucer-shaped objects, each 150–180 feet in diameter. The objects, which presented a color-changing corona effect as they accelerated, were in sight for eight minutes. The pilots were unable to get close enough to film the objects.

Following each mission, pilots were assigned new jet aircraft. Aircraft were routinely checked for radiation, and all instrumentation, cameras, and magazines were replaced upon landing.

On another mission, Noel and his squadron did manage to film the objects, but were never allowed to see the images they recorded. He understood that the film was taken elsewhere, possibly Wright-Patterson Field, for evaluation.

Following a third UFO encounter, in 1954, the pilots returned to Mountain Home Air Force Base, Idaho, suffering from symptoms akin to combat fatigue. They wondered if they had been exposed to dangerous radiation during the missions. If power unleashed by the craft was powerful enough to affect instruments, then what about humans?

The pilots were warned not to discuss their missions with anyone. They were threatened with long jail time and substantial fines if they ever talked.

Eight years later, Noel broke his silence by going on a radio show. He felt he was near enough to the ten-year statute of limitations prohibiting military personnel from discussing certain information. He was wrong.

Just before going on, two men approached him, flashing CIA credentials. They warned Noel to "cease and desist," adding that it could be "detrimental" to his health should he do the broadcast. Noel went ahead, anyway.[29]

"Suffice to say that there is no doubt in my mind that Mel was describing genuine encounters with UFOs, and his knowledge of aircraft and flying is beyond dispute," writes Good. "Since leaving the Air Force, Mel has continued to fly different types of aircraft in his capacity as a commercial pilot. He has also done a great deal of research into UFOs, sometimes in association with his friend Gordon Cooper, the ex-astronaut and Air Force pilot."[30]

In August 1949, the Air Force's Air Technical Intelligence Center (ATIC) concluded that UFOs constituted "no direct threat to the national security."[31] Later, in 1966, the Air Force commissioned a group of scientists at the University of Colorado to conduct a "scientific investigation of unidentified flying objects." The eighteen-month study concluded that UFOs were not extraterrestrial.[32]

The scientists, however, did not rule out the possibility that UFOs were actually supersecret military aircraft, as suggested in the 1947 Twining memorandum.

"We adopted the term 'conspiracy hypothesis' for the view that some agency of the Government either within the Air Force, the Central Intelligence Agency, or elsewhere knows all about UFOs and is keeping the knowledge secret," the final report concludes. "Without denying the possibility that this could be true, we decided very early in the study, that we were not likely to succeed in carrying out a form of counter-espionage against our own Government, in the hope of settling the question. We therefore decided not to pay special attention to it, but instead to keep alert to any indications that might lead to any evidence that not all of the essential facts known to the Government were being given to us.

"Although we found no such evidence, it must be conceded that there may be a supersecret government UFO laboratory hidden away somewhere of whose existence we are not aware...."[33]

*In short, the scientists refused to look at the man behind the curtain.*

# 3

# Let's Get Real

*Appearances often are deceiving.*
— Aesop

In 1950 — three years after private pilot Kenneth Arnold ushered in the "modern era" of UFOs — *U.S. News & World Report* made a startling claim: *UFOs were actually secret military aircraft*. The article wasn't based upon hearsay. It was published only after extensive interviews with scientists, engineers, and military personnel.

The article firmly stated that flying saucers — the objects we now call UFOs — were "not mysterious visitors from Mars." Instead, the article asserted: "They are actual planes, soundly engineered on principles developed by [the] U.S. in wartime. By using this new design, they can do things that no conventional aircraft can be expected to approach."[1]

*U.S. News* noted that prototypes of these secret craft were first built in 1942 by the American military. The United States apparently had some stiff competition. The article went on to say that Germany and Italy worked on similar designs during the same period.

"The first U.S. model," the article stated, "...was elliptical in shape, powered by two piston engines and driven by twin propellers. It had a maximum speed between 400 and 500 miles an hour. More important, it could rise almost vertically and its minimum speed for landing was only about 35 miles an hour, a great advantage in military and naval aircraft. And it was far more maneuverable than conventional military planes."[2]

Then there was this: "Official inquiry by the Air Force, in the face of overwhelming evidence that the saucers are real, was called off last December. This indicates clearly that top Air Force officials know where the saucers originate and are not concerned about them, as they would be if these aircraft were from Russia or Mars. These officials, at the same time, denied emphatically that a secret Air Force project is responsible."[3]

The Air Force's denial was partly correct—"plausible deniability," it's called today—because the craft was, in fact, acquired by the Navy. According to confirmed sources, the "flying saucer" was built by defense contractor Chance-Vought and thoroughly tested by Navy engineers. *U.S. News* confirmed that twice as much was spent in 1949 by the Navy as by the Air Force on secret "guided-missile" research. "There is no public accounting for these millions, the only Government funds aside from atomic-energy dollars that still are being spent *with great secrecy* [emphasis added]."[4]

Is this article, written during the burgeoning Cold War era, accurate? Has the American military had in its possession advanced, radically designed aircraft—*flying saucers*—since World War II?

There is every indication that *U.S. News'* reporting was dead-on. Compelling evidence in support of the article can be found in the U.S. Patent Office. There one can discover a cornucopia of "flying saucer" patents. A detailed patent submitted in 1953 by the Lockheed Aircraft Corporation—designers of the U-2 and SR-71 spycraft, as well as the F-117A stealth fighter—describes an "aircraft of circular plan-form and of bi-convex vertical cross section."[5] In short, a flying saucer.

Curiously, there is no mention of whether the craft ever flew. We now know, however, that one such device did in fact take to the skies— not once or twice, but on more than one hundred manned test flights. The remarkable craft, the V-173, so impressed the Navy that it approved construction of the XF5U-1, an improved fighter prototype of the craft that was reportedly capable of vertical takeoffs and speeds far in excess of any aircraft of the times.[6]

The Navy then claims to have scrapped the project. But did it?

In 1947, the Air Force, confronted with growing reports of "flying saucers," asked just that question in a classified memorandum. "Are you positive the Navy junked the XF5U-1 project?" the Air Force inquired.[7]

Declassified Air Force documents strongly suggest the Air Force got its answer. In late 1947, Major General L. C. Craigie ordered the establishment of a detailed project to investigate UFOs. The project, code-named Sign, was instructed to "collect, collate, evaluate and distribute to interested government agencies and contractors all information concerning sightings and phenomena in the atmosphere *which can be construed to be of concern to the national security* [emphasis added]."[8]

The following year, Project Sign investigators issued an "Estimate of the Situation," concluding that UFOs were real and interplanetary. The report was sent to Air Force Chief of Staff General Hoyt S. Vandenberg, who summarily dismissed the findings, strongly indicating that he knew something his underlings didn't.[9] He may, in fact, have eventually conveyed secret information about UFOs to the Project Sign staff which, by February 1949, had scrapped its original assessment. In their final report, classified secret, the investigators concluded: "Future activity on this project should be carried on *at the minimum level necessary* to record, summarize and evaluate the data received on future reports and to complete the specialized investigations now in progress [emphasis added]."[10]

In August 1949, Project Grudge, a follow-up to Project Sign, was even more blunt in its conclusions: "There is no evidence that objects reported upon are the result of an advanced scientific *foreign* development; and, therefore they constitute no direct threat to the national security [emphasis added]."[11]

In short, the Air Force couldn't have cared less about UFOs. They had concluded, in two separate studies, that the elusive disks weren't *somebody else's* technology and that they were of no threat to this country.

On the surface, this would seem a curious posture, considering the spate of bizarre cases recorded during the Sign-Grudge years. In the previous chapter, we noted the tragic case of Captain Thomas Mantell, who died in pursuit of a metallic, disk-shaped craft that easily outmaneuvered his fighter plane. Add to this the Chiles-Whitted case of July 24, 1948. In this incident, an Eastern Airlines DC-3, piloted by Captains Clarence S. Chiles and John B. Whitted, narrowly missed colliding with an unidentified craft that streaked past them at an estimated speed of 700 miles per hour, then turned sharply and shot straight up out of sight.[12]

We'll examine "UFO attacks" in subsequent chapters. For now, let's return to the matter of patents. As previously noted, the U.S. Patent Office has issued patents on numerous flying saucer-type aircraft.

Patent 2,772,057 was issued on November 27, 1956, to John C. Fischer for his designs of a "Circular Aircraft." Homer F. Streib's

"Circular Wing Aircraft" and "Circular Wing Aircraft with Universally Tiltable Ducted Power Plant" were patented—2,876,964 and 2,876,965, respectively—on March 10, 1959; Nathan C. Price's "High Velocity High Altitude V.T.O.L. Aircraft" was patented (3,103,324) on September 10, 1963; and J. C. M. Frost's circular aircraft, patented (3,124,323) on March 10, 1964.

As early as 1960, Archie L. Leggett was issued Patent 2,947,496 for a radically new rotating disk-shaped craft designed for flight within the earth's atmosphere as well as for interplanetary travel. In 1957, aircraft designer Constantin P. Lent was issued Patent 2,801,058 for a "Saucer-Shaped Aircraft" capable of instantaneously rising vertically, hovering, and traveling at supersonic speeds. Several years later, Heinrich Fleissner's "Rotating Jet Aircraft With Lifting Disc Wing and Centrifuging Tanks"—Patent 2,939,648—promised a revolutionary craft that "takes off from and lands vertically on any suitable ground or water surface and has the ability to remain in suspension at any point at any desired altitude regardless of weather conditions." The inventor further claimed that "acute angle turning is made possible by the fact that all the turning devices are in proximity to the center of the aircraft and further, the center body is the only portion that is turned in that the wing, extending outwardly therefrom, is continuously rotating and is not affected by the turning of the central body."[13]

Were these simply screwball inventions, or were these inventors onto something? It is interesting to note that most of these patents spoke of *jet-powered* craft, not propeller vehicles such as the Navy's XF5U-1. Surely, the governments of the world, with their vast resources, possessed the capability of designing jet-propelled flying saucers of their own.

One such craft is known to have been built. This was Weapons System 606A, otherwise known as the Avro Disk. As early as the 1950s Britain's Avro Aircraft, designers of some of World War II's most successful bombers, built a plant near Toronto, Canada, for the development of this craft. The saucer-shaped vehicle—closely resembling tabloid renderings and eyewitness sketches of "flying saucers"—exhibited highly efficient vertical lift capabilities.

The Canadian government originally funded the new project, but was soon forced to abandon it due to budget constraints. Enter the

U.S. military. By 1954, the highly classified program had evolved from theory into a full-blown research effort developed to produce a thirty-foot-diameter circular-winged jet aircraft that could easily reach speeds of 1,000 miles per hour.

But the craft proved to be unstable. During test flights it wobbled and had to be tethered to avoid damage. Declassified documents state that the U.S. military scrubbed the project in December 1961 after spending $10 million.[14]

In an article published in the January 1995 issue of *Popular Mechanics*, senior correspondent Abe Dane uncovered intriguing information that the design of saucer-shaped craft may not have died, as previously thought, with the disappointing Avro Disk. William Blake, an engineer at the Air Force's Wright Laboratory, told Dane that he had seen documents in the 1960s that discussed the design of a *nuclear-powered* craft, not wholly unlike the Avro Disk, that was four hundred feet in diameter and capable of carrying a million-pound payload. The craft was termed GEM, the ground-effect machine.[15]

Which brings us to the recent DarkStar fiasco. In June 1995, the Pentagon announced it had received from Lockheed Martin/Boeing the prototype of a $10 million saucer-shaped reconnaissance drone, dubbed DarkStar, that could be satellite-controlled and was capable of detecting "a basketball on the ground from 45,000 feet high." The media, disseminating information supplied by the Pentagon, provided specifications of the craft: fifteen feet long with a wingspan of sixty-nine feet and a cruising speed of 180 miles per hour.[16]

On its second flight, in April 1996, the drone smacked into the ground and was destroyed following a shaky takeoff from concrete Runway 04 at Edwards Air Force Base.[17] There had been indications of trouble during DarkStar's maiden flight the previous month. During that flight, the Tier-3 drone, funded by the Defense Airborne Reconnaissance Office and Defense Advanced Research Projects Agency (DARPA), experienced "premature main gear liftoff and wheelbarrowing," according to *Aviation Week & Space Technology*.[18] Harry Berman, DARPA Tier-3 program manager, had voiced concerns about the craft's electronic guidance system. "We struggled to understand how it interprets satellite data," he later stated. "We didn't know enough to ask the next questions...We got some strange...data in taxi tests..."[19]

Years ago, *Ideal's UFO Magazine* quoted a retired USAF officer who claimed that the Avro Disk was a "cover" for alien spacecraft the Air Force was secretly test flying. A cover, perhaps. But *alien spacecraft?*[20]

In any event, the "public execution" of the Avro Disk—and now, DarkStar—has *created the impression* that the military establishment is horribly inept at building saucers that fly. But is this really the case? What of the *U.S. News* revelations? What of the futuristic patents of the past? What of William Blake's disclosure?

Flying saucers—not the kind from outer space—may have originated in Nazi Germany, as suggested early on by *U.S. News*. In late 1944, Reuters news agency reported that German scientists had developed a secret air defense weapon that resembled "the glass balls that adorn Christmas trees. They have been seen hanging in the air over German territory, sometimes singly, sometimes in clusters. They are colored silver and are apparently transparent."[21]

The existence of such weapons was confirmed by the Associated Press. Appearing on the front page of the *New York Times* (January 2, 1945), an AP dispatch noted that these so-called "foo-fighters" were frequently observed by Allied bombing crews flying missions over the Reich. The eerie balls of light often followed Allied aircraft, as if taunting their crews, and easily evaded pursuit.

Lieutenant Donald Meiers told reporters: "A 'foo-fighter' picked me up recently at 700 feet and chased me twenty miles down the Rhine Valley. I turned to starboard and two balls of fire turned with me. I turned to the port side and they turned with me. We were going 260 miles an hour and the balls were keeping right up with us.

"On another occasion when a 'foo-fighter' picked us up, I dove at 360 miles per hour. It kept right off our wing tips for a while and then zoomed up into the sky.

"When I first saw the things off my wing tips, I had the horrible thought that a German on the ground was ready to press a button and explode them. But they don't explode or attack us. They just seem to follow us like will-o'-wisps."

Lieutenant Meiers was an observant airman. He described three classes of foo-fighters. Said Meiers: "One is red balls of fire which appear off our wing tips and fly along with us; the second is a vertical row of three balls of fire which fly in front of us, and the third is a group of about fifteen lights which appear off in the distance — like a Christmas tree up in the air — and flicker on and off."[22]

Shortly after the end of World War II, reports of secret Nazi aircraft began to surface in obscure German publications. One 1950s article claims that Rudolph Schriever, a Luftwaffe aeronautical engineer, designed, as early as 1941, a "flying top," which was tested the following year; another states that Schriever and three colleagues — German scientists named Habermohl and Miethe, and an Italian physicist, Dr. Bellonzo — went on to design a jet-propelled saucer-shaped craft. According to one source, the device had "adjustable wing-disks" and a "fixed, cupola-shaped cockpit." The 140-foot flying saucer could reportedly reach an altitude of 40,000 feet and had a cruising speed of 1,250 miles per hour.[23]

Another inventor, Victor Schauberger, is also said to have designed flying disks for the Nazis. According to researcher Renato Vesco, Schauberger narrowly avoided capture by the Russians following the war and later worked on top-secret projects for the American military.[24]

There is no concrete evidence that the Nazi's "Project Saucer" ever existed. However, in a 1955 CIA memorandum, W. E. Lexow, Chief of the Applied Science Division of the agency's Office of Scientific Intelligence, observed that John Frost, designer of the Avro Disk, "reported to have obtained his original idea for the flying machine from a group of Germans just after World War II...."[25]

In 1944, a year before the end of World War II, future CIA director Allen Dulles, then an intelligence agent with the Office of Strategic Service (OSS), secretly met with prominent Nazis, offering them safe haven in the United States in exchange for technological and intelligence information. Later that year, OSS agent Frank Wisner arranged for the airlift of American prisoners of war — and a large contingent of pro-Nazi intelligence specialists.

Dulles liked Nazis. The Dulles-affiliated law firm of Sullivan & Cromwell had refused to close its offices in Germany after the start of World War II, even as Nazi bombs were devastating Great Britain and France. Many of Dulles' business associates were, in fact, prominent Nazis.[26]

Barely a week after the war had ended, Dulles had Reinhard Gehlen, Hitler's master spy, secretly flown into the Washington D.C.-area aboard a U.S. Army DC-3. At Fort Hunt, near Washington, Gehlen met with Dulles, President Truman's national security advisor and generals working for army intelligence. Within a year, Gehlen was back in Germany, with the full blessing of Dulles and the Washington intelligence establishment. There he recruited former SS and Gestapo officials as the first step in organizing an American-sanctioned spy network to monitor the Soviets, whom Dulles had decided even before war's end were to be America's new enemy.

Gehlen's spy organization would later flourish under the auspices of the CIA. Klaus Barbie, the "Butcher of Lyon," was one of those hired by Gehlen. Others were Dr. Franz Alfred Six and Emil Augsburg, SS intelligence officers directly responsible for the extermination of numerous Jews during the Holocaust.

While the U.S. government was ostensibly hunting Nazi war criminals, the U.S. War Department was secretly importing Nazi scientists into the United States. Many of these men of science had been involved with fatal experiments conducted on concentration camp victims.[27]

What did the U.S. military learn from these scientists? What technology did we acquire from these "former" Nazis? Did John Frost, in fact, base his early saucer design on German technology, as the 1955 CIA memo suggests?

Following the war, Nazi scientists and avionics experts were subjected to intensive interrogations. Careful searches of SS units, factories, and technical facilities were conducted throughout Germany. Technical documents of every kind were scoured.

Colonel D.L. Putt, assistant commanding officer for the Technical Information Service of the Allied Military Government, issued a final report in July 1946, assessing the extent of German secrets then in Allied hands. Thorough searches of Peenemünde (the German V-2 rocket base) and elsewhere had produced a wealth of new aeronautical developments, according to Colonel Putt.[28]

In 1946, following the clandestine mass exodus of Nazi scientists to America, strange cigar- and spool-shaped objects with fiery tails suddenly appeared with frightening regularity in the skies over Scandinavia. Between July 9 and July 12, the Swedish General Staff received three hundred reports of "ghost rockets."[29] During one twenty-four-hour period in August, the number of sightings jumped to more than a thousand.[30] Some of the mysterious objects were seen to explode or crash.[31]

A Swedish astronomer was studying some clouds through a telescope when he observed one of the objects on the horizon. "I first believed it to be an airplane," he told the *New York Times*, "but soon I noticed it was traveling much too fast for that, and within ten seconds I got a full view of the projectile. I managed to get a clear view of the bomb's body and estimate that it was at least 90 feet long. The body was torpedo-shaped and shining like metal. No sound could be heard, although the bomb was only two kilometers away. At the explosion, a terrific light flashed up that for a moment completely blinded me. No fire, smoke or sparks were noticeable."[32]

In central Sweden, a newly built barn collapsed following sightings of the unknown objects. A sharp crack was heard and the barn fell.[33]

One eyewitness saw one of the objects explode overhead, raining down fragments. Another ghost rocket passed directly over Stockholm and reportedly crashed north of the city.[34]

The Swedish Army rushed experts to three crash sights on August 12. Afterwards, they refused to discuss the matter.[35]

The Swedish government attempted to acquire new radar units from the American military in the hopes of tracking and possibly recovering one of the objects. Curiously, the Americans refused the request of their World War II ally.[36] *Why?*

In America, shortly after the first appearance of ghost rockets over Scandinavia, the "modern era" of UFOs began.* People from all walks of life began to report the appearance of saucer-shaped and odd triangular-shaped, or batlike, craft soaring through the skies. Interestingly, during this same period, rumors were rife that secret aircraft facilities had been established in the sparsely populated, dense forests of Western Canada. Many early reports from the Pacific Northwest did, in fact, indicate that the reported objects were flying on a course toward

---

*The "modern era" includes UFO cases occurring after World War II. UFO enthusiasts are eager to point out that UFOs have been seen throughout history, thus the need for the "modern era" tag. Early UFO sightings, however, lack scientific authenticity and were, most likely, misidentifications of astronomical and terrestrial phenomena that would be easily identifiable today. Meteors, discounted by established scientists well into the eighteenth century, no doubt produced many such early accounts. So, too, comets and ball lightning.

Western Canada.[37] Other craft were seen in New Mexico, Nevada, and California, in the vicinity of top-secret military installations.[38]

In recent years, sightings of large, triangular-shaped "flying wings" have been sighted in growing numbers. On the evening of May 3, 1990, a triangular craft was seen by five witnesses in California over a four-hour period. The craft made multiple passes over Mojave, Lancaster, Tehachapi, and Palmdale. Tehachapi is near Edwards Air Force Base; Palmdale is the home of Lockheed's Advanced Development Projects division, the so-called "Skunk Works," where top-secret aviation research is conducted.

On June 19, 1990, a loud, deep-roaring device was sighted near Mojave. Other similar craft were spotted traveling in a northeasterly direction, passing close to Edwards Air Force Base and the China Lake Naval Weapon Center. This is the same general area where airline pilots have reported seeing high-speed vehicles at altitudes above 50,000 feet.

During this same period, fast-moving "bright lights" were seen in southern California, from Santa Barbara to George Air Force Base, near Antelope Valley. One observer saw an object streak across the evening sky, requiring less than twenty seconds to transit a seventy-degree arc overhead.

These and other cases were discussed in the October 1, 1990, issue of *Aviation Week & Space Technology*, America's premier avionics magazine. The publication did not treat the reports as evidence of alien spacecraft, but rather as proof of supersecret military aircraft. "Multiple reports from well-qualified observers," states *Aviation Week*, "lend substantial credence to the existence of numerous secret aircraft flying from remote bases in the southwestern U.S., regardless of the political, funding or technical arguments against that probability."[39]

The article notes: "Advanced secret aircraft developed at highly classified government facilities in the Nevada desert over the last decade are demonstrating and validating new technologies for the U.S.'s future fighters, bombers and reconnaissance platforms.

"Although facilities in remote areas of the Southwest have been home to classified vehicles *for decades*, the number and sophistication of new aircraft appear to have increased sharply over the last 10 years, when substantial funding was made available for 'deep black' projects.

"Vehicles now flying from these well-guarded sites include both manned and unmanned hypersonic-capable aircraft designed to perform strategic reconnaissance and other, less conventionally defined missions [emphasis added]...."[40]

The article goes on to conclude that observations by witnesses suggest the existence of two—perhaps more—distinct types of craft: a triangular-shaped craft that has been seen in flight with F-117A stealth fighters; a high-speed aircraft exhibiting a deep, rumbling roar that may be more than a hundred feet long; and, possibly, a high-altitude model that travels at extremely high speeds, often appearing as a bright, sometimes pulsating light.

*Aviation Week* notes that observed flight characteristics provide "substantial evidence" of wholly new craft that employ "exotic propulsion and aerodynamic schemes not fully understood at this time." A Fiscal 1986 Procurement Program document mentions "Aurora," a code name for black-budget projects that hides specifics even from members of Congress who authorize funding. According to the document, the Fiscal 1986 budget request for "Aurora"—$80.1 million—soared to almost $2.3 *billion* in Fiscal 1987.[41]

Timothy B. Reynolds, a computer system manager, claims to have seen one of these revolutionary new craft up close. He says he saw a triangular-shaped craft inside a hangar at Ellington Air Force Base in the late 1960s. The craft reportedly had a thirty- to forty-foot wingspan and was absolutely streamlined with tricycle landing gear. Two engine inlets were observed, and the aircraft was "very rounded—with a molded look—and gray-colored."[42]

Additional confirmation of man-made UFOs comes from aviation writer James Goodall. "We are test-flying vehicles that defy description," an Air Force officer told Goodall. "We have things that are so far beyond the comprehension of the average aviation authority as to be really *alien* to our way of thinking [emphasis added]." Goodall also claims to have heard rumors of "force-field technology," "gravity-drive systems," as well as "flying saucer" designs.[43]

Which brings us to the matter of the Place With No Name. This locale is so hush-hush that the American government refuses to acknowledge its existence. It adjoins Nellis Air Force Base in the sunravaged Nevada desert, about eighty miles north-northwest of Las

Vegas. It is an otherwise picturesque place, located near a dry lake bed and majestic mountain ranges. On a clear night, stargazers might easily become intoxicated by the sight of faraway stars glowing like flawless precious stones in the velvety sky. But just don't try to catch a glimpse of the Place With No Name.

Prior to April 1995, people flocked to Freedom Ridge, which offered an unobstructed view of this place with no name. CNN's Larry King, Montel Williams, and other media types have conducted live remotes from the area and, like so many others, were placed under military surveillance. On numerous occasions, Freedom Ridge "pilgrims" have been subjected to verbal abuse and ordered off theses public lands by gun-toting military security officers.

Well, Freedom Ridge *used* to be on public lands. In October 1993, the Air Force asked Interior Secretary Bruce Babbitt to withdraw Freedom Ridge and White Sides Mountain, another frequent viewing spot, from public lands, citing the need to protect "the safe and secure operation" of the 3.5-million-acre Nellis Air Force range complex. In its extraordinary move to snatch up four thousand acres of public land, the Air Force was forced, at least obliquely, to acknowledge the existence of the Place With No Name, referring to it simply as "an operating location near Groom Dry Lake."

A year and half later, the Air Force got its wish. Freedom Ridge and White Sides Mountain were officially transferred from the Bureau of Land Management to the Air Force until at least November 2001. So much for snoopy taxpayers glimpsing the far-off hangars, barracks, antennas, and runways of the Place With No Name.

Or so the Air Force thought. Freedom Ridge viewers continue to view the strange goings-on of this place from another vantage point, Tikaboo Peak, thirteen miles away. Instead of binoculars, they now use telescopes which, despite the military's best efforts, provide a clear view of the secret facility.[44]

So why would anyone — anyone with a life, anyway — want to spend time watching the Place With No Name?

The answer is simple: it is rumored that UFOs — *recovered alien craft* — are being tested there. It is a fact that numerous sightings of saucer- and triangular-shaped craft have occurred in the area. It is also true that the Place With No Name has served as the home of American spy craft—specifically, the U-2 and SR-71. There are also rumors that the new generation of Aurora craft, backed by drastic increases in funding, are tested and flown there.[45]

In *Revelations* (Ballantine Books, 1991), astrophysicist Jacques Vallee speculates that the ballyhoo over UFOs here may be a deliberate disinformation campaign, orchestrated by the American military to distract the public's attention away from the true nature of the facility. Reports of flying saucers, back-engineered from captured alien craft, and the presence of "little bodies" at the top-secret installation are, according to Vallee, "planted by the military in an effort to thoroughly discredit the reports made by anyone who would observe the strange maneuvers of [the Aurora] aircraft, a development which they knew could not be effectively hidden from civilians in the vicinity."[46] Vallee adds that those spreading such disinformation should be viewed as *agents provocateur.*[47]

It is no secret that "UFOs" have frequently appeared in the skies over the Soviet Union, China, and Cuba, as well as high-profile trouble spots around the globe. These craft have shown up precisely where one would expect to find spy craft.

In 1978, news of a strange event that allegedly took place two decades earlier over Cuba was leaked by a security specialist, then attached to the 6947th Security Squadron at Homestead Air Force Base in Florida. The 6947th's mission was to monitor all Cuban Air Force communications and radar transmissions. According to this security man, in March 1967, 6947th intercept operators, fluent in Spanish, heard the voices of Cuban air defense radar controllers proclaiming that an unidentified object had been detected flying toward Cuba from the northeast. The UFO reportedly breached Cuban air space at an altitude of 33,000 feet and a speed of more than 600 miles per hour. Two Soviet-built MIG-21 jet fighters were scrambled.

The Cuban pilots approached to within three miles of the object. The flight leader reported to ground control that he could see a bright metallic sphere with no visible markings or appendages.* Ordered to destroy the craft, the leader armed his missiles and prepared to open

---

*U.S. intelligence agencies commonly "sterilize" spy craft. All insignia, serial numbers—even name tags on crew uniforms—are removed to avoid incrimination of the United States in the event of a crash. Weapons used are foreign-made, "sterilized" at special overseas facilities.

fire when, suddenly, his aircraft exploded. A wingman reported that the craft had simply disintegrated; no smoke or flames were observed. The object then accelerated and climbed to almost 100,000 feet (a favorite cruising altitude of spy craft) where it quickly streaked away from the tiny island on a south-southeast heading.

An Intelligence Spot Report was sent to National Security Agency (NSA) headquarters. Such reports are required in cases of suspected aircraft losses by hostile nations. The 6947th awaited a reply from NSA, also a part of standard operating procedures. But the 6947th never received a response; the detachment was told only to transfer all tapes and relevant information of the incident to NSA headquarters.

Robert Todd, a researcher opposing official UFO secrecy, found out about the case and formally requested confirmation from the Air Force, Navy, CIA, and NSA. He received no replies and, months later, informed the Air Force and NSA of his intentions to contact the Cuban government directly.

Two weeks later, two men identifying themselves as FBI agents visited Todd's home. Todd was read his rights and asked to sign a statement that he had been so advised. He waived his rights, whereupon the agents informed him of existing espionage laws. The agents asserted that violation of these laws carried penalties of life imprisonment, even death. They hinted darkly that Todd might be tried as a spy.

The agents grilled Todd on his sources for the Cuban incident. Todd refused to answer. By this time, perhaps unknown to the agents, the story had already been released to UPI.

Todd then asked some questions of his own. Was the Cuban story classified? The older of the two agents answered, "Some of the information is classified. Most of it is bullshit!"[48]

Which part of the story was bullshit? *The part implying the object was a UFO, not an American spy craft?*

Why would the government get so bent out of shape over just another UFO report? Hadn't the military establishment made it perfectly clear that it considered UFOs to be of no threat to national security? Had Todd, caught up in the zeal of ufology, inadvertently stumbled onto a secret spy mission of the U.S. military?

Let's consider some other "UFO" reports:

• **Tehran, Iran.** In the late 1970s, around the time of the attack on the American embassy by Muslim fundamentalists and the ensuing hostage crisis, an F-4 fighter plane was scrambled to intercept an unidentified flying object. As the Iranian pilot bore down on the object, his instrumentation and communications equipment went dead. When the F-4 turned away, the electronics returned to normal.

Another F-4 was sent aloft. As the fighter approached, the object released a large glowing mass. The ball of light — half the size of the full moon — sped toward the F-4. The F-4's pilot attempted to fire an AIM-9 missile at the light. But no go. Like the F-4 before it, weapons control and other electronics on board the fighter became inoperative.

The pilot broke off his pursuit, turning his aircraft away rapidly. The globe of light then returned to the original object.

Later another glob of light shot out of the object and appeared to settle on or just above the ground. A civil airliner approaching the area during the sighting also experienced electronic malfunctions.*[49]

• **Gorky, USSR.** Air-traffic controllers at Gorky Airport observed a grayish cigar-shaped object approaching them on the evening of March 27, 1983. The unknown object was about the size of a conventional aircraft, with no discernible wings or tail structure. Failing to respond to radio contact, the "UFO" coasted along at a speed up to 125 miles per hour at an altitude of 3,000 feet. Witnesses stated the object behaved erratically, flying forty-five miles to the southeast, then turning back toward the airport before finally vanishing twenty-five miles north of Gorky. The device was tracked on radar for forty minutes.[50]

• **Lanzhou, China.** On the evening of June 11, 1985, a Chinese Civil Aviation Administration Boeing 747 was in flight from Peking to Paris when the pilot and crew spotted an elliptical craft zipping across the jumbo jet's path. The object reportedly had an extremely bright spot in its center and was lined with three rows of bluish-white lights.

---

*Details of this case are contained in a U.S. Army Defense Intelligence Agency (DIA) message dated August 31, 1977. The DIA document was sought under a Freedom of Information Act (FOIA) request filed by teacher Charles Huffer. Initially, the DIA refused Huffer's request but, upon appeal, was forced to release contents of the previously classified document. See *The UFO Cover-Up* (Fireside, 1984).

According to the flight crew, the object illuminated an area of twenty-five to thirty miles.[51]

• **Chernobyl, USSR.** The catastrophe at the Chernobyl nuclear facility took place on April 26, 1986. The incident, with its global implications, was reported widely in the media. But five years later, another "accident" occurred at the power plant that received little publicity. On the evening of October 11, 1991, gas in a generator overheated, eventually causing an explosion. Fire swept through the facility. Before flames were extinguished, the nuclear plant's roof was severely damaged.

Just prior to the explosion, several witnesses sighted a glowing object hovering over the facility. Following up on the disaster, a Soviet reporter arrived on the scene to photograph the building housing the damaged generator. He later had the film developed and observed a large, disk-shaped object hovering in the sky over the building. Soviet internal affairs investigators examined the film, ruling out film or processing defects as the cause of the image.[52]

Are aircraft and weapons systems known to the public simply a cover for even more advanced and exotic technologies? Are monies appropriated for current technologies being rechanneled into "black" — off-the-books — projects? Is the American public, perhaps even Congress, being hoodwinked by the American military establishment?

Former Navy jet mechanic Tony Gonsalves, for one, thinks that at least one item of military hardware — the controversial B-2 bomber — is as phony as a three-dollar bill.

The Air Force has publicly claimed that its on-and-off-again-funded bomber represents a "quantum leap in aviation technology." But does it?

Gonsalves has scrutinized specifications of the B-2. And therein, according to Gonsalves, lies the rub. In a May 1990 report, he pointed out that the maximum weight of the bomber is supposed to be 367,000 pounds, a weight too massive for the plane's ten tires. It is a fact that during the bomber's planned maiden flight, it never made it down the runway, its nose wheel sinking into the tarmac.

Gonsalves noticed something else. The B-2 is supposed to store 28,000 gallons of fuel. This in itself would take up 227,000 pounds of weight, leaving too little room for the actual aircraft structure, flight crew, and bomb payload.

Commenting on Gonsalves' report, British UFO researcher Graham Birdsall notes: "Since the B-2 aircraft was rolled out, it has had flight-control problems. It does not have the flight range as previously claimed. With a top speed of 500 mph, it's impossible to achieve what the Air Force claimed, namely, the B-2 can deliver its armed payload anywhere in the world within five hours.*

"The amount spent on research [and] development of the B-2, according to official figures, is $22.4 billion — that translates to $100 for every American man, woman and child...."

Birdsall adds that during the B-2's initial roll-out ceremony, it was announced that by 1992, forty-four of the aircraft would be in service. "Two years after the B-2 was unveiled," he points out, "only four aircraft have been built, and between them, [have] recorded only 600 flying hours."[54]

Birdsall made these remarks in England in 1991. Since then, the entire B-2 program is estimated to have skyrocketed to $70 billion.[55] *Where has all the money gone?*

Gonsalves claimed that the B-2 program is a "cut-and-paste job," with much of its funding having been sunk into another, altogether different version of the aircraft. This secret version of the B-2, possibly nuclear-powered, is capable of performing maneuvers "beyond our current understanding," says Birdsall, referring to Gonsalves' findings.[56]

Military spending, for sure, continues to skyrocket. In 1991, the year we "won" the Cold War, U.S. military expenditures reached $311 billion. Since that time, the budget has not decreased significantly, despite the lack of any real threat.

*Vanity Fair* contributing editor Andrew Cockburn has sounded a cautionary note with respect to the military-industrial complex. Notes Cockburn: "With such meager budget cuts, how is it that our actual combat forces are disappearing at a much faster rate?"

---

*The problems apparently don't end there. According to the U.S. General Accounting Office, the bomber has radar that can't distinguish a rain cloud from a mountainside, has not passed most of its basic tests and may not be impervious to radar, as claimed. After fourteen years, "the Air Force has yet to demonstrate that the B-2 design will meet some of its most important mission requirements," a GAO draft report concludes, according to the *New York Times* (July 16, 1995).

Cockburn points out that the Army has lost about forty percent of its combat battalions since 1990. Air Force strength, he states, is down even more — fifty percent. Furthermore, the Navy's active fleet has shrunk from 546 ships five years ago to 361 today.

Says Cockburn: "The problem is that the apparent goal of our defense effort is to direct as much money as possible into corporate coffers. The Pentagon is thus spending huge sums on high-tech research and development projects....

"Back in the Reagan days, such raids on the Treasury drew obloquy from the press and Congress. Nowadays almost no one seems to care, especially those in the Pentagon and White House."[57]

In 1995 the military received from Congress even more money than it requested. Curiously, this was one of the few department budgets receiving swift White House approval that year.

On December 15, 1995, the first C-130 aircraft, loaded with American peacekeeping troops, took off from Germany and *attempted* to land in war-torn Tuzla, Bosnia. Poor visibility over the touchdown area forced the plane to return to base. The plane carrying those troops was *twenty-five years old* and its radar system was so antiquated that its crew was unable to execute a landing that even commercial airliners are able to accomplish with relative ease.[58]

Tragedy was averted this time, but not four months later when Commerce Secretary Ron Brown and thirty-two others died aboard a military transport plane that slammed into a mountainside while on final approach to Dubrovnik airport in Croatia. Although weather conditions were poor, at least two other aircraft — commercial flights — had landed safely at the airport in the half-hour before the military jet's approach. The twin-engine CT-43, the military version of the Boeing 737-200, was not equipped with modern flight data or cockpit voice recorders and had been in service for *twenty-two years,* admitted a Pentagon spokesperson.*[59]

Military funding certainly isn't being invested in our enlisted men and women. Or in the military hardware that's responsible for

---

*This ill-fated CT-43 was attached to a fleet assigned to transport military and industry personnel with top-secret clearances. According to the *Air Force Times,* CT-43s routinely ferry top-level officials from McCarran Airport in Las Vegas to the secret Groom Lake facility.

transporting them and others safely around the globe. It's going somewhere else.

As Goodall put it: "We are flying vehicles that defy description...." Or, to put it another way — *costly flying vehicles that remain hidden from the American taxpayer.*

# 4

# Warning: It Has Been Determined That UFOs May Be Hazardous to Your Health

*Let us remember that "if we suffer tamely a lawless attack upon our liberty, we encourage it, and involve others in our doom." It is a very serious consideration...that millions yet unborn may be the miserable sharers of the event.*

—Samuel Adams

On the morning of June 30, 1908, a thermonuclear explosion—equivalent to a ten-megaton hydrogen bomb—destroyed a vast section of the Tungus forests in Siberia. In the wake of the explosion, a voluminous mushroom-shaped cloud billowed high overhead. The blast could be heard in Kansk, five hundred miles away. Windows were shattered and roofs were blown off houses. Huge waves lashed the banks of the Angara River. Seismographs around the world recorded earth tremors and, for three nights, an eerie glow lit up the night sky across Europe. In Moscow, one could take photos at midnight.

Local villagers reported seeing an enormous ball of fire—as dazzling as the sun—traveling slowly through the sky just prior to the explosion. Eyewitnesses said that the object slowed down and changed course as it passed overhead. The enormous fireball consumed tens of millions of trees, incinerated vast herds of reindeer, and left lifeless twelve million square miles of soil.

Trees at the explosion's epicenter were twisted and mangled, bereft of branches and foliage. Some trees, their tops turned to charcoal, remained rooted, jutting up like dead poles. Trees further away from the epicenter lay on the ground, with the tops of the trees uniformly pointing away from the epicenter, confirming the blast's horrendous shock wave.

Early on, Soviet scientist V. Fessenkov concluded that the Tungus explosion was the result of a meteorite, but this theory was quickly

41

discounted as expeditions to the site failed to uncover any fragments of the killer bolide. A comet, then? Scientists latched on to this theory as well. But the theory, like the one before it, was seriously flawed. If a comet had crashed into the earth, it surely would have been sighted by astronomers — or casual observers of the heavens, for that matter — long before plowing into the frozen forests of Siberia. No such luminous body was sighted anywhere prior to the explosion. Furthermore, a comet — or meteorite — would not slow down and change course within the earth's atmosphere.

Whatever ripped into the Siberian Tungus was powerful and *highly radioactive*. Physicist Clyde Cowan and Nobel prize-winning chemist Willard Libby confirmed the presence of radioactivity in trees as far away as Arizona. There, tree rings of old Douglas firs, corresponding to the time of the Tungus explosion, were found to contain significantly elevated levels of radioactive carbon-14.

Additional evidence of radioactivity caused by the Tungus event was presented in 1969 by Soviet scientists conducting flora studies of the area. They discovered that forty- to fifty-year-old trees — those that had germinated in the wake of the explosion — had attained heights normally expected to occur only after the passage of two hundred to three hundred years, indicating severe radiation effects. Furthermore, trees surviving the explosion were found to have undergone a four-fold increase in girth after 1908.

But most astonishing are the findings of the Valga Geographical Institute. There Soviet scientists examined more than one hundred sections of trees from the disaster area. The outer ten to fifteen rings of each section, corresponding to 1908 and thereafter, showed unmistakable signs of radioactivity. Not just radioactivity, but evidence of *artificial radioactive isotopes,* key man-made components of nuclear weapons.[1]

Are we, therefore, to conclude that a thermonuclear device was detonated in Siberia in 1908, nearly forty years before the creation of the Manhattan Project and the subsequent destruction of Hiroshima and Nagasaki?

There is compelling evidence that numerous advances in weapon systems have, in fact, become operational long before their existence has been made public. Consider the case of inventor Nikola Tesla, a pioneer in the field of electrical energy. In July 1934, Tesla, then seventy-eight, met with *New York Times* reporters at the Hotel New Yorker. During the interview, he made a startling claim: he had invented a weapon capable of generating and transmitting highly concentrated particles of energy, which could "kill without trace." He further boasted that the weapon "will bring down a fleet of 10,000 enemy airplanes at a distance of 250 miles from a defending nation's border and will cause armies of millions to drop dead in their tracks."[2]

Was Tesla just blowing smoke, or was he perhaps seeking potential buyers for a new deadly technology — particle-beam weaponry — that would only be hinted at publicly by the American military a half-century later?

In 1905, Tesla was granted U.S. Patent 787,412 for a device capable of transmitting "electrical energy through the natural mediums."[3] He had already invented, in the late 1880s, the power source known as alternating current (AC). In 1915, the *New York Times* reported that Tesla had filed patent applications for a weapon that was akin to "Thor's shooting thunderbolts." Tesla claimed that the weapon was capable of transmitting electrical energy that could "produce destructive effects at a distance."

Said Tesla: "I have already constructed a wireless transmitter which makes this possible…. With transmitters of this kind we are enabled to project electrical energy in any amount to any distance and apply it for innumerable purposes, both in peace and war. Through the universal adoption of this system, ideal conditions for the maintenance of law and order will be realized, for then the energy necessary to the enforcement of right and justice will be normally productive, yet potential, and in any moment, available for attack and defense."[4] In another *New York Times* interview, conducted in 1940, Tesla reiterated that his "teleforce" was capable of destroying aircraft at a distance of 250 miles. The "beam," he added, actually consisted of four separate inventions, *"two of which already have been tested* [emphasis added]."[5]

Was Tesla letting the proverbial cat out of the bag?

Science writer Oliver Nichelson is convinced that an energy beam unleashed by Tesla was, in fact, responsible for the devastation of the Tungus forests. According to Nichelson, Tesla, after being rebuffed by financial backer J. P. Morgan, directed his energy device — located on Long Island, New York — toward Admiral Peary and his expeditionary force approaching the North Pole. His intention may have been to put on a dramatic light show for the expedition in order to garner attention for his free-energy device.

Nichelson and International Tesla Society president J. W. McGinniss both assert that Tesla succeeded with his demonstration. Perhaps too well.

Nichelson and McGinniss speculate that Tesla may have miscalculated the effects of gravity on the directed beam of energy, causing it to pass over the North Pole and, instead, rip into Siberia. Nichelson points out that Tesla's research facility on Long Island, the North Pole, and the Tungus forests of Siberia form a straight line, strongly suggesting a Tesla connection to the 1908 disaster.[6]

Tesla, after all, boasted that his "death ray" had been tested. Resulting in the Tungus incident, one wonders?

We may never know if Tesla was involved, for in 1943, the day after his death, FBI agents broke into his home and illegally confiscated all his scientific papers and effects. All his files disappeared that day and have not been seen since, giving rise to speculation that the U.S. government went on to develop Tesla's revolutionary — and deadly — weapons system.[7]

It is with Tesla in mind that we must consider one of the more disturbing aspects of UFOs — namely, the deleterious effects of the elusive objects upon people and man-made devices. There are numerous UFO incidents involving incapacitated aircraft, automobiles, electrical power stations, and air-traffic control facilities, as well as significant injuries — sometimes fatal — to humans. These occurrences, which have steadily increased since the close of World War II, cannot be easily dismissed.

On June 16, 1948, amid growing U.S.-Soviet hostilities, one of the Soviet Air Force's most highly decorated pilots, Arcade Apraksin, was testing a new jet aircraft when he reportedly encountered a "cucumber-shaped" object emitting strange beams of light. Apraksin notified ground control, which instructed the pilot to approach and fire on the object if it refused to land.

Apraksin soared ahead and suddenly the light beams "opened up in a fan," temporarily blinding the airman. The aircraft's electrical systems then shut off, forcing Apraksin to glide to safety as the UFO shot off into the clouds.

The following year, Apraksin was on another test flight when he sighted a similar object. The object directed beams of light toward him, causing his jet to again experience electrical malfunctions. But this time, the "UFO attack" was more severe—the cockpit canopy of Apraksin's jet was damaged, resulting in a loss of air pressure. The pilot managed an emergency landing and then lost consciousness.[8]

Previously secret documents, released recently under the Freedom of Information Act, reveal that the CIA actively monitored Soviet responses to such incidents. One classified memorandum, sent from the CIA's assistant director of operations to Allen Dulles on August 22, 1952, reported on the results of a two-year search of Soviet press reports on UFOs. The memo recorded comments made during a Moscow broadcast the previous year in which it was stated that a U.S. Naval Research Bureau chief had allegedly concluded that UFOs were secret American devices used to "fan war hysteria in [the Soviet Union]."* On September 11, 1952, H. Marshall Chadwell, CIA Assistant Director of Scientific Intelligence, fired off a classified memorandum to then-CIA Director General Walter Bedell Smith, stressing intelligence "problems," including the "present level of Russian knowledge regarding these phenomena" and "possible Soviet intentions and capabilities to utilize these phenomena to the detriment of US security interests."[9]

During the summer of 1982, China—another of America's adversaries—was inundated by reports of UFOs. On June 18, five Chinese Air Force pilots on patrol over North China's military frontier suddenly encountered a UFO the size of the full moon. It grew even larger as it approached the startled pilots.

One pilot reported that the object generated "rings of light." He described what appeared like fire at the core of the rings. During the encounter, the Chinese jet fighters experienced electrical malfunctions, affecting navigation and communications systems.[10]

Strange aerial encounters have continued over the Soviet Union in recent years. On March 21, 1990, Soviet Defense Forces jets were

---

*It should be noted that the authors of the USAF's Project Grudge Report (1949), discussed in the previous chapter, secretly urged the sharing of findings with the "Psychological Warfare Division and other government agencies interested in *psychological warfare* [emphasis added]." You will recall that the Robertson Panel, convened later by the CIA, was particularly intrigued by psychological warfare and UFOs.

dispatched to intercept a fast-moving object over Moscow. The speed of the unknown device was estimated to be 3,000 miles per hour. Soviet Army General Ivan Tretyak, then Deputy Minister of Defense, later stated that the pursuit was broken off for fear the object might possess "formidable capabilities for retaliation." He added that radar aboard one of the interceptors became inoperative. Tretyak immediately suspected that the object was a product of American stealth technology, noting darkly that *"measures which we are now taking [to counter the American stealth program] will simultaneously promote the solution to the UFO riddle* [emphasis added]."[11]

On June 30, 1987, the U.S. Department of State released a cable claiming that "Soviet authorities have constructed an SDI [Strategic Defense Initiative] research station near the Radio-Physics Institute in the area of Stavropol. The research station apparently is focusing its work on electromagnetic methods of shooting down satellites. When tests are run, the resulting microwaves can be detected by scientists working at the Radio-Physics Institute. *Perhaps of equal interest is that this area has the largest number of UFO sightings in the USSR* [emphasis added]...."[12]

Were these the countermeasures alluded to by General Tretyak? Was this the Soviets' response to brazen overflights by advanced American surveillance craft, perhaps? Has a secret aerial conflict been ongoing between East and West?

In June 1982, a particularly destructive pair of UFOs was allegedly sighted over the Soviet space center at Baikonur. If true, the incident is one of the most bizarre ever reported. According to Soviet scientists Drs. Alexei Zolotov and Vladimir Azhazha, one of the two UFOs appeared suddenly and hovered briefly over the principal launch pad. The following day, support towers were found to be severely damaged — bolts and rivets had somehow popped out, and welds had come apart. The other UFO reportedly hovered over the facility's housing complex, shattering thousands of panes of glass.[13]

In her book *The UFO Controversy* (Barnes & Noble, 1993), Jenny Randles tells of an equally harrowing incident, this time over Great Britain's Rendlesham Forest, the site of secret NATO operations and a virtual mecca for UFO sightings. According to Randles, a Britten-Norman Trislander cargo plane, en route from Stansted to Amsterdam, was in stable flight at 5,000 feet when suddenly the pilot felt a "bump" in the controls. One of the aircraft's four engines then inexplicably seized up.

When the aircraft landed in Holland, an inspection showed substantial damage to the engine. Metal fragments were imbedded in the plane's fuselage.

Britain's Civil Aviation Authority noted that one of the holes was "four inches by one-half inch" and that "three items" were recovered from the plane's hull, one of which was magnetic. The CAA could offer no explanation as to the cause of the damage, adding that ground radar had picked up no other aircraft or "identifiable objects" at the time of the disruption. "Of course, that means there *were* other targets on the radar," writes Randles, "...and that one of these 'unidentified objects' may have been of considerable interest." Speculation followed that "military objects" may have been involved.[14]

In the summer of 1995, the flight crew aboard an Aerolineas Argentinas passenger plane, during final approach to Bariloche Airport in Argentina, spotted a luminous object rapidly approaching their position. The pilot, fearing a collision, took evasive action. The object then fell in alongside the airliner. As the airliner and UFO approached the runway, all electrical power at the airport failed and a nearby town was plunged into darkness. With the runway lights suddenly extinguished, the plane aborted the landing and was able to land only during a tense second approach.*

---

*Throughout 1995, radar systems at America's largest commercial airports experienced an unprecedented number of power failures. During the summer, airports in New York, Chicago, Washington, and elsewhere "went black," greatly imperiling airline passengers and crews, according to union officials representing air-traffic controllers. In Miami, seven outages were recorded during a single three-week period. On July 16, radar complexes at airports in six states inexplicably malfunctioned. Lauren McCormack, an air-traffic controller at O'Hare Airport in Chicago, resigned in protest over the aggravated blackouts. And the outages continued in 1996. On January 6, according to the Associated Press, a massive power failure struck Seattle Center, affecting at least fifty airplanes flying over the Pacific Northwest and causing flight delays on the ground. During the outage, Seattle controllers were out of contact with aircraft over a 286,000-square-mile area, including Washington, most of Oregon, northern Idaho, western Montana, and part of Northern California. The FAA said the cause of the severe outage "remained under investigation."

Eyewitnesses said the mystery object was about the same size as the airliner. Bright flashing lights shone from the belly of the craft. The object was reportedly seen by the flight crew and most of the passengers on board, as well as military personnel and observers in the airport's control tower. The UFO disappeared after shooting straight up into the sky at a tremendous speed.[15]

Years earlier, in September 1959, tragedy struck the crew and passengers of Braniff Airlines Flight 542 during a late-night commute from Houston to Dallas, Texas. Southeast of the farming community of Buffalo, the Electra airliner suddenly exploded and crashed in flames. All twenty-seven passengers and a crew of six on board were killed.[16]

Wreckage of the plane was strewn along a fourteen-thousand-foot path. Pieces of wing, propellers, engines, stabilizers, gear boxes, and unrecognizable, seared shapes lined the pathway of destruction. All that remained of the forward fuselage were crushed metal remnants, two feet square or smaller, which fanned out for a distance of two hundred feet. The nose of the airliner was stuffed in a four-foot-deep crater. The plane's cockpit was thoroughly demolished.[17]

The accident site presented a grisly scene. Hunks of wreckage and bodies, grossly mutilated, hung from large trees along the crash path. Braniff's chief of operations, R. V. Carleton, later told newsmen: "I've investigated lots of crashes, but I've never seen one where the plane was so thoroughly demolished, the wreckage so widely scattered and the people so horribly mangled. And there was nothing among the wreckage which indicated a fire or bomb aboard the plane."[18]

One eyewitness reported the sudden appearance of a "white light" just before the airliner exploded in flames and crashed. The sound of the explosion rattled the ground like a sonic boom.

The official report of the Civil Aeronautics Board noted:

> That the aircraft broke up violently is self-evident. That the breakup process was both quick and with little or no warning is also clear for two reasons. First, only one of the 37 aircraft's passenger seats recognizable as such was found with the safety belt fastened, and this probably means there was no time to order their fastening. Second, the final radio message preceded the breakup by an interval of something less than two minutes and that message gave no hint of trouble.

A definite sequence of failures and breakages appears discernible.... Separation of the left wing and the No. 1 gear box propeller...occurred at about the same time; it is impossible to say which went first. The horizontal stabilizer then broke up under the impact of parts coming from the wing; wing planking from the right wing tip came free; the No. 4 power plant tore loose; and the right wing outboard of No. 4 separated. All of these events happened in a short period of time. Somewhat later, at much lower altitudes, the fuselage broke in two separate portions at a point about halfway back....

CAB investigators concluded that there was "no positive indication of the cause" of the crash. Examination of hydraulic and electrical system components of the downed Electra revealed no indication of operational stress. No abnormal heat patterns, indicating excessive braking action, were noted, and no evidence of fire or overheating was observed during the inspection of recovered radio components. Sabotage was also ruled out.

"Much of the information...is of a negative nature insofar as the probable cause of this accident is concerned," the CAB report added. "The aircraft itself was virtually new and had not needed appreciable maintenance work; that which had been accomplished had been signed off in accordance with established practices." As for the white light sighted before the crash, investigators conceded that its appearance "cannot be reconciled."[19]

Equally baffling is the case of Meal 88, a USAF B-52 bomber that vanished off the Texas coast amid a flurry of UFO reports. On the day of the bomber's disappearance, several people working in downtown Corpus Christi saw a strange object hovering over the Gulf of Mexico. One witness observed that the object was gigantic and shaped like a "huge dome." The object was shrouded in a peculiar cloudy vapor. Soon single-engine jets reportedly burst onto the scene and began circling the massive object. As the principal witness put it, the jets appeared "like gnats circling a turtle."[20]

Meal 88 departed Carswell Air Force Base, Fort Worth, at 6:30 P.M. CST on February 28, 1968. The bomber's crew was assigned to the 7th Bomb Wing, Strategic Air Command. Meal 88's mission: to proceed to Matagorda Island, near Corpus Christi, and simulate bombing runs over a designated target site.

Shortly after 7:00, Meal 88 was over the target. Command pilot Frank Salavarria eased the giant bomber upward. The crew was now ready for its first simulated high-level bomb release over Matagorda Island.

But then trouble hit. Radar aboard the aircraft went haywire. Matagorda Ground Control was advised of the situation, but Salavarria was nevertheless instructed to carry out the bombing run. Navigator Charles Roberts, meanwhile, struggled unsuccessfully to repair the malfunction.

Salavarria next positioned the plane for a mock low-level bomb release. Suddenly the radar failed completely. A radio call went out to Matagorda.

> MEAL 88: Meal 88 is going to abort. I've lost my radar picture.... I'm aborting for safety, aborting for safety. Over.
> MATAGORDA: Roger. Type I abort for safety.
> MEAL 88: That's affirmative. We have no radar picture. We are IFR. I'm maintaining 1,200 feet. Have you got a drop line to Houston center?
> MATAGORDA: Roger. Go ahead with info. I'll relay.
> MEAL 88: Roger. Tell them we'll fly our normal departure.... We're canceling our other two releases due to radar. Over.

Salavarria received clearance to climb to 5,000 feet. At 2,500 feet, the radar snapped back on. The crew completed two bombing passes around 11:00. Meal 88 again radioed Matagorda.

> MEAL 88: Are we cleared off heading bomb plot?
> MATAGORDA: Roger. You're cleared from heading...88, how do you read this radio check, please?
> MEAL 88: Loud and clear. 88.
> MATAGORDA: Roger. You're loud and clear also. Thank you.
> MEAL 88: Rog. 88.

That was Meal 88's last transmission. The bomber and its crew were never seen again.[21]

An extensive search of the area was conducted by the Coast Guard, U.S. Navy, and a rescue team headed by Colonel William M. McDonald of the Search and Rescue Center at Roberts-Gebaur Air Force Base.

Nothing was found. No oil slicks or verifiable wreckage of any kind. A tiny raft — the only item spotted by rescue planes — turned out to be from a boat. Meal 88 had vanished.[22]

Less than two weeks after the disappearance, several pieces of metal were found near Padre Island and Port Isabel, southwest of the target site.[23] The Boeing Company, designers of the bomber, examined the specimens, concluding that they were fragments from an upper-wing structure of a B-52.[24]

Carswell Air Force Base officials stated that the pieces of metal were not ones that could come loose during normal flight. Furthermore, Colonel McDonald noted that one of the metal fragments was jagged and scorched on the edges. The fragment showed signs of a violent explosion.[25]

It is apparent that electrical systems of all kinds react adversely to UFOs. This may be due to the propulsion systems these unknown devices employ, or perhaps something more sinister.

Electrical power grids seem to be a favorite target of UFOs. In early November 1965, the northeastern United States and portions of Canada were suddenly thrust into darkness as a massive electrical power grid, invulnerable even to nuclear attack, mysteriously failed. The Great Blackout engulfed an eighty-thousand-square-mile area, leaving thirty million people groping in the dark. New York, Buffalo, Rochester, Albany, Providence, Boston, and Toronto were without power for hours. In New York alone, losses as a result of the blackout hit a staggering $100 million.

*Key military commands located in the area, including Strategic Air Command and North American Air Defense Command bases, were unaffected by the devastating blackout, and no alert was issued, despite real concerns that the blackout had been the result of sabotage.*[26]

At the precise moment of the blackout, Weldon Ross, a private pilot and instructor, and a student pilot were preparing for a landing at Syracuse when they observed a large red ball of light — about one hundred feet in diameter — hanging in the sky directly over two 345,000-volt power lines at the New York Power Authority's Clay substation, the source of the massive disruption, according to reports issued that evening. The Federal Power Commission later said they would investigate the sighting, but issued no follow-up announcements.[27]

A plague of blackouts struck the world that year. On November 16, only days following the Great Blackout, a series of power outages struck England, including numerous sections of London.[28] Then on November 26, power failures hit St. Paul, Minnesota, occurring simultaneously with the appearance of bluish-glowing lights just north of the city. House lights and appliances in the vicinity of the object went dead, and a motorist reported that his car lights and radio went out. The blackout was never explained.[29]

Later, on December 2, Juárez, Mexico, and portions of Texas and New Mexico lost all electrical power and, again, on December 4, sections of East Texas — more than forty thousand homes — were plunged into darkness.[30] On December 26, Buenos Aires went dark, trapping hundreds in the city's subways, and, across the globe, Finland experienced widespread blackouts.[31] Earlier that year, in September, electrical power in Cuernavaca, Mexico, failed just as a disk-shaped object was sighted hovering low over the city.[32]

On the evening of September 12, 1979, amid a flurry of UFO activity, a complete power failure blacked out Xuginglong and Huaihua City in the Hunan Province of China. Within moments of the power failure, a bright flying object appeared overhead, emitting downward rays of white light. Then, suddenly, the object raced silently away.[33]

Which brings us to the matter of UFO vehicle-interference cases. Since the early days of Kenneth Arnold, a deluge of reports involving severe electromagnetic effects on vehicles — automobiles, trucks, motorcycles, boats — has been recorded. One extensive study, conducted by Mark Rodeghier, lists well over four hundred cases.[34] Of all the cases listed by Rodeghier, eighty-two percent involved electromagnetic interference — i.e., failure of engines, lights, or other electrical equipment, such as radios.[35] A smaller percentage involved loss of command of the vehicle or, in some cases, the outright destruction of engines and/or electrical equipment.[36] Rodeghier's study lists thirty-one cases where the affected vehicle was hit with a light beam[37] and, in nearly one hundred cases, witnesses experienced odd physiological effects, ranging from heat effects to paralysis.[38]

Researcher James McCampbell has suggested that microwave radiation, emitted by UFOs, may be the cause of the extraordinary effects observed in vehicle-interference cases. He has demonstrated his theory by exposing filaments of headlights—commonly affected in these cases—to microwaves. With intense enough radiation, he has successfully interrupted current flow and caused the lights to extinguish.[39]

Let's now take a look at some vehicle-interference cases.

• **Levelland, Texas (November 2–3, 1957).** Two witnesses, driving north of the city, spotted a glowing, torpedo-shaped object approaching them. As the object passed overhead, the car's motor and lights failed. The witnesses got out of the car and experienced a tremendous heat wave that forced them to "hit the ground." When the object finally departed, the automobile functioned normally.[40]

An hour later, a witness driving along the outskirts of town noticed a peculiar object resting in the middle of the road. The object, about two hundred feet across, was egg-shaped and glowed brightly. As he approached the device, the car's engine and lights failed. The object then shot off into the air and disappeared. Five minutes later, another driver, several miles away, reported that he, too, had sighted a two-hundred-foot-long object on the road. Similarly, his car's engine and lights failed and did not function normally until the object departed.[41]

About the same time, a college student was driving outside Levelland when his car's engine and lights suddenly failed. Getting out to check under the hood, he was startled to see an egg-shaped craft, seventy-five to one hundred feet long, resting on the road. The object then disappeared, and the student was able to again start his car. Fifteen minutes later, still another witness spotted the same or a similar object resting on a dirt road nine miles north of town. His car stalled. The glowing object then raced up into the sky and disappeared. Following the object's abrupt exit, the witness was able to start his car.[42]

Numerous other witnesses reported sightings of strange glowing craft that evening. A truck driver in the area reported seeing an object—also egg-shaped and about two hundred feet long—on the ground that glowed "like a neon sign." As in the other sightings, the truck driver's engine and lights shut off but returned to normal when the object departed.[43]

More than a dozen witnesses—including police and sheriff's deputies—sighted strange objects or flashes of light that evening.[44]

• **Sanlucar de Barrameda, Spain (March 23, 1974).** A bright, metallic object approached an automobile driven by the chauffeur of the president of the Cadiz Provincial Commission. The driver reported that the object "moved up with great brilliancy." As the UFO drew nearer, he experienced an odd sensation. The car inexplicably slowed and wavered back and forth "like a feather."

Richard Fox, Acting U.S. Defense Attaché in Madrid, sent a report of this and twenty-eight other Spanish UFO incidents from 1973 and 1974 to the Defense Intelligence Agency (DIA), the U.S. military's equivalent of the CIA.[45]

• **Jessup, Maryland (July 8, 1977).** A farm worker was operating a tractor when a round, silver-domed object with "green windows" passed overhead. He reportedly watched the strange object for almost half an hour while it moved erratically over the area. The tractor then stalled, and the device flew away. The worker observed that the tractor was not prone to stalling and that it could idle for hours.[46]

• **Stephen, Minnesota (August 27, 1979).** Ten miles west of town, a thirty-five-year-old policeman saw a light hovering just above the ground near a grove of trees. Curiously, he drove toward the unknown object and, suddenly, it zoomed toward him and hit the car. The policeman then lost consciousness.

When he awoke, he discovered that his car's windshield was broken and the radio antenna was bent. The car was sprawled across the roadway. His eyes stung.

Inexplicably, both the car clock and his wristwatch were running fourteen minutes slow.[47]

• **Uttoxeter, England (early 1995).** A young man was riding his motorcycle on the way to work when he began to encounter engine problems. He pulled off the quiet country road, seeking a pay phone to summon help. Immediately, he was bathed in a vivid white light. Looking up, he saw a "huge square," filled with "superstructures and spotlights," hovering about thirty feet overhead.

The square dimmed slightly and began to move away. As it departed, the cyclist observed that the object was actually pyramid-shaped. He had been underneath its base, he concluded.

The motorcycle refused to start and the young man was forced to walk it home. A later examination, with witnesses present, revealed that the motorcycle, still inoperative, had somehow become magnetized. A Zippo lighter held nearby leaped out of its owner's hand and stuck to the bike's gas tank.

The day following the harrowing encounter, the young man fell ill and, two days later, developed a curious rash. As time passed, his condition worsened. Severe fatigue set in, his vision became distorted, and his fingers tingled. Although exhibiting classic symptoms of radiation poisoning, he was told by an attending physician that he had "a virus."[48]

This incident brings to mind the case of Stephen Michalak. Shortly after noon on May 20, 1967, Michalak, a fifty-year-old industrial mechanic, was enjoying some weekend prospecting near Falcon Lake, Manitoba, when he was distracted by the squawking of nearby geese. Looking up, he was surprised to see two disk-shaped objects descending from the southwest. One of the objects began to hover near the ground, while its companion landed about 160 feet away.

Michalak noted that the objects were domed and about forty feet in diameter. The landed craft changed colors from glowing red to the iridescence of hot stainless steel. An intense purplish light shone from apertures around the dome. The craft had no markings.

Observing the craft, Michalak began to notice wafts of warm air and the smell of sulfur. An odd hissing sound emanated from the object.

Michalak eventually approached the craft and heard humanlike voices from within. Assuming it was a secret American device, he called forth in English. Getting no response, he tried again, this time in Russian, German, Italian, French, and Ukrainian. The voices suddenly ceased.

The mechanic poked his head inside the craft's hatch and observed honeycombed interior walls that were about twenty inches thick. A panel then slid over the hatch, cutting off his view.

Michalak next touched the craft with a gloved hand, causing the fingertips of the gloves to become burned. Abruptly the craft tilted slightly and started to spin rapidly. As it spun, an exhaust vent on the craft gushed forth heat, burning his upper abdomen and setting his shirt and undershirt on fire.

Panicked, Michalak tore off his upper garments, threw them to the ground and stamped out the fire. His shirt was all but destroyed, but he succeeded in saving remnants of his undershirt. A cap he was wearing was also burned.

Soon thereafter, the craft took off, disappearing in the direction from which it had come.

Michalak began to feel ill. His head ached and he experienced cold sweats and nausea. Weak and vomiting, he struggled to a nearby highway for help. There he requested assistance from an RCMP constable who was driving by. Thinking that Michalak was drunk, the constable refused assistance. Michalak then returned to his motel and took a bus home to Winnipeg.

His condition worsened. He also became aware of a wretched stench from his lungs. His appetite withered, and he experienced a rapid loss of weight.

Two days following his encounter, he sought medical assistance and was hospitalized. During the next seven days, he lost twenty-two pounds.[49]

Blood tests confirmed that the mechanic's lymphocyte count was down from twenty-five to sixteen percent, only returning to normal after four weeks. Medical reports also documented the presence of "hive-like areas with impetiginous centers" on his body, as well as "atypical lymphoid cells in the marrow." The "awful stench" lingered, and he continued to feel nauseated, dizzy, and fatigued. He furthermore experienced numbness and chronic swelling in his joints.

In August 1968, Michalak visited the Mayo Clinic in Minnesota. There it was confirmed that he had neurological dermatitis and syncope (fainting spells), caused by exacerbation of a preexisting heart condition. Psychiatric testing showed no signs of psychotic or other emotional disorders.[50]

Michalak was examined by numerous physicians and medical specialists in Canada and the U.S. None was ever able to offer any logical explanation for his condition.*

---

*In 1978, I was informed by a Canadian government official that Michalak continued to feel ill ten years after his encounter. About this same time, I visited the offices of the National Research Council in Ottawa and was able to secure the release of previously secret Canadian UFO files, considered "missing" for thirty years. Among the

Dr. Horace Dudley, former chief of the Radioisotope Laboratory at New York's U.S. Naval Hospital believes that the symptoms displayed by Michalak are "a classical picture of severe whole body [exposure to] radiation...."

"I would guess," said Dr. Dudley, "that Mr. Michalak received in the order of 100-200 roentgens. It is very fortunate that this dose of radiation only lasted a very short time or he would certainly have received a lethal dose...."[51]

Another well-documented case also involves possible radiation poisoning by a UFO. The date: December 29, 1980. The place: Southeast Texas.

On that evening, Dayton resident Vickie Landrum, fifty-seven, her seven-year-old grandson, Colby, and a friend, Betty Cash, fifty-two, were driving on a lonely rural road about twenty miles northeast of Houston when they suddenly noticed a bright light in the sky ahead of them. As they drove closer, they could now see that the light was actually an immense metallic, diamond-shaped craft.

The object swooped down over the road in front of them. The sky lit up.

Betty, the driver, slammed on the brakes. The three then got out of the car to look at the object. As they gawked skyward, they were bathed in scorching heat as the object roared and emitted a curious beeping sound.

Colby became terrified and Vickie returned with him to the car. Betty remained outside. When she finally returned to the car moments later, she had to use a jacket to hold the door handle, which had become red hot. The car's interior was sweltering, despite the crisp forty-degree temperature outside.

Eventually the object rose and moved away from the frightened trio. As the fiery intruder departed, a contingent of twenty or more large helicopters appeared on the scene. The helicopters stuck with the object as it shot off toward the southwest and disappeared.

---

documents was a voluminous file on the Michalak case, revealing that no fewer than ten official Canadian government agencies had conducted thorough investigations of the case. Each agency independently concluded that the case was utterly perplexing and definitely not a hoax.

That same evening the three became violently ill. Betty, exposed the longest to the object, developed blisters on her head and face, and her neck, eyelids, and earlobes swelled. Her eyes closed shut and she was unable to see for several days. She also experienced headaches, nausea, vomiting, and diarrhea. Large patches of her hair fell out, and her face began to peel.

Vickie and Colby suffered similarly. Colby was "sunburned" from the encounter, and he experienced debilitating eye problems. Vickie began losing hair and felt as though her scalp was "asleep." Both suffered from nausea and diarrhea.

Several days later, appearing near death, Betty was rushed to Parkway Hospital in Houston, where she was hospitalized, complaining of a persistent headache, nausea, swelling, and lack of appetite. Her illness continued, even after her release from the hospital.

Too ill to work, she lost her small business and was forced to move to Alabama to receive care from her mother. Headaches and chronic fatigue persisted for months.

All three witnesses experienced deteriorating eyesight. Betty, who previously had excellent vision, was forced to wear glasses. Colby, too, had to acquire corrective eyewear, and Vickie experienced temporary blindness in one eye, which oozed frequently.

Physicians who examined Betty were unable to diagnose her ailments. They concluded, however, that her symptoms were suggestive of radiation poisoning.

Spokesman for military bases in the area steadfastly denied that any helicopters were aloft the night of the incident. They also stated that no military exercises had taken place anywhere in Southeast Texas that evening. The U.S. Defense Department denied any knowledge of the event.[52]

Vickie remains skeptical. "I don't believe for a minute that the UFO was from another planet," she told the *Dallas Times Herald*. "I just don't believe in it."[53]

"UFO attacks" have been particularly virulent in Brazil. There scores of peasants in the area of Parnarama have reportedly fallen ill or have died after being exposed to intense beams of light directed at them by strange, buzzing craft seen often in the skies. Some victims have been burned, experiencing nausea, diarrhea, and headaches before lapsing into fatal comas. According to Jacques Vallee, who has personally investigated these cases, the Brazilian Air Force has closely followed the situation and has told witnesses not to discuss what they have seen. "Many of the injuries described in Brazil," Dr. Vallee concludes, "are consistent with the effects of high-power pulsed microwaves."[54]

So what do we have here? What can we make of these disturbing events?

There are only three possible conclusions:

1. The incidents are all hoaxes and/or the product of grossly disturbed minds.

2. Extraterrestrials are conducting a not-so-kind invasion of earth.

3. The American military and intelligence community are using the planet as a testing ground for its secret arsenal of technologically advanced aircraft and weapon systems.

The first possibility is absurd, unless one believes that our planet is beset by some rampant psychosis, spreading even more virulently than the AIDS virus. Too many honest, sane people have experienced these events to be either hoaxes or hallucinations.

So what are we left with — bug-eyed monsters from outer space? You've seen the evidence. Clearly, extraterrestrials are not visiting earth. If they were here, we would know it by now.

Which leaves us with our final supposition. Compelling evidence suggests that the American military-industrial complex has more than a few flying saucers up its sleeve. It is disturbing to think that this powerful cabal is conducting covert testing, sometimes with lethal results, on an unsuspecting world populace. Perhaps the incidents detailed in this chapter represent only unintentional damage caused by the propulsion systems of the military's latest space-age hardware. *Perhaps not.*

# 5

# Death From Above

*Weapons change but man who uses them changes not at all. To win battles you do not beat weapons — you beat the soul of man...*

— General George S. Patton

The collapse of communism in the Soviet Union has paid off big for the Pentagon.

Recently the Soviets delivered to the United States a mobile, fifteen-million-watt generator that has the military-industrial complex salivating. *Aviation Week & Space Technology* reports that the generator can "operate electricity-hungry, directed-energy weapons from hidden sites on remote battlefields or from space."

U.S. defense insiders suggest that the device — the Pamir-3U magnetohydro-dynamic (MHD) electrical power generator — will be used "to drive long-range lasers or high-power microwave (HPM) weapons," capable of scrambling computer memories and frying electronic systems. "Even at 20 tons," *Aviation Week* reports, "the self-contained, Russian power system is light enough to be taken into remote areas for military operations, small enough to be hidden from enemy observation and powerful enough...to power a steady-state weapon like a laser...for 6-10 [seconds]....Or, with some sort of power conversion, it could be used to fire a high-powered microwave [weapon]....In fact, the MHD system is so reliable and autonomous that both Russia and the U.S. have considered it to power space-based weapons." The generator has already been modified by the Pentagon to produce even more lethal results, as much as fifty percent more power.

The United States Air Force concedes that the Soviets may have already employed such devices for classified military projects, possibly directed-energy weapons. If so, this would seem to lend further credence to the boasts of Soviet General Tretyak, discussed in the previous chapter.

The lethal device was delivered to Edwards Air Force Base in California after completing a series of *eight test shots* at an Aerojet Corp. facility in Sacramento.* The Soviet MHD was originally purchased by Textron Defense Systems, a defense contractor that made billions of dollars in profits from the sale of helicopters to the U.S. military during the Vietnam War. The project officer for the generator's acquisition was David Price, a member of the high-energy plasma division of Phillips Laboratory's advanced weapons and survivability directorate at Kirtland Air Force Base, New Mexico.

"The Russian's MHD system could be a key component for electromagnetic pulse (EMP) or HPM weapon designs because of its resistance to countermeasures," *Aviation Week* notes. "Since the system has no microelectronic components, it cannot be electronically overloaded or upset by defensive blasts of electromagnetic pulses or high-power microwaves."[1]

But this announcement, like that for the Pentagon's DarkStar "flying saucer," may be old — perhaps, *ancient* — news. Nikola Tesla, you will recall, claimed to have invented such a weapon more than a half-century ago. Then there is the strange document located in the Imperial War Museum in London. Dated October 3, 1945, the document contains interviews of Japanese army officers conducted by Allied agents. It notes that Japanese scientists during World War II were close to developing a "death ray," capable of causing "paralysis or death to any human being upon whom the beam was focused." Although specifically intended as an antiaircraft weapon, it was reportedly tested on animals. Allied interrogators concluded: "With the development of higher-power and shorter-wave length oscillators, which has become possible through the Allied research on radar, it is possible that a death ray might be developed that could kill unshielded human beings at a distance of five to ten miles if these Japanese experiments are reliable indications of the potentialities of the death ray."[2]

---

*Two events do not necessarily show cause-and-effect. However, it should be noted that the testing of this device coincided with the onset of widespread power disruptions at major commercial airports across the United States.

Furthermore, scientist Robert Ley, head of the Labor Front in Nazi Germany, announced to Martin Bormann and other prominent Nazi officials in the closing days of World War II that he, too, had developed a "death ray." According to Albert Speer in his book *Inside the Third Reich,* Ley proclaimed: "Death rays have been invented! A simple apparatus that we can produce in large quantities. I've studied the documentation; there's no doubt about it. This will be the decisive weapon!"[3] Soon thereafter, Ley was captured by the Allies. While awaiting the start of the Nuremberg Trials, he was found dead, an apparent suicide.[4]

Carnegie Mellon University engineering professor H. Keith Florig is an expert in the field of HPM weaponry. Writing in *Spectrum,* the official publication of the Institute of Electrical and Electronics Engineers, Florig notes: "High-power microwaves could upset any system that depends on electronic signals for its operation. At high energy fluences, they burn out sensitive semiconductor components in electronic systems. *Components most at risk are receiving diodes in radars and communication units…and perhaps even the semiconductors in the electronic ignition systems of ground vehicles. Very high energy fluences might even detonate missile warheads, bombs, or artillery shells* [emphasis added]."[5]

In the summer of 1961, near Rybinsk, about ninety miles from Moscow, a huge disk-shaped object, surrounded by numerous smaller objects, suddenly appeared over a Soviet missile defense battery. Missiles were reportedly fired at the intruder. About a mile from the target, they inexplicably exploded. The battery commander ordered another launch against the devices, but to no avail. The installation was hit by a complete electrical blackout, scuttling the launch. When the objects departed, power was restored.[6]

About this same time, several cars near Moscow stalled when a UFO hovered momentarily over an overpass, according to the USSR Academy of Sciences Institute of Space Research. The cars did not restart, the Soviet scientists observed, until the object sped away.[7]

In the 1960s and '70s, numerous Strategic Air Command (SAC) bases and Minuteman nuclear missile sites were visited by UFOs. In the spring of 1966, the command consoles at a missile launch-control center in Great Falls, Montana, reportedly experienced a severe electrical malfunction. Nuclear missiles, monitored at the site, became inoperative, registering a "no-go fault condition." Personnel outside observed UFOs at the time of the malfunction. Again, in March 1967, radar at Malmstrom Air Force Base, near Great Falls, detected an unknown object near the base just as nuclear missiles there became lifeless in their silos.[8]

In the fall of 1975, Malmstrom Air Force Base security personnel were reportedly dispatched when remote sensors at the missile launch facility were triggered. An orange glowing disk the size of a football field illuminated the missile site. F-106 jet interceptors were scrambled, but were unable to keep up with the device, which suddenly "blinked out." Afterwards, missile specialists who visited the silo were astonished to discover that warhead-targeting data for one of the missiles had somehow been reconfigured. The missile had to be removed and replaced.[9]

The 24th NORAD Region confirmed later sightings of unidentified objects over Malmstrom. On November 7, Captain Roscoe E. Moulthrop advised the Air Force Office of Special Investigations (AFOSI) that two adjacent launch-control facilities near Lewiston had also reported moving lights in the sky.[10]

Despite NORAD's confirmation of the sightings, the Air Force refused to respond to public inquiries. Said the Air Force: "All documentation at Malmstrom AFB has been destroyed in accordance with Air Force directives for the dates of the UFO sightings mentioned...."[11]

The above cases are curious in light of Florig's statements on the potential of HPM weapons to disrupt missile warheads. Has the military been secretly testing the effects of this new technology on its own defense installations? Have the Soviets been involved?

Let's look at another series of strange events that occurred a few years after the Malmstrom sightings. During the winter of 1977–78, a spate of loud booms emanating from the upper atmosphere shook the Eastern United States from Connecticut to South Carolina. The explosions—"skyquakes"—broke windows, set off smoke detectors, disrupted streetlights, and shook houses. In some instances, brilliant flashes of light were observed.

Scientists at the Lamont-Doherty Geological Observatory in Palisades, New York, estimated the blasts produced energy equivalent to one hundred tons of dynamite. Only nuclear detonations had recorded higher yields.

The Mitre Corporation, an engineering firm in Virginia, conducted a study of the odd explosions. Its findings? According to Mitre researchers, two-thirds of the incidents were attributable to supersonic aircraft; the source of the remaining third—about two hundred cases—could not be determined.[12]

On April 2, 1978, following the outbreak of skyquakes, an ear-splitting blast rocked the tiny Canadian community of Bell Island, Newfoundland. Eerie streaks of blinding silvery-white light shot out of the sky, shaking homes for miles around. A television set exploded, electrical outlets were blown off walls, and several chickens were incinerated at one locale.

The devastating bombardment was detected by satellite, registering as a "potential nuclear blast." The St. John's *Evening Telegram* reported that soon after the incident two military attachés from a U.S. military facility in Los Alamos, New Mexico, visited Bell Island and "carefully avoided the news media."

"Defense department observers in Washington, D.C.," the newspaper stated, "have confirmed that the U.S. armed forces base which is interested in the [blast] is none other than a weapons laboratory....A spokesman for the Center for Defense Information in Washington said...that Los Alamos researchers are *designing the most highly classified weapons, including the new death-ray style laser weapons* [emphasis added]."

The light that struck the Bell Island home of James Bickford was described as "a straight beam, like that of a flashlight, coming down from the sky at a 45-degree angle to the ground." Bickford reported that the bolt of light was accompanied by a blast "louder than 300 sticks of dynamite."

The *Evening Telegram* stated that satellite tracking stations in the United States reported the blast to the Los Alamos facility. "It is uncertain, however, why a potentially dangerous and supposedly unexpected event should be reported so immediately to scientists engaged in long-term research."[13]

More recently, in early December 1995, explosions from unidentified low-flying objects shook the self-proclaimed republic of Somaliland. "A few days after the explosions, inhabitants came down with various ailments such as coughing, diarrhea, breathing difficulties and headaches," a government minister told a Reuters reporter. Several children died, and animals ran "wild and uncontrolled," some clawing at trees, after the blasts. Numerous windows were shattered.[14]

In November 1977, a few days before the first skyquake rocked North America, mysterious radio signals forced cancellation of the scheduled launch of Meteosat 1, a European weather satellite. The signals were detected by ground personnel at Cape Canaveral during a routine test of the booster's command-destruct system. Had the satellite been launched, officials said, the signals could have triggered the destruct system, causing the booster and its payload to explode.[15]

Several months earlier, the American satellite Pegasus 1 inexplicably "came to life" after nine years of total silence. As if responding to a radio command, the derelict satellite began to transmit signals back to earth. Pegasus 1 was switched off, but the following month it again started up, interrupting the transmission of another satellite.[16]

In 1988 — seven years before the acquisition of the Soviet-built Pamir-3U MHD generator — the American military's experiments with electromagnetic weapon systems had become so widespread that the Foundation on Economic Trends, a Washington, D.C.-based environmental group, was able to obtain a temporary court injunction requiring such experiments to be stopped or moderated at laboratories in Virginia, Maryland, Alabama, and New Mexico. The environmental group successfully argued that even the mere operation of these facilities — without weapons actually being fired — posed serious health risks to those in the area. Jeremy Rifkin, president of the foundation, hailed the settlement as "an historic first" because "a federal court recognized the potential hazard of electrical pollution in our society."[17]

But the courts are fickle, particularly when it comes to the issue of "national security." In July 1988, Robert Frost crawled out of his car in front of his Las Vegas-area home and began to scream. His face was burned and noticeably swollen. Later his skin split and bled. Each day, he grew sicker; his internal organs began to fail. Sixteen months later, he was dead at the age of fifty-seven.

Frost, a sheet metal worker, had erected buildings and installed air-conditioning units at the Air Force's hush-hush Groom Lake facility. Other workers there had also fallen ill, complaining of respiratory difficulties, burning skin, and impaired motor ability. There were also elevated levels of cancer, according to Jonathan Turley, a George Washington University law professor who sued the government on behalf of Frost and the other afflicted workers.[18]

Something at the base, Turley contends, killed Frost and disabled the others. Most of Turley's motions, however, were denied. Although the Air Force did commission an inspection of the facility by the Environmental Protection Agency, it immediately moved to classify the final report, citing "national security reasons." A U.S. District Court ruling, nevertheless, ordered the Air Force to either release the report or acquire a presidential exemption preventing disclosure.[19] Curiously, President Clinton, who has championed environmental causes in the past, signed an exemption order, in effect blocking release of the report to the public.[20]

New Mexico is home to many military bases and research facilities conducting supersecret weapons development and testing, including EMP and HPM technology. These include Kirtland Air Force Base, Sandia National Laboratories, Phillips Laboratories, the Defense Nuclear Agency, as well as other research and development facilities at White Sands and Los Alamos.

Is it possible, then, that this confluence of high-energy weapons testing has caused the skies over New Mexico to literally hum?

This may seem like a ludicrous question. But a growing number of New Mexicans aren't laughing.

Since 1991, residents of the tiny desert hamlet of Taos have detected the presence of a continuous, low-level hum that appears to have no identifiable source. Those who first complained of the hum were brushed off by physicians who dismissed the afflicted listeners as "hysterical." That is, until scientific instruments set up on the edge of town confirmed the presence of the persistent hum. Listening posts were established by the University of New Mexico and Sandia National Laboratories.*

A Denver audiologist has discovered that the hum seems to vibrate steadily at a frequency of seventeen cycles per second with a harmonic

---

*Sandia scientists are in the habit of showing up at the most curious times. Sandia, a weapons research firm, is housed at Kirtland Air Force Base, a virtual disinformation mill when it comes to the subject of UFOs. Sandia senior engineer Dick Spaulding and Mark Boslough, a Sandia scientist specializing in "experimental impact physics," spawned the story that the mystery blast in Bell Island, Newfoundland, discussed earlier, was likely nothing more than a meteorite, despite a lack of evidence to support the claim. We'll take a closer look at Sandia in the next chapter.

range to seventy cycles per second. The normal low range of human hearing is twenty to thirty cycles per second, thus explaining why everyone in Taos hasn't heard the hum. Only those with acute hearing seem to be able to sense it.

Tom Sharpe, a reporter with the *Albuquerque Journal,* confirms that the hum has become so agitating that some Taos residents have fled the area. One resident, Sara Allen, likens the mysterious sound to "a refrigerator running two rooms away," or "a diesel truck idling in the distance." Winona Whitted terms the hum "life-threatening," adding that she lost her job due to the hum's debilitating effects; she believes that the military may be conducting mind-control experiments.

Investigative reporter Chuck DeCaro suspects that a "nonlethal" military weapon may be involved. "There are a lot of studies in the military and other parts of the government about the effects of radio-frequency energy...on human behavior and physiology," says DeCaro.

Doris Quarles, another Taos resident affected by the hum, is convinced the military is involved. "The Defense Department knows what it is," she states. "I don't understand why they're not telling us what it is."[21]

Back in 1959, an ex-Navy pilot, who encountered three circular UFOs while flying in his Cessna 170 over New Mexico, was reportedly warned by a Kirtland Air Force Base officer that he might develop "radiation sickness" as a result of his close proximity to the objects. Following the sighting, the pilot had been ordered by the FAA to land at Kirtland, whereupon he was immediately whisked to a debriefing room. There the Air Force officer instructed him that, in the event of illness, he should notify the Air Force, which would secure care for him at a "government hospital." Said the pilot in a signed affidavit: "He [the Kirtland Air Force Base officer] warned me to keep this secret from everybody but my wife and to make sure she kept quiet too."[22]

On June 2, 1964, another odd incident occurred in New Mexico, in the town of Hobbs. Eight-year-old Charles Keith Davis was standing outside his grandparents' laundry when he suddenly began to scream. Mrs. Frank Smith, the boy's grandmother, flung open the door and rushed outside, where she was shocked to see a strange object hovering over Charles' head. Moments later, the object shot away.

Mrs. Smith buried Charles' head in her apron. His hair was singed and there were second-degree burns on his face, ears, and neck. Mrs. Smith later stated that one of Charles' ears looked "like a piece of meat" and his face was so swollen that "you couldn't see his nose."[23]

A year earlier, the Associated Press carried an article on Dr. Leo J. Baranski, an experimental psychologist at North American Aviation. The article stated that Dr. Baranski was working on a "ray" that was capable of prolonging a person's life or destroying entire populations. Baranski theorized that if one could discover the microwave frequency of adenosine-triphosphate (ATP) — organic molecules essential for the proper functioning of the body's muscular system — and control the release of this energy, then one might be able to produce superhuman strength in an individual or, conversely, cause "complete irreversibility of function or lethality."

Baranski added: "Using masers [microwave amplifying devices], we could extend the range of effectiveness to almost any distance on earth and in space. A weapon that incorporates ATP's critical microwave releasing frequency could produce effects ranging from completely reversible traumatization [temporary paralysis] to virtually instant lethality.

"Such a weapon is within the present state of the art, all even down to the size of a handgun, since all the necessary components are already on the commercial market."[24]

In his *Spectrum* article, Florig also addresses the biological implications of microwave weaponry. "The most familiar biological effect of microwaves is that they *heat tissue*," Florig writes. "Microwave-induced changes in brain temperature of only a few degrees have been shown to cause convulsions, unconsciousness, and amnesia in rats [emphasis added]."[25]

Florig adds: "HPM weapons that merely stun the nervous system temporarily seem, like short-acting chemical agents, to be more humane than lethal force. But HPM weapons that blind, burn, or bake people to death are likely to be viewed as an abhorrent addition to the arsenal."[26]

Operators of the egg-shaped craft that zapped ten-year-old Sharon Stull apparently had no qualms about dispensing destructive energy. In April 1964, Sharon was playing with friends in Albuquerque — the

THE GREAT UFO HOAX

home of Kirtland Air Force Base — when she received first-degree burns under her eyes and on the nose. She later told her attending physician that the object — slightly smaller than an airplane — had struck her with a "ray." Thereafter, police chief A. B. Martinez warned Albuquerque residents to stay away from mysterious objects, adding that they should be treated with "respect and caution."

Sharon was treated for burns at Bataan Memorial Hospital. Incredibly, in the four weeks that followed, she allegedly grew more than five inches and gained twenty-five pounds.

"A month ago she was just a child who liked to play with dolls," Mrs. Stull said. "Now she is suddenly mature and grown-up, cooks meals by herself, cleans house, and takes care of the younger children."

Mrs. Stull told reporters that Sharon's eyes had healed, but that prolonged reading made her eyes hurt. Outdoors, she had to wear dark glasses.

Mrs. Stull admitted consternation over her daughter's growth spurt and radical change in personality.

"I know she definitely saw something in the sky, but I don't know what," she said. "It has been a nightmare for us ever since. I wish I had kept her inside that day."[*][27]

Another odd physiological response to a ray-spewing UFO occurred on September 3, 1965, on Highway 36, near Damon, Texas, southwest of Houston. Brazoria County Sheriff's Deputies Bob Goode and Billy McCoy were proceeding south in their patrol car when McCoy noticed a peculiar purplish glow westward beyond a pasture in the San Bernard River area. As the glow became brighter, McCoy and Goode observed a smaller blue light separate from the main light source and move a short distance to the right.

---

*Only a few days prior to Sharon's unnerving encounter, New Mexico highway patrolman Lonnie Zamora was pursuing a speeding motorist near Socorro when he saw a bright light descending from the sky. Breaking off the chase, he drove into the desert where he observed an object — also egg-shaped — resting on four legs. Two figures, dressed in white coveralls, were standing alongside the craft. Several minutes later, the craft, with its occupants, took off and disappeared. Zamora noticed a distinctive insignia on the side of the craft. Leon Davidson, a scientist, later examined a drawing Zamora made of the insignia. Viewing it from different perspectives, Davidson was able to make out the merging of three unmistakable letters: *C-I-A*. Military interrogators reportedly told Zamora to keep quiet about the odd insignia.

Goode was convinced the bright glows were merely oil field lights. McCoy wasn't so sure.

Deputy Goode pulled off to the side of the road and pointed the car in the direction of the glowing lights. The lights had risen slightly and now appeared as two side-by-side luminous orbs.

Then, suddenly, the lights raced toward the idling patrol car, stopping about a hundred yards from the highway. An eerie purplish glow filled the car. As McCoy and Goode gaped upward, they saw that the lights were on opposite ends of an immense, cigar-shaped craft. The device, skimming the pasture below, had no markings, portholes, or protrusions.

"It had a left side [with a] purple light that was longer than it was wide and a blue light on the right side, not as brilliant as the purple light," McCoy later reported. "It appeared to be about 200 feet across from one light to the other, and was about 40 to 50 feet thick in the middle, tapering off at the ends."

During the sighting, Goode felt a blast of heat on his left hand through the open window. He panicked, pulled the car onto the highway and jammed the gas pedal to the floor. McCoy peered back at the lighted object as Goode pushed the patrol car to 110 miles per hour. The object then snapped back like a ball on a giant rubber band to its original position and shot upward out of sight.[28]

Prior to the sighting, Goode had been severely bitten by a baby alligator he had brought home to show his children. "I had him all tied up so he couldn't bite anyone," Goode told the *Brazosport Facts*, "but when I went to let him loose—I don't know what I was thinking—I reached down to pick him up by the tail and he whirled around and bit me. He nearly took my finger off."

It was time to go to work, so Goode had bandaged his bloody, badly gnawed left index finger and joined McCoy on patrol duty. His finger throbbed.

Following the sighting, Goode removed the bandage and was surprised to see that his finger was no longer swollen.

"The finger looked like it was almost healed—instantly," Goode's companion observed. This was the same hand that had been bathed in the warm purplish light. The next day, light scarring on his finger provided the only evidence of the alligator attack.[29]

Exposure to various levels of electromagnetic radiation is known to cause a wide range of symptoms among humans. Often the effects are harmful; on occasion, as in the previous case, the effects seem beneficial. In his study of UFO vehicle-interference, Mark Rodeghier observed that in almost one-fourth of all such incidents, physiological effects, varying greatly, occurred in witnesses. While most effects tended to be disconcerting or even frightening, a tiny number of cases involved pleasant responses to the presence of UFOs. Several witnesses included in the study noted they felt a "feeling of peace."

Peaceful does *not* describe the feelings of Alaskans toward the increasing military presence in the "Last Frontier." One military venture in particular has a growing number of Alaskan activists fuming. Many feel this project, if allowed to flourish, could spell disaster for not only Alaska but for the entire world.

# 6

# Terror in the Arctic

*Of the despotism to which unrestrained military power leads*
*we have plenty of examples from Alexander to Mao.*
— Samuel Eliot Morison

Each year, the Sonoma State University journalism department releases a list of the ten most censored stories. In short, *real* news that the media — for reasons only it knows — collectively ignores.

In 1994, while members of the Fourth Estate swooped down on Los Angeles like starving crows feeding on the latest O. J. Simpson rumors, the Pentagon was *quietly* — thanks to the media — installing high-tech gadgetry in the Last Frontier. This latest spending romp is known as Project HAARP (High Frequency Active Auroral Research Program), and it was one of the ten most censored stories of 1994, according to Sonoma State's media watchdogs.[1]

The Fall 1994 issue of *Arctic Research,* published by the National Science Foundation, describes Project HAARP this way:

As part of a Joint Service [Air Force-Navy] research effort, entitled High-Frequency Active Auroral Research Program (HAARP), a unique, high-power, HF ionospheric heating facility will be constructed in Alaska. The heater will be capable of providing sufficient energy densities in the ionosphere to enable investigations to be conducted on the modulation of auroral currents to generate ELF/VLF waves, the acceleration of electrons to produce optical emissions, the production of field-aligned ionization to scatter radio waves, and other phenomena triggered by the interactions of very-high-power radio waves in the ionosphere. A ground-based heating instrument having effective radiated powers in excess of 1 gW (90 dBW), with HF tuning over the 2.8–12 MHz band and

73

beam steering agility, is planned. In addition a wide variety of diagnostic instrumentation will also be acquired, including: ELF/VLF/HF receivers, HF ionospheric sounders, HF/VHF radars, UHF scintillation receivers, optical and IR cameras, and an incoherent scatter radar. Construction of the facility is expected to begin in early 1994.[2]

*Say what?*

No wonder the media never covered the HAARP story. They couldn't make out what the military was saying. Perhaps the Pentagon planned it that way.

In plain English, Project HAARP will transmit a beam of high-frequency energy into the ionosphere, thirty-five to five hundred miles above the earth, as a way of improving military communications, according to its designers. Ramy Shanny, president of Advanced Powers Technologies, Inc. (APTI), the Washington-based firm building the $160-million Alaska project for the U.S. military, has dismissed concern over the venture as "paranoia."* Yet Shanny admits that the project—eventually to consist of 360 seventy-two-foot antennas spanning a vast section of the Alaskan frontier—could disrupt television and radio reception and, far more serious, could scramble the electronics of airplanes.**[3]

A growing number of physicists have expressed grave concerns about HAARP. They are convinced that the project is actually an exotic weapon system, capable of blowing spacecraft out of the sky, disrupting communications over vast regions of the planet, and even affecting—either purposefully or accidentally—global weather patterns.

Physicist Richard Williams, a consultant to the David Sarnoff laboratory in Princeton, alleges HAARP is "an irresponsible act of global vandalism." He and other scientists believe that HAARP could

---

*The *Washington Post* of April 17, 1995, purports that "rumors are buzzing across the Internet that [Project HAARP] has a secret purpose—digging up bodies of UFO aliens." Where did the *Post* come up with this? None of the anti-HAARP activists in Alaska and elsewhere have ever fostered such an outlandish claim. The "rumors" smack of disinformation, designed to distract attention away from HAARP's operational agenda and to furthermore discredit opponents of the project.

**Curiously, these are the same effects often observed in close-encounter UFO cases.

eventually produce "a severe disruption of the upper atmosphere" and may "produce effects that spread rapidly around the Earth for years."[4]

Another vociferous critic is physicist Bernard Eastlund, who originally devised the HAARP concept as a consultant to petroleum-giant Atlantic Richfield (ARCO), which was seeking new and profitable methods of extracting Alaskan natural gas. His work led to the design of systems capable of generating extraordinary power — equal to a nuclear blast — that could destroy incoming enemy missiles and disrupt satellite communications.

The Pentagon quickly got wind of the project and threw research funding Eastlund's way. In 1987, he was granted three patents — one of which was immediately classified — for his weapon-system designs.

Then a curious thing happened. According to the *Washington Post*, Shanny fired Eastlund, noting the physicist's "way out" ideas as the grounds for dismissal.[5] Eastlund remembers it differently. The physicist says that relations with ARCO turned sour after Robert Hirsch, ARCO vice president, met with Edward Teller, the so-called "Father of the H-Bomb" and leading proponent of the Reagan-era Strategic Defense Initiative (SDI). Thereafter, Eastlund claims, "new [secret] initiatives began which I was not privy to, and I declined further involvement."[6]

In 1994, ARCO sold APTI to Dallas-based defense contractor E-Systems, designer of ultrasecret military electronics systems and the President's E-4B "doomsday plane."* Giant defense contractor Raytheon, an original bidder for HAARP, then acquired E-Systems and assumed exclusive ownership of Eastlund's "way out" patents. HAARP is jointly managed by the USAF's Phillips Laboratory and the Office of Naval Research.

The government steadfastly claims that Project HAARP, with its mission of churning up the aurora borealis with electromagnetic energy,

---

*E-Systems has been the subject of scrutiny by the *Washington Post* and CBS's *60 Minutes*. The October 24, 1994, issue of the *Post* reported that E-Systems is "part of the central nervous system for the nation's intelligence community." CBS and the *Post* discovered that most of E-Systems' business, in fact, comes from the National Security Agency, military intelligence organizations, and the CIA. The company is so much a part of the "black world" that employees are permitted to discuss their work only with individuals with a "need to know." E-Systems has designed, among other things, sophisticated eavesdropping systems for law enforcement agencies and the government.

is not a weapon system, and that its effects will be fleeting and otherwise benign. But others see it differently.

"Many of us are not happy with the prospect of [the military] altering the Earth's neutral atmospheric properties," native Alaskan Charles Edwardsen, Jr., wrote President Clinton in 1994. "We do not want to be anyone's testing ground...."[7]

Eskimo leaders have reason to be concerned about HAARP. They recall how in the 1950s, the Department of Energy and other federal agencies subjected Eskimos to radiation without their knowledge. Numerous natives from various villages stretching across Alaska's oil-rich North Slope were exposed to high levels of iodine 131 and other radioactive materials — the equivalent of seven hundred chest X-rays — in order to observe the effects of such exposure on the immune system.*

In May 1995, the North Slope Borough, the official native government representing a vast section of Alaska above the Arctic Circle, sued the federal government on behalf of seventy residents said to have been subjected to this experimentation. The claim was filed against the U.S. Air Force, Department of the Interior, Department of Health and Human Services, Atomic Energy Commission, and Department of Energy.

Borough mayor George Ahmaogak, Sr., has expressed outrage over what he sees as stonewalling by the government, even today, forty years later.

"The government has not released all the documents that might help us identify every victim," he told the *North Slope Sentinel,* adding: "This is a shameful episode in the history of federal government relations with our people. Innocent people may have died before their time. Others may have contracted serious illnesses, and those who are still healthy have to live with the fear of cancer or some other disease from that radiation."[8]

---

*This is not the first time that the American military and intelligence community has endangered the lives of Americans in the name of technological progress. While the Department of Energy was dosing Eskimos with deadly radiation in the 1950s, the U.S. Navy was busy conducting open-air experiments with toxic serratia bacteria on unsuspecting residents of San Francisco. The U.S. government conducted more than three hundred open-air germ tests on the American public between 1950 and 1969, a lawsuit filed against the government subsequently revealed.

The North Slope Borough isn't waiting for the federal government to respond to its request. At a December 1995 meeting, the NSB Assembly allocated more than $400,000 to conduct a thorough investigation of the matter, including medical screenings of the experiments' unwitting participants. David Harding, a spokesman for mayor Ahmaogak, notes that about fifty of the original test subjects are still alive, while others have died of cancer. Says Harding: "They were basically...used as guinea pigs."[9]

Then there is Project Chariot. In 1958, scientists from Lawrence Livermore Labs announced their intention of using nuclear explosives to excavate a harbor on Ogotoruk Creek near Cape Thompson, a region that continues to be widely used by natives for subsistence hunting and fishing. The idea had originally been put forth by Edward Teller. The venture was part of the Atomic Energy Commission's Plowshares Program, designed to explore "peaceful" uses for nuclear explosives.

A nuclear test-ban treaty between the Soviet Union and the United States forced cancellation of Project Chariot. However, a study to trace movements of radioisotopes through the soil and water at the proposed site was carried out in 1962. Thirty years later, it was revealed that atomic waste had been spread in the area without proper permits. The Alaska Department of Environmental Conservation moved to have the site placed on the state's Hazardous Waste Site list.

Nevertheless, the ADEC sided with the federal Department of Energy, stating that "the department did not find any indication that people using the area for subsistence...would receive a dose [of radiation] significantly above background [levels] to cause harm." The ADEC chose not to restrict use of the site.[10]

"Despite these reassurances," the *Arctic Sounder* reported, "the villagers continue to express concerns about the high rate of cancer in their community. Residents and the state have asked that all documents dealing with Project Chariot be declassified for public scrutiny."[11]

Alaskans' protestations over Project HAARP have also apparently fallen on deaf ears. The Clinton administration, despite its overt support of environmental protection, has approved increased funding for HAARP, authorizing testing at the Gakona, Alaska, site. HAARP is expected to be fully operational by 1998.[12]

Drs. Gael and Patrick Flanagan do not trust the government's pub-licly avowed good intentions. "When first viewed from a limited exte-rior viewpoint, [HAARP] looks like a harmless research project," they observe. "When viewed from a wider perspective, we begin to see that HAARP is a secret undertaking that is not unlike the Manhattan Pro-ject which gave us the atomic bomb....

"Under ordinary conditions, certain minerals and substances can-not harm our cells because they cannot pass across [the cell and blood-brain barriers] and enter where they don't belong.... The power levels proposed by the HAARP manifesto are so great that these circularly polarized waves will be amplified by using solar energy and the ampli-fication by the maser effect. This means these types of signals could be focused over large areas of the planet. *Whole populations could be adversely affected by these signals* [emphasis added]."[13]

The Flanagans further warn that the ozone layer and Van Allen Radiation Belt that protect us from harmful cosmic rays could be adversely affected by HAARP.

"If this barrier is weakened, we have a lot more to worry about than a little extra sunburn," they assert. "The entrance of high-energy particles could cause severe damage to the DNA blueprints of virtu-ally all life on our planet."

They add: "These changes could also have a profound effect on our already rapidly shifting weather patterns. For example, a change in the ionic make-up of the upper atmosphere could potentially alter the infrared transmission windows which control the heat energy reach-ing our planet from the Sun. This, in turn, could cause an acceleration of the melting of the polar [icecaps] which is already underway. The partial melting of the Antarctic [icecap] alone could raise sea levels all over the world by at least 150 feet. This would devastate the entire civ-ilized world."[14]

The Flanagans also warn of the potential misuse of HAARP tech-nology for the "implementation of electronic global mind control." They note: "Certain types of electromagnetic signals can induce visual and auditory effects when the field around the head or body is at the right frequency, intensity and modulation levels. We are not accus-ing the developers of HAARP of amoral intentions for the use of this technology, but the potential for abuse is there."[15]

Actually, high-frequency heaters have been operated for decades by researchers around the globe. There are currently transmitters located in Norway, the Soviet Union, Puerto Rico, and another in Alaska, near Fairbanks. But HAARP will be the granddaddy of them all, with a power output twice that of any other ionospheric heater.[16]

Alaska governor Tony Knowles, who eked out a razor-thin campaign victory thanks largely to Alaska native support, seems to be in the dark about HAARP. When recently asked about the project by *Popular Science* writer Mark Farmer, a Knowles spokesman replied, "We have no idea what you are talking about." State Representative Jeanette James, whose district surrounds the HAARP site, has queried Air Force officials about the project, only to be told "not to worry."

"My gut feeling is that it is frightening," says James. "I'm skeptical. I don't think they know what they are doing."[17]

In their book *Angels Don't Play This HAARP* (Earthpulse Press, 1995), Dr. Nick Begich* and Jeane Manning note that Alaskan activists opposed to HAARP have also been frustrated in their efforts to find out more about the project. HAARP opponents have discovered that personnel at the site seem to know little about the project; information requests have been routed to command centers out of state. On one occasion, a response to general queries came directly from Kirtland Air Force Base, the New Mexico base heavily involved in "black" weapons research.[18] Favorable reports on HAARP issued by the Mitre Corporation, furthermore, have been severely criticized by NO-HAARP activists. Says one Mitre critic: "They're NSA [National Security Agency] owned, operated, signed, sealed and delivered. Mitre Corporation is the main defense communications contractor for the United States government."**[19]

---

*Author Begich is the son of former U.S. Congressman Nick Begich, Sr., who in 1972 was aboard a private plane that disappeared mysteriously over Alaska. Also aboard this flight was Hale Boggs, U.S. House Majority Leader, who had served on the Warren Commission investigating the assassination of John Kennedy. Prior to his disappearance, Boggs had become a staunch critic of the FBI, claiming that the agency had wiretapped his telephone and those of other Congressmen. He publicly charged the FBI with "Gestapo tactics." On November 22, 1973, the *Los Angeles Star* reported that Boggs had "startling revelations on Watergate and the assassination of President Kennedy."

**The Mitre Corporation has conducted studies on the biological effects of highly concentrated microwave frequencies. You will recall that Mitre was also asked to "investigate" the Mystery Booms of 1977-78.

HAARP opponents clearly do not trust government assurances that the project is safe. They continue to raise specific concerns about HAARP. Let's take a closer look at some of these issues.

## *Weapon Capabilities*

HAARP opponents are convinced the project is actually a new "nonlethal" weapon system, currently being pushed by the White House and Congress. The term "nonlethal" is misleading, as the Department of Defense itself admits. A policy report issued in July 1994 by the Office of the Assistant Secretary of Defense concedes that "as lethal weapons do not achieve perfect lethality, neither will 'non-lethal' weapons always be capable of precluding fatalities and undesired collateral damage."[20] In short, property and humans in the path of energy released by these weapons might well be wiped out.

In November 1993, about four hundred scientists gathered at the Johns Hopkins University Applied Physics Lab to discuss research efforts in nonlethal technologies, including radiofrequency radiation (RF), electromagnetic pulse (EMP) and extremely low-frequency (ELF) fields. Sponsored by the Los Alamos National Laboratory, the gathering focused on military — and law enforcement — uses of nonlethal weaponry. Scheduled keynote speakers were Edward Teller and U.S. Attorney General Janet Reno.[21]

One of the presenters was Dr. Clay Easterly of Oak Ridge National Laboratories. When later asked about his work, Easterly stated that he was exploring the effects of ELF/EMFs on humans. He would say nothing more, adding that specific applications of his research were classified by the military.[22]

U.S. House Speaker Newt Gingrich is a big fan of nonlethal weapons. He advocates their use in domestic law enforcement, arguing that such weapon systems will provide "new options to local police and law enforcement authorities." In the foreword to *Low-Intensity Conflict and Modern Technology,* an Air Force publication on potential military uses of HAARP-related technology, Gingrich endorses the use of nonlethal weapons against radicals around the globe.[23]

In this same publication, Captain Paul Tyler observes: "The potential applications of artificial electromagnetic fields are wide-ranging and can be used in many military or quasi-military situations.... Some of these potential uses include dealing with terrorist groups, crowd control, controlling breaches of security at military installations, and antipersonnel techniques in tactical warfare. In all of these cases the EM systems would be used to produce mild to severe physiological disruption or perceptual distortion or disorientation.

"In addition, the ability of individuals to function could be degraded to such a point that they would be combat ineffective. Another advantage of electromagnetic systems is that they can provide coverage over large areas with a single system. They are silent and countermeasures to them may be difficult to develop."[24]

The deleterious effects of EM exposure have been demonstrated in laboratories around the world. Scientist Arthur Guy of the University of Washington exposed rats to low levels of electromagnetic radiation. The result? He observed that exposed rats suffered immunological stress and tumor formations at a rate four times higher than rats not exposed to the radiation.[25]

Likewise, Howard Wachtel and fellow researchers at the University of Colorado have observed "a brief depression in the electroencephalograms of rodents exposed to [microwave] pulses." The researchers have demonstrated that the activity of nerve cells can be temporarily altered by a single microwave pulse.[26]

In 1994, the International Committee of the Red Cross issued a report dealing with nonlethal technologies. The report notes that EM pulses, capable of being generated by HAARP, can (1) overheat and damage animal tissue, (2) affect the nervous system, (3) create a threshold for inducing microwave "hearing," (4) cause bit errors in unshielded computers, and (5) burn out unprotected receiver diodes in antennas.

The report observes that the Chemical Weapons Convention specifically bans — with exceptions — the use of such weapons. One of these exceptions, the Red Cross committee points out, is in the area of domestic law enforcement. The report adds that the focus of EM weaponry is shifting — from an instrument of war to "riot control."[27]

As early as the 1960s, geophysicist Gordon J.F. MacDonald observed that accurately timed "electronic strokes" could lead to a "pattern of oscillations" capable of producing high power levels over the earth. He further noted that "one could develop a system that would *seriously impair the brain performance of very large populations in selected regions over an extended period* [emphasis added]."[28]

MacDonald's comments appeared in Zbigniew Brzezinski's book, *Between Two Ages: America's Role in the Technetronic Era* (Penguin Books, 1976). As early as 1970, Brzezinski, who served as President Jimmy Carter's national security advisor, predicted a "more controlled and directed society" dominated by a powerful elite in the future. Furthermore, he envisioned that both liberals and conservatives would be inclined to employ technology toward this end. Liberals, Brzezinski stated, would use the technology at hand in the name of progress, while conservatives would opt for such measures, given the group's preoccupation with public order and its fascination with "modern gadgetry."[29]

In June 1995, the Council on Foreign Relations (CFR), an elite organization created by David Rockefeller and others that reportedly receives regular briefings from the CIA, issued a document urging the use of nonlethal weapons against terrorists and drug traffickers. The report recommends that such attacks be carried out clandestinely.[30]

Brzezinski is himself a prominent member of CFR, as well as the even more exclusive Trilateral Commission. Was the former national security advisor, in his book, slyly sending up a trial balloon?

"The current emphasis on these technologies reflects the level of interest of the government," Begich and Manning write, "and the increased visibility the government is giving these areas indicates an intention to use these systems in a more open manner. It is common practice to let things like these types of technological advances come out in small bits in order to 'test the waters' of public opinion. In this way the population can be co-opted into accepting greater levels of intrusion by governmental agencies. The idea is to indoctrinate by being taught to *believe*, rather than being given all of the facts so that a prudent person could *think* about the issues and make reasoned decisions."[31]

In April 1995, the U.S. Department of Defense's Directorate for Civil-Military Programs conducted a two-week military deployment exercise in Kotzebue and other nearby native villages. The exercise, dubbed Operation Kotzebue Care '95, was carried out by the U.S. Public Health Service and the Alaska National Guard, with the aid of Marine Reserve units from as far away as Florida and Washington, D.C. Ostensibly, the exercise was to enhance military medical readiness by providing natives with medical and dental services. However, the exercise seemed more purely military in design. During one exercise, soldiers pretended to shoot people in the head with their fingers, after which they would drop a card reading "head wound" beside the "body."[32] Earlier that year, Gov. Knowles had established a board of inquiry to investigate allegations of widespread racial discrimination in the Alaska National Guard.[33] About this same time, the Anchorage office of the FBI advertised on cable-access stations the hiring of five hundred "special agents," an extraordinary increase in workforce given the current federal budget crunch and Alaska's sparse population.

That same year, President Clinton announced massive base closings. Interestingly, no Alaska bases were affected. Fort Richardson, originally on the base-closing list, inexplicably received a last-minute reprieve from the president. Located in Anchorage, it is the largest army base near Project HAARP.[34]

## *Threat to Aircraft*

HAARP officials concede that HAARP can scramble the electronics of planes flying nearby. In the spring of 1993, the Federal Aviation Authority began warning commercial pilots of the potential risks of HAARP.[35] Despite bitter protests of FAA engineers and Alaska bush pilots, HAARP was given the go-ahead. HAARP's transmitters, assures the military, will be shut down when sensors indicate a plane is in the vicinity.[36]

Has the plan worked?

In 1995 a record number of civilian and military aircraft pelted the Alaskan countryside. Through July, there were one hundred aviation accidents, up from sixty-two the previous year. In all, thirty-three people died, compared to just five fatalities during the same period in 1994.[37]

In April, a DC-4, hauling freight, crashed while landing in the Alaskan community of Kivalina. The plane was delivering gasoline and propane to the Kivalina Native Store. The previous month, another plane—a Cessna 207 owned by Yute Air Alaska—crashed while delivering soda pop and pastries to the same store. Pilot Sean Sonntag died in the crash.[38]

On July 14, two pilots spotting for fish about twenty miles west of King Salmon were killed when their planes collided in midair. The planes plunged into Halfmoon Bay. National Transportation Safety Board investigators were uncertain as to the cause of the crash; they noted that weather, at the time of the midair collision, was good, with clear skies and light winds.[39] About this same time, a pilot flying home from a fishing trip with his sons had to execute an emergency landing after his floatplane's engine quit at two thousand feet. The engine, pilot James Borden later stated, sputtered on and off before finally shutting down.[40]

The following month, search and rescue pilots for the North Slope Borough located the wreckage of a Piper SuperCub on the side of a mountain, in the Brooks Range, about 120 miles southeast of Deadhorse. Both occupants of the plane were dead. NTSB investigators could offer no immediate explanation for the crash.[41]

On September 22, an Air Force AWACS radar plane crashed on takeoff at Elmendorf Air Force Base in Anchorage, killing all twenty-four military personnel aboard. Colonel Charlie Lambert, an interim Air Force crash investigator, stated that the crash was so catastrophic that it was difficult to distinguish one piece of wreckage from another. He told reporters that "minor parts" were recovered from the route the plane took before it plunged into a valley about a mile and a half from the runway.[42]

Early the following year, a nine-pound Air Force investigation report claimed the aircraft had sucked geese into its engines, causing it to lose thrust and crash. The final report failed to explain why Elmendorf's goose-control system had failed.[43] Actually, geese counts on the base were down. Colonel Wayne Heskew, reprimanded after the incident, refuted the Air Force's official conclusion, stating that on his own weekly inspection flights he "never saw any geese at all in the flight pattern."

"Not once did any pilot say to me that any of them thought there was a problem," Heskew told *Anchorage Daily News* columnist Mike Doogan.[44]

Two other crashes involving military aircraft occurred the following month. On October 10, an Air Force pilot was rescued after his A-10 Thunderbolt jet fighter crashed onto a military training range about fifty miles southeast of Eielson Air Force Base. Two months earlier, another plane—an F-15 also out of Eielson—crashed about 109 miles east of Fairbanks. The pilot, Captain Garth Doty, ejected safely.[45]

## Disturbance of Animal Migrations

Alaska natives are concerned about the possible effects of HAARP EM emanations on migration patterns of wildlife. Many rely upon subsistence hunting for their very survival. Diminished wildlife can spell disaster for these native peoples.

During the summer of 1995, hunters from Anaktuvuk Pass, south of Barrow, came up empty-handed in their quest for caribou, the mainstay of the Nunamiut Eskimos there. Hunting parties were dispatched as far away as Umiat in search of the normally plentiful herds. The village is the last inhabited Nunamiut community on the North Slope, with most of its people solely dependent upon subsistence foods.[46]

That same summer, more than 1,100 dead caribou were discovered near the native village of Point Hope and Kivalina, the site of plane crashes earlier in the year. Department of Wildlife officials concluded that the herd had died from starvation. But many area natives remain unconvinced.

Point Hope mayor Ray Koonuk, Sr., told reporters: "People from Point Hope and Kivalina are concerned because of the past activities of the Atomic Energy Commission and of the Department of Energy.... We are very concerned. Just because the dead caribou are skinny does not mean they died only of malnutrition. Something might have caused them to not eat. The feeding grounds are very rich. This is the first time this year a lot of caribou have died. We will wait for the facts...."[47]

## Climatological Upheaval

In August 1974, the CIA's Office of Research and Development prepared a lengthy report on global weather patterns in the wake of a series of weather disasters that began in 1960. CIA researchers concluded that it was likely that we were in the midst of a major climatic shift.

Said the CIA: "Any nation with scientific knowledge of the atmospheric sciences will challenge this natural climatic change. The potential for international conflict due to controlled climate modification can be a reality in the 1970s.... *Any country could pursue a climate modification course highly detrimental to adjacent nations in order to ensure its own economic, political, or social survival* [emphasis added]."[48]

The report further stated that it was incumbent upon man to "effectively modify the climate."[49]

"Leaders in climatology and economics are in agreement that a climatic change is taking place and that it has already caused major economic problems throughout the world," the CIA observed. "As it becomes more apparent to the nations around the world that the current trend is indeed a long-term reality, new alignments will be made among nations to insure a secure supply of food resources. *Assessing the impact of climatic change on major nations will, in the future, occupy a major portion of the Intelligence Community's assets* [emphasis added]."[50]

The report stressed that the intelligence community must "understand the magnitude of international threats which occur as a function of climatic change."

"These methodologies," the report continued, "are necessary to forewarn us of the economic and political collapse of nations caused by a worldwide failure in food production. *In addition, methodologies are also necessary to project and assess a nation's propensity to initiate militarily large-scale migrations of their people* [emphasis added]...."[51]

The CIA pointed out the preponderance of crop failures in the Soviet Union, China, and small developing nations during this period. This, the agency reasoned, could be America's trump card.

"The world's increasing dependence on American surpluses portends an increase in U.S. power and influence, especially vis-à-vis the food-deficit poor countries," the report stated.[52]

A 1977 *Saturday Review* editorial warned of weather warfare, in response to the release of the CIA report. The editorial described the deadening of our collective conscience from the endless procession of superweapons. Mass insanity, it said. "If the collective conscience does not now respond, then all our philosophy and religion and education...have been abstract, irrelevant, futile."

The *Saturday Review* then offered a disturbing suggestion. "It is difficult to read the CIA report," the editorial boldly observed, "without wondering whether some of the climatic aberrations in recent years may not have been part of *military experimental programs* [emphasis added]."[53]

It is interesting to note that the CIA report was made available to the public. Did the Company issue the report as a cover — *justification* — for its own weather modification efforts?

Weather modification experiments have been conducted in the United States since 1946. That year, General Electric researcher Vincent Schaefer successfully caused snow to fall in a small weather simulator.[54] In 1957 the President's Advisory Committee on Climate Control found that cloud seeding could increase rainfall by as much as seventeen percent.[55] And during the 1960s and '70s, the Department of Defense employed advanced seeding methods as an instrument of war. In June 1971, the U.S. military caused seven inches of rain to fall on the Ho Chi Minh trail, Hanoi's main supply channel during the Vietnam War.[56]

It is interesting to note that the CIA report spoke of an impending *ice age*. Today, twenty years later, we are experiencing severe ozone depletion and global warming. How could conditions have changed so in such a short period of time? Was the CIA assessment, backed by the latest scientific data, horribly off the mark, or can this environmental flip-flop be accounted for in some other way? *Weather modification that worked a little too well, perhaps?*

Critics fear that HAARP's transmitters can accidentally — or intentionally — alter the world's climate, as well as shake up the ground below. One thing's for certain. Since the inception of HAARP, earth's tectonic plates have been on the move and the weather has turned really freaky.

• **July 1995.** Ten Chinese provinces experienced record rainfalls, causing flooding and the death of 1,200 people. The provinces are prime rice-growing areas. In all, some 900,000 houses collapsed and more than 2.7 million acres of crops were wiped out.[57] At the same time, Mexico experienced its worst drought in decades. Millions of dollars in wheat and livestock were destroyed by the blistering dry heat.[58]

• **Summer 1995.** Moscow's hottest summer this century caused automobiles to break down in clouds of steam. Cracks lined the concrete runway of the city's Sheremetyvevo-2 International Airport. A powerful tremblor also shook Russia's Kamchatka Peninsula, killing as many as two thousand people. The region's oil-production facilities were severely damaged.[59]

• **September-October 1995.** Torrential rains across Southeast Asia ruined an estimated seventy per cent of Laos' rice fields and killed at least sixty-two people in Thailand. That same month, a 7.2 earthquake jolted Mexico; earth movements were also felt worldwide—in Japan, Siberia, China, Iran, Indonesia, Pakistan, Afghanistan, Sumatra, Turkey, Ecuador, Chile, Colombia, Peru, Costa Rica, Greece, Algeria, Hungary, Romania, the French Alps, Australia, New Zealand, western Montana, Las Vegas, Los Angeles, and the San Francisco Bay Area.[60] *Virtually everywhere on the globe.* Several weeks later, a 6.2 earthquake jolted Fairbanks.[61] This unprecedented activity coincided with simultaneous energy releases by HAARP and HIPAS, the mini-HAARP facility in Fairbanks. The heaters beamed energy at the same point high in the ionosphere. The event was reportedly recorded by sensors set up in Anchorage, Fairbanks, and Glenallen.[62]

• **January 1996.** Fierce blizzards struck a wide area from the Ohio Valley to Atlantic Canada. The areas received record snowfalls, and approximately one hundred people died from the wintry conditions. Cold air from the storms swept south to Cuba, where the lowest temperatures in fifty years were recorded. Meanwhile, in Somalia, drought conditions worsened, causing the forced migration of 800,000 nomads and the death of a half-million head of livestock.[63]

And who can forget 1995's deluge of hurricanes? This was the first year that the National Weather Service ran short of letters to name the pesky storms. Then there were the killer floods in the Northeastern United States in the opening days of 1996. The weather seems to be getting weirder—and harder to explain.

Meanwhile, the U.S. government continues to perturb the planet's upper atmosphere. In early February 1995, two rockets, carrying undisclosed chemicals, were launched from the Poker Flat Research Range, north of Fairbanks, directly into an aurora borealis located at an altitude of 150 miles. According to the Associated Press, the rockets also carried "weather experiments."[64] Another rocket was launched from Poker Flat the following month. This time, a rocket released barium and calcium 340 miles into the atmosphere.[65]

Furthermore, scientists from Sandia National Laboratories propose to establish a vast complex — the Atmospheric Radiation Measurement (ARM) program — near Barrow. Sandia has conferred with North Slope Borough and school district officials, promising to share "scientific and technical education" associated with ARM's "climate studies." Sandia has not discussed specifics of the program, and North Slope educators who have met privately with company officials are mum about their discussions.

In an ARM report, dated April 1995, Sandia officials express concern over the North Slope Borough's "regulatory environment." The report warns that "lack of support by the community could impede or prevent the granting of required permits. It could also create an environment in which achievement of ARM goals would be more difficult and/or more costly."[66]

Some area residents are unnerved by the sudden appearance of Sandia, a weapons contractor that has had many a contract thrown its way by the Department of Energy. Natives of the North Slope have not forgotten the DOE projects of the fifties that began with grins and handshakes. Nor are they sure that ARM is not somehow connected to HAARP. Posters, critical of Sandia's presence, have begun to crop up in Barrow.

Then there is the matter of sprites and jets. Recently pilots flying at high altitudes have reported seeing immense red and blue blobs flickering atop thunderstorms, above the stratosphere. These eerie blobs have been videotaped. But even so, scientists are at a complete loss to explain the phenomenon, other than to say that some unknown electrical force is at work.

"Every explanation has holes in it," said John Winckler, a University of Minnesota physics and astronomy professor, at a meeting of the American Geophysical Union in San Francisco. "We're in the beginning of a new aspect of science here."

The largest lights — red sprites — have been spotted towering sixty miles into the night sky, while the smaller, pulsating blue lights —

jets — have been seen shooting upward from thunderstorms at speeds in excess of 100,000 miles per hour. Radio signals generated by the mysterious phenomenon sound like "eggs hitting a griddle," according to Davis Sentman of the University of Alaska Fairbank's Geophysical Institute, which is actively involved with the Poker Flat rocket program and other Pentagon projects, including HAARP.

It has even been suggested that these strange bursts of light might endanger space shuttle astronauts. Walter Lyons of the Mission Research Corp. is currently studying sprites and jets for NASA. Says Lyons: "I would not volunteer to be the first astronaut to fly through one."[67]

Curiously, amid the flurry of Pentagon activities in Alaska, a UFO plunked down on the frozen Arctic Ocean off the coast of Barrow. The dome of pulsating orange and blue lights showed up at an opportune time — on New Year's Day, 1995. About sixty cars and trucks lined the beach near the town's gravel pit as Barrowites gawked at the shining intruder. Others, on foot, peered through the telescopic sights of hunting rifles, hoping for a closer look.

North Slope Borough Search and Rescue director Chuck Caldwell saw the lights, as well.

"I'm not prepared to believe it was a UFO," he said. "But that raises an interesting question…What would we have done if it was something up there? I'm glad we didn't have to find out." He told reporters that unknown lights had been seen over the ocean about a month earlier.[68]

Alaska Island Air pilot Jerry Jordan later reported that he had seen a bright light streak past his plane on New Year's Eve. There were no known aircraft in the area at the time.[69]

Many Barrow residents expressed hopes that the UFO they sighted was real. Even Tom Opie, the city's volunteer fire chief.

"I wanted to believe it as much as the next guy," he observed.[70]

Documented sightings — at least ones involving so many witnesses — have rarely, if ever, occurred in Barrow. The timing of the sighting is also strange. Can Barrow expect to see more "UFOs" as the activities of HAARP and ARM expand?

It is apparent from press reports that inhabitants of the Arctic *want* to see more of them. Which is a shame. While they're looking "out there," they'll most assuredly miss the Wizard's sleight of hand behind the curtain.

# 7

# Abductions of the Mind

---

*What makes Western civilization worth saving is the free-dom of the mind, now under heavy attack from the primitives…who have persisted among us.…*
— Elmer Davis

I gave a revolver to an elderly and readily suggestible man whom I had just hypnotized. The revolver had just been loaded by Mr. H. with a percussion cap. I explained to [the subject], while pointing to Mr. H., that Mr. H. was a very wicked man whom he should shoot to kill. With great determination he took the revolver and fired a shot directly at Mr. H. Mr. H. fell down pretending to be wounded. I then explained to my subject that the fellow was not yet quite dead, and that he should give him another bullet, which he did without further ado.[1]

This is how Ludwig Mayer, a German hypnosis researcher, described an experiment he conducted more than forty years ago. It is a landmark case that challenged the widely held belief that hypnotized subjects cannot be coaxed into committing criminal acts.

In 1951, Danish hypnotist Bjorn Nielsen went one-up on Mayer. His shenanigans would later become known as the Palle Hardrup Affair, which has been discussed widely in clinical treatises including Peter Reiter's *Antisocial or Criminal Acts and Hypnosis* (Charles C. Thomas, 1958). Hardrup, a hypnotic subject of Nielsen's, killed a guard while robbing a bank — all on the suggestion of Nielsen, according to evidence later brought out in court. In an effort to nix any inklings of conscience in Hardrup, Nielsen told the subject — under hypnosis — that his actions were guided by his "guardian angel." This guiding spirit was represented by the letter X. When Hardrup was presented with an X, he blindly obeyed any suggestion given him by the hypnotist. This extended to murder, robbery, and the offering up of his girlfriend's sexual favors to Nielsen.[2]

In March 1988, a "UFO Abductions Workshop" was held at the Whole Life Expo in Los Angeles. One lecture concerned UFO abductees, accounts of people allegedly accosted by strange-looking creatures and subjected to weird medical experiments aboard alien spacecraft. In one now-famous encounter, the audience was told, an abductee recalled being given a gun—a regular weapon, not a ray gun—and told by his alien captors to shoot a man tied to a chair in front of him. The aliens told the abductee that the bound man had done "evil on the earth."

"He's a bad person. You have to kill him," the aliens pushed. The abductee *considered* shooting the man, but instead turned the gun on the aliens.

"Fine," one of the creatures muttered, and quickly snatched up the weapon.[3]

What do these cases have in common?

Perhaps nothing. *Perhaps everything.*

The above abduction case is eerily similar to covert experiments carried out as early as 1950 by the CIA under various code names— BLUEBIRD,[4] ARTICHOKE,[5] MK-DELTA,[6] MK-SEARCH,[7] and MK-ULTRA.[8] Even earlier, the Pentagon began its own series of experiments, tucked away from public scrutiny under the classified headings of CHATTER,[9] THIRD CHANCE,[10] and DERBY HAT.[11] The goal of these top-secret programs, which frequently involved the use of unwitting human test subjects, was to devise methods of gaining control of the human mind and ultimately, in certain experiments, to create a so-called Manchurian Candidate, a brainwashed assassin programmed to kill on command.* The experiments also had something else in common: they were illegal under the laws of the United States, and they were in violation of the Nuremberg Code adopted by the international tribunal that sat in judgment of Nazis after World War II. In fact, many

---

*The term Manchurian Candidate was first coined by writer Richard Condon in his novel of an ex-Korean War vet who is programmed to assassinate a U.S. presidential candidate. A film, based upon Condon's best seller, featured Laurence Harvey as the brainwashed GI Raymond Shaw.

of the early mind-control experiments carried out by the CIA and U.S. military were based upon ghoulish experiments carried out at Dachau by Nazi "researchers."[12]

Snagged by Senate investigators in the 1970s, the CIA funded a propaganda campaign as a cover for its nefarious research. Communists, CIA officials told Senate committee members, were the real culprit when it came to brainwashing. The CIA explained that it had been forced into pursuing its own line of research to stem the communist threat.

The CIA proffered the same explanation to the FBI. In 1956, CIA head Allen Dulles sent a secret memorandum to FBI director J. Edgar Hoover excoriating the evils of "communist control." The memo supported "training" individuals to resist communist brainwashing efforts.[13]

However, in a secret memorandum sent to J. Lee Rankin, general counsel to the Warren Commission, CIA Deputy Director of Plans Richard Helms, who had personally authorized assassination attempts against Fidel Castro and other world leaders, admitted that Soviet mind-control studies lagged far behind the West.[14] In fact, the whole business of communist brainwashing may have been cooked up by the CIA and U.S. military as a cover for its own nasty deeds carried out during the Korean War.

At war's end, the International Scientific Commission for the Facts Concerning Bacterial Warfare in Korea and China (ISC) found that numerous Korean and Chinese communities had suffered unexplained outbreaks of bubonic plague and other diseases coinciding with the appearance of insects not then common to these areas. The ISC accused the American military of using types of bacteriological warfare, originally developed by the Japanese during World War II. The organization stated that the Americans had "deliberately protected the Japanese bacteriological war criminals" and had spread plague germs in Korea and China by means of "flea bombs," germ-laden canisters filled with fleas carrying bubonic plague like the ones dropped during World War II on Chinese cities by Japan's infamous Unit 731, known as the Ishii Corps. These revelations seemed to confirm the confessions of American prisoners of war — extracted by communist brainwashing, the American military claimed — that the U.S. had indeed used germ warfare against the Koreans and Chinese.

Peter Williams' and David Wallace's book *Unit 731: The Japanese Army's Secret of Secrets* (Hodder and Stoughton, 1989) explores these allegations. The book appeared in many countries but, curiously, the chapter detailing America's alleged use of bacteriological warfare during the Korean War was conspicuously missing in the American edition. These charges have been around since the 1950s, but have been lambasted by the American press. On March 15, 1952, the *New York Times* dismissed the allegations under the banner headline "REDS' PHOTOGRAPHS ON GERM WARFARE EXPOSED AS FAKES—EVIDENCE IS CONCLUSIVE."*[15]

It is from this bubbling cauldron following the Korean War that the CIA and U.S. military plucked forth the notion of mind control. United States Senate investigations may have, in fact, bolstered government efforts to push forward with mind-control research. Covert government researchers, by "coming clean" with Senate committees, accomplished what has become known in spook vernacular as a "limited hangout." Yes, the CIA and military admitted to wrongdoing. Yes, they had conducted research involving pharmaceuticals and hypnosis on unwitting human subjects. Yes, they were sorry.

But this is a story of omission. While the offending parties freely admitted to slipping soldiers LSD, causing some to go crazy or commit suicide, they failed to talk much at all about their most cherished area of study—psychoelectronics. In fact, virtually all documents released to date have dealt with the use of drugs in mind control; according to one estimate, as many as twenty-five percent of all MK-ULTRA projects were part of the "black" world, impervious to Congressional scrutiny or Freedom of Information requests. Many of these projects likely dealt with psychoelectronics.**[16]

Psychoelectronics is the stimulation of the brain by microwaves or other electromagnetic sources that causes changes in human behav-

---

*At the 1925 Geneva Convention, most of the world's global powers signed an agreement banning the use of biological weapons. There were two abstainers: the United States and Japan.

**We may never know the full extent of the CIA's involvement in mind-control experiments. According to the authors of *Acid Dreams: The CIA, LSD and the Sixties Rebellion* (Grove Press, 1985), in the early 1970s CIA director Richard Helms ordered the destruction of many secret MK-ULTRA documents due to "a burgeoning paper problem."

ior that can be controlled. This is not science fiction. It is science — a technology that was given birth by the U.S. intelligence community back in the 1950s, at a time when Mayer and Nielsen were performing parlor tricks. Little did they know, their mind-control methods were already obsolete.

In 1953, during the early years of the Cold War, scientist John Lilly, known for his work with marine mammals, was asked by the director of the National Institute of Mental Health (NIMH), then a major conduit of CIA funds, to brief the CIA, FBI, NSA, and various U.S. military intelligence services on his research involving electrodes and brain-stimulation. Lilly says he refused, noting: "I feel that if this technique got into the hands of a secret agency, they would have total control over a human being and be able to change his beliefs extremely quickly, leaving little evidence of what they had done."[17]

At the National Institutes of Health (NIH), Lilly pounded up to six hundred electrodes into the skulls of monkeys and, through the use of electrical stimulation, was able to discover precise sites in the brain that produced pain, fear, anxiety, anger, even sexual arousal. Lilly's "brain maps" attracted widespread interest in the intelligence community. Much to his chagrin, his work with dolphins was subsequently applied to warfare in a joint CIA-Navy program known as Swimmer Nullification.*[18]

It was also in the 1950s and early 1960s that a neurosurgeon named José Delgado, a recipient of NIH funds, began to implant radio transmitter-receivers in the brains of animals — and humans — in order to control these test subjects from afar. In one experiment, Delgado reportedly imbedded an electrode in the brain of a bull and then, stepping unprotected into a Madrid bullring, he challenged the bull to attack. This the bull did, but, just before reaching him, Delgado pressed a button on a black box — a stimoceiver, he called it — and the angry beast suddenly halted.[19]

In this and other experiments, Delgado demonstrated that emotions and behavior could be electronically induced. An experiment involving "radio stimulation" produced a variety of effects in human

---

*Interestingly, Lilly claims in *The Scientist* (Ronin Publishing, 1988) to have interacted with alien forces that he dubs "solid state entities."

test subjects, including elation, deep concentration, relaxation, and "colored visions" (remotely induced hallucinations).[20]

In the future, Delgado observed, "ESB [electronic stimulation of the brain] could possibly become a master control of human behavior."[21] He added: "The contention that an ideal society should be 'well behaved' requires a clarification of meaning. In some old plantations slaves behaved very well, worked hard, were submissive to their masters, and were probably happier than some of the free blacks in modern ghettos. In several dictatorial countries the general population is skillful, productive, well behaved, and perhaps as happy as those in more democratic societies." Then, almost as an aside, he said: "It is doubtful, however, that slavery or dictatorship should be our models."[22]

In the 1970s, Robert Heath, chairman of the Tulane University Medical School's Department of Neurology and Psychiatry, conducted numerous ESB experiments, some for the CIA and United States Army. A fierce anti-marijuana crusader and proponent of lobotomies, Heath believed ESB just might cure society's ills. Especially homosexuality.

In one experiment, Heath "wired" a twenty-four-year-old male homosexual. When electrodes in his brain were stimulated, the subject said he felt relaxed, self-confident, and euphoric. The stimulation also aroused him sexually. He was encouraged to masturbate while watching a stag film and, later, was even supplied with the services of a prostitute.[23]

Heath soon discovered that he could control his patients' memory — producing, in effect, incidents of "missing time" — and, furthermore, that he could produce a wide range of emotional responses, even hallucinations, in patients.[24] Heath claims that he was asked to conduct more extensive ESB research for the Army, but that he refused, concerned with the ethics of such a proposal.[25]

Computer specialist Joseph Meyer had no such qualms. Meyer worked for the National Security Agency, the most secretive of all American intelligence agencies. Meyer proposed that electronic tracking devices be attached to "subscribers" — "criminal recidivists," as well as those free on bail or on parole. He argued that such an "electronic surveillance and command-control system [would make] crime pointless."[26]

He added:

The aim of the transponder surveillance scheme is to constrain criminals and arrestees into behaving like law abiding citizens. If this aim is fulfilled, then most of the subscribers will do ordinary things like get up in the morning and go to work. At night they will stay close to home, to avoid being implicated in crimes. At their place of work, a human surveillance system will operate. Low-powered transceivers in their domiciles can monitor them indoors. Alarm transceivers in banks, stores, and other buildings would warn security personnel of their approach. Almost all subscribers would be following predictable routine patterns, so that even if the surveillance lost an individual for a time it would pick him up again, or have him automatically paged.[27]

Meyer further envisioned the infiltration of subscriber groups by informants and undercover agents who would provide advance warning of "mutinies and large-scale confrontations, or massive destruction of transponders." He stressed that riots and revolts would be futile, because tampering with a transponder would be a felony.[28]

In a little known book entitled *Were We Controlled?* (University Books, 1967), the author — writing under the pseudonym Lincoln Lawrence — revealed details of what he claimed to be radical new methods in mind control. Specifically, he referred to RHIC-EDOM technology. Together RHIC (Radio Hypnotic Intracerebral Control) and EDOM (Electronic Dissolution of Memory), Lawrence claimed, could induce a hypnotic trance, deliver suggestions to a subject and, with the use of EDOM, erase all memory of the hypnotic session and the particular act the subject was instructed to perform. Post-hypnotic suggestions could be "triggered at will" by a radio transmission, received via a miniaturized radio receiver implanted in the subject's brain.

Lawrence went on to say that "there is already in use a small EDOM generator-transmitter which can be concealed on the body of the person. Contact with this person — a casual handshake or even just a touch — transmits a tiny electronic charge plus an ultrasonic signal tone which for a short while will disturb the time orientation of the person affected."[29]

Ten years after the publication of *Were We Controlled?*, Senator Richard Schweiker, speaking during committee hearings exploring CIA abuses, asked Sidney Gottlieb, science advisor to then-CIA deputy director Richard Bissell, about MK-ULTRA, the CIA's mind-control program.*

> SCHWEIKER: Did any of these projects involve radio hypnotic intracerebral control, which is a combination, as I understand it, in layman's terms, radio transmissions and hypnosis?
> GOTTLIEB: My answer is no.
> SCHWEIKER: None whatsoever?
> GOTTLIEB: Well, I am trying to be responsive to the terms that you used. As I remember it, there was a current interest, running interest, all the time in what affects people's standing in the field of radio energy have, and it could easily have been that somewhere in many projects, someone was trying to see if you could hypnotize someone easier if he was standing in a radio beam. That would seem like a reasonable piece of research to do.

Senator Schweiker then mentioned that he had heard that radar (i.e., microwaves) had been used to erase the memory of animals. Gottlieb responded dryly: "I can believe that, Senator."[30]

Gottlieb may have been struggling not to commit perjury. He may have gotten away with it. According to one CIA source, the agency concentrated on psychoelectronics *after* the reported termination of MK-ULTRA in 1963.[31] Other sources, including Lincoln Lawrence, asserted that psychoelectronics was properly a product of *military* research.[32] Gottlieb was asked only about the CIA. As such, he *technically* provided truthful testimony.

But back to Lawrence's book. If RHIC-EDOM itself wasn't weird enough, Lawrence went on to make another astonishing claim: He asserted that Lee Harvey Oswald had been implanted with a tiny radio receiver and, by means of RHIC-EDOM, had been "instructed" to kill President Kennedy. Oswald, Lawrence claimed, had been implanted

---

*Gottlieb wore many hats at the CIA. He was heavily involved in MK-ULTRA and other mind-control programs. In addition, Richard Helms (before ascending to the CIA's top post) requested that then-CIA director Allen Dulles set up a program under Gottlieb for the "covert use of biological and chemical materials." Gottlieb was also asked to research assassination techniques for Bissell, who was deeply involved in CIA-mob efforts to assassinate Cuba's Fidel Castro.

in the Soviet Union during his supposed defection but was later taken over by another unnamed intelligence apparatus.[33]

Sound crazy? CIA director John McCone, appointed by President Kennedy before his death, was apparently privy to the same information as Lawrence. In a secret memorandum sent to Secret Service chief James Rowley, McCone speculated that, following minor surgery in Minsk, Oswald might have been "chemically or *electronically* 'controlled'...a sleeper agent. Subject spent 11 days hospitalized for a 'minor ailment' which should have required no more than three days hospitalization at best [emphasis added]."[34]

Something in the book also tipped off Oswald's mother, Marguerite, that Lawrence knew Oswald personally. She wouldn't confirm what had raised her suspicions. She did, however, note that the texture of hair on the back of Oswald's head had changed after returning from the Soviet Union.[35] Oswald's brother noticed something odd about Lee, too. His brother's hair, he observed, had thinned considerably on top and the texture had changed from "soft to kinky."[36]

Martin Cannon, author of a fascinating and well-researched paper on government mind-control experiments and UFO abductions entitled *The Controllers: A New Hypothesis of Alien Abductions*, claims to know who Lawrence is. According to Cannon, the author is a "former FBI agent turned journalist."[37]

Investigative journalist Dick Russell did manage to locate the individual—radio announcer Art Ford—who, he was told, ghostwrote *Were We Controlled?* Ford told Russell that he had only done research for the elusive author and had no clue as to Lawrence's identity, adding that he always deposited his material at a mail drop. Ford asserted, however, that Martin Scheiman, Lawrence's attorney, was found dead in the Time-Life Building with a bullet through his head after the book was published. His death was reportedly ruled a suicide.[38] Also turning up dead was Damon Runyon, Jr., who wrote a condensation of the book for the *National Enquirer*, which was never published. Runyon was the only person who had ever received a written communication from Lawrence. The *New York Times* of April 15, 1968, reported that the son of the famed writer had fallen from an overpass. The police tentatively ruled his death a suicide.[39]

The CIA is supposed to have written a 350-page report on RHIC-EDOM following Kennedy's assassination. The claim was made by journalist James Moore in the August 18, 1975, issue of *Modern People*.[40]

We can only speculate about Lawrence's book. Surely, whoever wrote it had an intimate knowledge of government mind-control research. It provided information that became public knowledge only after the convening of a special U.S. Senate committee a decade later.

But what does all this have to do with alien abductions? Consider, for a moment, the commonalties — the glue, if you will — that bind abductions and mind-control research. There are the accounts of "missing time" reported by mind-control test subjects *and* UFO abductees. There are the "forgotten memories" that resurface only after intensive hypnotherapy. There are the "odd" sensations, as Delgado called them — the feeling of floating, for one. Then there are the hallucinations — the "colored visions" — that are reported by both test subjects and abductees. The "abductees" see aliens; test subjects see what they are *told* to see.

Martin Cannon is convinced abductions are real. He rejects the notion that all abduction accounts are the product of disturbed minds, or the result of encounters with visitors from Zeta Reticuli.

Says Cannon: "The kidnapping is real. The fear is real. The pain is real. The instruction is real. But the little grey men from Zeta Reticuli are *not* real; they are constructs, Halloween masks meant to disguise the real faces of the controllers. The abductors may not be visitors from Beyond; rather, they may be a symptom of the carcinoma which blackens our body politic."[41]

Microwave radiation, the power behind the military's powerful EMP weapons, seems to be inexorably linked to the abduction phenomenon. In 1970, the RAND Corporation, a private think tank with cozy ties to the intelligence community, conceded that microwaves could be used to promote insomnia, fatigue, irritability, *memory loss,* and *hallucinations.*[42] Even Nikola Tesla, early in this century, observed behavioral effects associated with electromagnetic exposure, according to author Margaret Cheney.[43] As early as 1934, E.L. Chaffee and R.U. Light published a paper on "A Method for the Remote Control of Electrical Stimulation of the Nervous System."[44]

In 1973, Joseph Sharp, an Army researcher, was able to "hear" and understand spoken words delivered on a pulsed microwave beam. Researcher Robert Becker comments that "such a device has obvious applications in covert operations designed to drive a target crazy with 'voices' or deliver undetectable instructions to a programmed assassin."[45] *Or to make a suggestible subject see aliens?*

Interestingly, in the USAF's publication *Low-Intensity Conflict and Modern Technology* (see chapter six), Captain Tyler mentions the use of EM weapons in "enhancing abilities for *anomalous phenomena.*" Julianne McKinney, director of the Association of National Security Alumni's Electronic Surveillance Project, says she has received numerous reports from private citizens who have been subjected to EM harassment by the military and leading defense contractors. Her research suggests that nonlethal technology may lie at the core of "applied anomalous phenomena" — specific mental images and perceptions created by exposure to electromagnetic radiation.[46]

Since November 1994, dozens of people have inexplicably moved to Taos, New Mexico, after receiving "the call." Taos, you will recall, is the site of a strange humming presence that has unnerved many residents. Those who have moved here, after *hearing* "the call," claim that Taos, the hippie mecca of the sixties, is a center for "extraterrestrial energy." They are at a loss to explain their move to the area or their heightened sense of awareness, stating only that they felt *compelled* to relocate to this small desert locale. Some of these emigrants have left behind jobs and successful businesses to come to Taos.

One woman claims that she came to Taos after spotting a UFO that approached her as she was washing a window in her son's bedroom.

"I knew it couldn't possibly be an airplane," she told the *Taos News.* "It came closer...then a very tired feeling overcame me. I felt compelled to lie down on the bed. What's more, I felt a weight right over my chest, pushing me down." She said she fought the urge to sleep, but soon dozed off.

She then explained what happened next.

When I was asleep, I had the strangest dream, one that recurs every now and then. Something closely resembling a cash register tape kept running upwards. I kept seeing rows and rows of green numbers. After a long time, the numbers started changing color. They became green on top and orange on the bottom. The running tape on the second set of numbers didn't run very long. When the numerical action stopped and I thought the experience was over, then some more numbers started coming up. These were orange. This experience seemed quite lengthy, just like the one with the green numbers. When the numbers quit registering in my mind, I wanted to get up, but again I was powerless to do so.[47]

When she awoke, she felt dazed and disoriented.

"I tried to see the flying craft," she noted, "but the sky looked like a blur to me." For two days, she experienced a "strange numbness."

"It felt like I was experiencing a *brain rape*," she stated. "That's pretty strange for me, because I have a [literal] mind and I'm not that fond of numbers [emphasis added]."[48]

Through the years, individuals have come forward claiming to have been the victims of government-run mind-control experiments. Curiously, these apparently sincere men and women have been ignored by the press. Even the term given to these individuals is derogatory. Wavies, they're called.

Valerie Wolf, a Louisiana social worker, has worked with many who claim to be survivors of inhumane government experiments. On March 15, 1995, Wolf presented her findings to the President's Committee on Radiation, convened to study radiation experiments conducted on children by the Atomic Energy Commission. Wolf is one of a growing number of activists concerned about such apparently widespread experimentation.[49]

By contrast, when UFO abductees come forward, their accounts are widely reported in the media. Recent books on alleged abductions have garnered surprisingly good reviews from the mainstream media, including the *New York Times*, which, curiously, froths at the mouth at such notions that the JFK assassination was a conspiracy.

Is it really more plausible to believe in prurient bug-eyed monsters from space than the idea that Lee Harvey Oswald didn't act alone? Or are "abductions" somehow more believable than the accounts of MK-ULTRA survivors?

An immense shift in attitudes among Americans regarding UFOs has taken place in the last fifty years. In the late 1940s, when UFOs first appeared on the scene, you could find few people who believed that the objects were from "out there." Most assumed they were secret military devices. Strange, but terrestrial, nonetheless.

Then in the '60s, twenty years after Kenneth Arnold's classic sighting, attitudes began to change dramatically. It was now the Age of Aquarius. Young people, often buoyed by psychedelics, began to speak of a New Age, universal love, and *the cosmos.\** Public opinion polls showed that many now believed that UFOs were "real," presumably from outer space.[50]

A recent survey, conducted in June 1995, reveals that belief in UFOs is at an all-time high. According to the Scripps Howard-Ohio University poll, fifty percent of all Americans now believe that UFOs are real. The Scripps Howard News Service reported the results in newspapers across the country in early August, emphasizing that "half of America's adults believe flying saucers could be real and that the federal government is covering up what it knows about extraterrestrial beings."[51]

Interestingly, the generations that were raised on television — age fifty-four and under — were the most likely to hold such beliefs. Fifty-six percent of Generation Xers polled said they believe in UFOs; Baby Boomers logged in a similar figure. By contrast, those 65 and older — the so-called Class of '46 — registered a no-vote for UFOs.

---

*The CIA had a fondness for LSD predating the Age of Aquarius. Time-Life magnates Henry and Claire Booth Luce, both more than cozy with the CIA, were frequent "trippers" during the early '60s. Henry claims to have had a chat with God on a golf course during one memorable trip. According to the book *Acid Dreams: The CIA, LSD and the Sixties Rebellion* (Grove Press, 1985), "Nearly every drug that appeared on the black market during the 1960s — marijuana, cocaine, heroin, PCP, amyl nitrate, mushrooms, DMT, barbiturates, laughing gas, speed, and many others — had previously been scrutinized, tested, and in some cases refined by the CIA and army scientists." The CIA and U.S. Army were particularly fond of LSD which, by their own admission, they administered to about one thousand unwitting people during the 1950s. According to an originally classified document of November 16, 1953, the CIA ordered ten kilos of LSD — thirty million doses — from Swiss manufacturer Sandoz. When Sandoz refused to comply, the CIA asked the Eli Lilly Company to make its own LSD. Soon thereafter, Lilly assured the CIA that "LSD would be available in tonnage quantities." Since one ton of LSD yields more than *2.5 billion* doses, it would seem only natural to ask the CIA what it did with all that acid. The establishment media, so far, has not seen fit to raise this disturbing question.

Only thirty-four percent of those polled in this age group believe UFOs are real.[52]

This strongly suggests that UFO belief systems are media-driven. Those exposed to the most television — Generation Xers and Baby Boomers — believe the most strongly in UFOs. Television has spun a veritable web around viewers, enticing them with repeated references to the "extraterrestrial phenomenon." Shows like *The X-Files, Sightings,* and a deluge of specials on the "alien presence" fill the airwaves.

At the same time, the government is portrayed as conducting some master cover-up. A cover-up of the "truth" — that UFOs are real and from "out there." But might another kind of cover-up exist, one even more insidious than the one proposed by the media and Hollywood? Is the media-driven "implant" that a government cover-up exists nothing more than a limited hangout, obfuscating the *TRUTH* with the truth?

In any event, the UFO abduction movement is beginning to come apart at the seams. *Despite the media and government's best efforts.*

On December 1, 1995, a small Salt Lake City newspaper called the *Deseret News* ran a story that could vie for a spot on Sonoma State's Most Censored list of news stories. To my knowledge, no other newspapers — large ones, anyway — ran the story.

A quick glance at the headline offers an explanation: ABDUCTED BY ALIENS — *AND* BY SECRET MILITARY? Zack Van Eyck, *Deseret News* staff writer, threw his readers a bombshell.

> MESQUITE, Nev. — Space invaders aren't the only ones kidnapping unsuspecting Americans and forcing them to undergo medical examinations, according to one of three alleged alien abduction victims who spoke here Thursday.
>
> Melinda Leslie, an Orange County, Calif., woman who leads a support group for self-described abductees, said more than three dozen people who believe they have been taken aboard alien spacecraft — including herself — have been re-abducted *by apparent military personnel and subjected to physical examinations and interrogation.*
>
> Leslie, addressing an audience of about 300 here at the fifth annual International UFO Congress, said *humans in a 'flying triangle'* abducted her and took her to an underground testing facility. There, men in hazardous-material jumpsuits performed an extensive gynecological exam and other medical procedures on her, she

said. *She was abducted by humans a second time and interrogated by a red-haired 'military captain' who demanded that she tell him everything she knew about the aliens.*

*Men in uniform also have been present during some alien abduction experiences, including one of the half-dozen Leslie has had, she said. She and other abductees have been targets of continued surveillance and harassment by these same people, she added* [emphasis added].

Leslie, the article continues, has formally requested the government — specifically, Health and Human Services in Washington — to investigate the military kidnappings. She rightly pointed out that those involved in scientific research must first be provided an implied consent form, notifying them that they are indeed test subjects. In reply to a letter sent by one of the abductees, Lana Skirboll, director of the National Institute of Mental Health's Office of Science Policy and Program Planning, said she needed additional information from the correspondent — address and social security number — before the agency could proceed.[53]

These are by no means isolated cases. Leah Haley, a mother of two from Mississippi, also claims to have been abducted by "aliens" *and military personnel.* Under hypnosis, she has recalled military officials subjecting her to electroshock in order to *revive* her memories of alien abductions.[54]

Since September 1990, Haley claims, she has been "followed by military types in navy blue or white cars" and has also been buzzed by unmarked black helicopters. Furthermore, she reports hearing "Morse-Code-type beeps" in her ears, adding that she has occasionally become disoriented.[55]

Psychiatrist Thomas G. Shafer, who attended to Haley in 1992, concluded that Haley manifests "no evidence of organic psychoses such as schizophrenia, organic brain syndrome, or bipolar illness." A Fantasy Prone Test given to Haley revealed that she is "less likely than the normal person to be fantasy prone."[56]

In another case, a Northern California abductee — we'll call him Peter — told investigator Cannon that he had encountered a *human being* during one encounter. He called this man "a doctor." He was able to describe the individual in great detail, and even drew a portrait of him.[57]

A short while later, an abductee from Southern California told Cannon a similar story, including a description of the same "doctor." "The physical details were so strikingly similar as to erase coincidence," says Cannon.[58]

Another intriguing account comes from Lucia Davidson, whom Cannon describes as thoughtful and articulate.

"In an interview with me," he writes, "she described an unsettling recollection of a human being, dressed normally, holding a black box with a protruding antennae. This odd snippet of memory *did not* coincide with the general thrust of her abduction narrative. Could this remembrance represent an all-too-brief segment of accurately-perceived reality interrupting her hypnotically-induced 'screen memory'? Peter (mentioned above) clearly recalled seeing a similar box during his abduction."[59]

Cannon points out that Lucia lives in the Los Angeles suburb of Tujunga Canyon, a frequent abduction site that is located near a supposedly abandoned Nike missile base. Witnesses in the area have described peculiar military activity at the site.[60]

The close proximity of this incident to the Nike base brings to mind the strange research of Louis West, now known for his participation in MK-ULTRA LSD experiments.* West received considerable CIA funding while serving as chairman of the UCLA Psychiatry Department and director of the Neuro-Psychiatric Institute, known for its work in the field of ESP. An expert in brainwashing, he testified at the trial of Patty Hearst.[61]

West was obsessed with the idea of curbing the violent impulses within man. In 1973, he proposed the creation of the Center for the Study and Reduction of Violence, where potentially violent individuals could expect to receive "drug therapy" and electrical jolts to the brain. The proposal was backed by then-California governor Ronald Reagan. Eventually West's idea was shot down by opponents. An important factor contributing to the center's demise was, no doubt, West's odd request to J.M. Stubblebine, director of the California State Department of Health. In a letter dated January 22, 1973, West pro-

---

*West has the dubious distinction of being the only man ever to kill an elephant with LSD.

posed that the controversial center be housed in an *abandoned Nike missile base* located in the Santa Monica Mountains, near Los Angeles.[62]

"The Voice of Authority tells us that MK-ULTRA belongs to history," says Cannon. "It threatened once, but no more. Anyone insisting otherwise must be silenced by glib rationalization or selective inattention.

"Yet these two topics—UFO abductions and mind control—have more in common than their mutual [ostracism]. The data overlap. If we could chart these phenomena...we would see a surprisingly large intersection between the two circles of information."[63]

Basically, abductions fall into one of two categories: Abductions of the Unpleasant Kind, like the shoot-on-command cases discussed at the opening of this chapter, and Abductions of the Pleasant Kind. This second variety is probably the more common of the two. Typically, those experiencing an APK abduction come away with feelings similar to those expressed by the Flower Children of the sixties. They talk of seeking higher levels of consciousness, of preparing for the arrival of the "Space Brothers."

Their banter is strictly New Age.

Although not generally known, the term New Age has a very disturbing origin. In 1942, a Tokyo University professor Chikao Fujisawa first used the term as a subtitle to his booklet *On the Divine Mission of Nippon*. The subtitle: *A Prophecy of the Dawn of a New Age.* His booklet was subsequently reprinted as part of a larger work, *Tokyo Record,* written by Otto Tolischus. In his treatise, Fujisawa espoused what one would not normally associate with the New Age movement. Fujisawa was, in fact, an unrepentant fascist who was convinced Japan had a "divine mission for the salvation of *disoriented mankind.*"[64]

Otto Tolischus summed up Fujisawa's views this way:

It bluntly announced that Japan was fighting by command of the Japanese gods to "reunite" all nations under the rule of the Japanese Emperor "as it was in the beginning." According to this leading light of Japanese science, Japan was the original motherland of all nations and the cradle of civilization, from which other nations have strayed, and to which they must return. The whole warring world, he proclaimed, must be converted into one large family under the divine rule of the Japanese Emperor, in which each nation will take its own proper place. This, he blandly announced, is the goal of "the divine mission of Nippon," and the objective which Japan has been pursuing throughout her history....

The capitalistic individualism prevalent in the United States, he declared, runs "counter to cosmic truth," and so does the Communism of Russia, but Nazism and Fascism are closer to the "truth." The latter had much in common, Fujisawa wrote, "with Musubi principle of one in many." And this "spiritual solidarity" of Japan, Germany and Italy prompted "a common front against the desperate offensive launched by those powers defending the old order."[65]

Fujisawa yearned for a New World Order, a term often used by Adolf Hitler and, most recently in this country, by George Bush and Bill Clinton.

Says Cannon: "A spectre haunts the democratic nations — the spectre of *technofascism*. All the powers of the espionage empire and the scientific establishment have entered into an unholy alliance to evoke this spectre: Psychiatrist and spy, Dulles and Delgado, microwave specialists and clandestine operators.

"A mind is a terrible thing to waste — and a worse thing to commandeer."[66]

Cannon warns that abductees are particularly susceptible to cults. Some abductees, he notes, have actually been "directed" to join certain religious-philosophical sects.

"The leaders of these groups tend to be 'ex'-CIA operatives, or Special Forces veterans," writes Cannon. "They are often linked through personal relations, even though they espouse widely varying traditions. I have heard disturbing reports that the leaders of some of these groups have used hypnosis, drugs, or 'mind machines' on their charges. Members of these cults have reported periods of missing time during ceremonies or 'study periods.' "[67]

One such group, Cannon contends, is led by former Apollo astronaut Virgil Armstrong who, he points out, is an ex-CIA employee and Green Beret. According to Cannon, Armstrong, who espouses the doctrine of "love and light," is a close friend of General John Singlaub of Iran-Contra fame and leader of the right-wing World Anti-Communist League.[68]

Cannon states that one abductee he knows was told by "voices," during an abduction episode, to seek out Armstrong and join his "sky-watch" activities. This abductee later reported back that the sky-watch she attended included a mass channeling session intended to send debilitating "negative vibrations" to Konstantin Chernenko, then Secretary General of the Soviet Union.[69]

Another shadowy organization is the I AM group, founded in the 1930s by those with strong Nazi sympathies. Following World War II, William Pelley, head of the American Nazi Silver Shirts, became a driving force behind the I AM movement. He later went on to head an occult organization called Soulcraft which, it so happened, employed George Hunt Williamson, a well-known "contactee" of the fifties who claimed to have a special relationship with the Space Brothers. Williamson co-authored a book, *UFOs Confidential,* which claimed that the solution to the UFO mystery was being stymied by a Jewish banking conspiracy. George Van Tassell, another famous contactee of the fifties, was also associated with Pelley and Rev. Wesley Swift, who founded the group that would eventually evolve into the Aryan Nations.[70]

Another prominent contactee from this period was George Adamski. Adamski reportedly had connections with Pelley and Williamson. Furthermore, he admitted that four U.S. government scientists were responsible for launching his emissary-to-the-Space-Brothers career. These scientists were allegedly from Point Loma Naval Electronics Laboratory near San Diego and a similar facility in Pasadena. Abroad, Adamski was said to have the backing of a former intelligence officer in the British Army. According to information developed by Jacques Vallee, the contactee had a passport bearing special privileges.[71] Even CIA director Allen Dulles may have intervened on behalf of Adamski in a court proceeding, a document from the fifties suggests.[72]

Researcher David Stupple asserts that most contactee groups today are offshoots of the I AM group. One of the most famous of these is Elizabeth Clare Prophet's Church Universal and Triumphant, a group that purportedly has a massive arms cache in underground bunkers.*[73] The Summer 1988 issue of the *Covert Action Information Bulletin* states that

---

*If this allegation is true, one must wonder why this "church" has not been targeted by the Bureau of Alcohol, Tobacco and Firearms (BATF), as was the Branch Davidian complex in Waco.

the organization is CIA-funded and, according to researcher John Judge, has ties to the World Anti-Communist League.[74] Prophet is active in abduction research and has sponsored presentations on the subject.[75]

In 1991 the Roper Organization posed questions to nearly six thousand Americans to determine the estimated number of UFO abductions nationwide. Those included in the poll were asked if they had ever had certain experiences which, according to the UFO buffs who had sponsored the poll, indicated a strong likelihood of abduction. These experiences were:

- Waking up paralyzed with a sense of presence nearby

- Experiencing "missing time"

- Seeing unusual lights in a room

- Finding marks or scars on your body that you could not explain

- Feeling that you were flying

Those who answered yes to at least four of the five questions were considered "probable abductees." Nearly 120 people fell into this category. Therefore, the pollsters concluded, nearly four million Americans have experienced alien abductions.

James Gleick, among others, considers this survey ridiculous. Writing in the *New Republic,* he states: "Most healthy people can answer yes to a few of these [questions]. I certainly can. They are well-known feelings and dream types. Even the sinister-sounding scar question is an easy yes for many people (take a moment to examine your body carefully and you'll see what I mean)."[76]

Gleick is equally critical of the use of hypnosis in abduction research.

"Hypnosis is all about suggestion," he asserts. "It has always been a fringe practice, as useful to carnival magicians and moviemakers as to clinical psychiatrists, and for every genuine buried memory unearthed by hypnotists, many more false memories have been implanted."[77]

Cannon agrees: "We *cannot* assume the accuracy of abduction descriptions given during subsequent hypnotic regression.... Indeed, responsible skeptics have argued that hypnotic regression may prove inadvertently harmful, in that it may *lock in place a false remembrance* [emphasis added]."[78]

Abduction researchers employing hypnosis have fallen under increasing criticism. One researcher, John Mack, came close to being ousted from Harvard University for his work with abductees. In his book *Abduction: Human Encounters With Aliens* (Ballantine Books, 1994), the psychiatrist recounts thirteen of the seventy-six cases that comprise his "abductee caseload."*

But Mack's cases involve not only abductions but *sexual interaction* with aliens. In *Abduction,* he recounts the story of "Ed," who, under hypnosis, recalled having sex in a "pod" with a silvery-blond alien.[79] "Catherine," he reports, was forced to lie naked on a table while aliens rammed an unknown instrument into her vagina.[80] And "Eva," according to Mack, was groped by three extraterrestrial "midgets."[81]

But Mack sees no harm in these intergalactic sexual romps. Cosmic rape aside, he feels that "the intelligences at work do not wish us ill."[82] He feels the entities really have our best interests at heart, and the indignities to which abductees are subjected are a small price to pay for all the consciousness-raising going on. Yes, Mack says his abductees have all been lectured by their sexual tormentors about the need for a New Age. You know — peace, love, and all that. Never mind the coerced gynecological examinations and forced sex.

Mack's Center for Psychology and Social Change has the strong financial backing of Rockefeller family members. The professor is defensive when asked about the $300,000 a year — most of it from the Rockefellers — that flows into the center. According to the *Boston Globe,* Laurance Rockefeller, nephew of Nelson, gives $250,000 annually, in addition to the $194,000 grant he made to start up Mack's Program for Extraordinary Experience Research. Laura Rockefeller Chasin, Alida Rockefeller, and Abby Rockefeller have also donated many thousands of dollars to Mack over the years, not counting $86,000 in reported gifts from the Rockefeller Family Fund (which a fund staffer denies). When presented with a list of these donations, on file at the Massachusetts

---

*Time* magazine took a look at Mack's use of hypnosis with abductees. It quoted one of the psychiatrist's subjects as saying she was given UFO literature to read before being hypnotized.

State Office of Charities, Mack exclaimed, "This is all wrong," but he refused to elaborate.*[83]

Interestingly, the same month Mack escaped censure by the Harvard Medical School, a licensed psychologist named Richard Boylan — an abduction researcher with no big-name backers — got the boot from the California State Licensing Board. Boylan, the psychology board concluded, had "abused his role as a therapist when he imposed his personal views on the existence of extraterrestrials into the dreams and memories of two patients."[84]

Says Gleick: "Of course, what really makes Mack different from the standard flying-saucer nut is that he's got authority.... The promotion surrounding his new book leans heavily on his professional trappings. There is his status as a medical doctor and psychiatrist...his Pulitzer Prize**...[and] Harvard University, where Mack enjoys the comfort of academic tenure."[85]

Mack is also active in the Human Potential Foundation, founded by retired Navy officer Scott Jones. In May 1995, the group, comprised of UFO true believers, met in the nation's capital to discuss the earth's "inevitable" large-scale meeting with alien cultures.[86] Laurance Rockefeller has reportedly contributed $700,000 to HPF.†[87]

Then there is the matter of "hybrids." Under hypnosis, many abductees recall being impregnated by aliens and having hybrid fetuses removed from their bodies. Abductees have reportedly seen half-human/half-alien fetuses in containers aboard the spacecraft. In some

---

*The New York Post of February 26, 1996, reports that Laurance Rockefeller has forked out even more money for "Unidentified Flying Objects: The Best Available Evidence," a 150-page report that he has distributed to one thousand world leaders, including Henry Kissinger, Walter Annenberg, and Colin Powell.

**Mack won a Pulitzer Prize for his biography of Lawrence of Arabia.

†Human Potential Foundation. It has a familiar ring to it, according to Mack critic Julianne McKinney. In the 1950s, an organization known as the Society for the Investigation of Human Ecology served as a front for mind-control experiments, heavily funded by the CIA and the Rockefeller Foundation. "Depatterning" — the breaking down of a human subject's ongoing behavior patterns by means of intensive electroshocks and LSD — was routinely employed by the research scientists working under CIA cover. Some subjects suffered brain damage and severe psychological disabilities. One sued the government and later, in 1988, accepted an out-of-court settlement.

cases, abductees — children and adults — have been encouraged by their alien captors to interact with hybrid tots.

UFO abduction enthusiast David Jacobs states that "there has been a great increase in hybrid activity." In an interview in Britain's *UFO Magazine,* Jacobs notes that hybrid toddlers "look odd…very different from either aliens or humans." He adds that reports of adult hybrids have also begun to surface in recent years. Says Jacobs: "I'm beginning to get the idea that something is happening."[88]

*Perhaps it is.*

Years ago, conspiracy *grande dame* Mae Brussell stunned her radio show audience when she proposed that UFO abductions might be a cover for secret government genetic experiments. She suggested that "aliens" might actually be "genetically mutilated" humans. She also seriously questioned the role of psychiatrists and others who hypnotize abductees, casting suspicion on the "cast of characters" involved in UFO research.[89]

Eugenics — the effort to breed "better people" — was an obsession of the Third Reich and later, following World War II, research efforts in this highly controversial area fell to American universities and private laboratories. One of the earliest efforts, the Eugenics Records Office (ERO) — a think tank for eugenicists — was funded by societal elites, including David Rockefeller.[90]

In recent years, numerous facilities have begun work on the Human Genome Project, designed to map the molecular sequence of human genes. Researchers say publicly that such research will give rise to new vaccines and other beneficial discoveries. But research at one Department of Agriculture facility has reportedly already taken another course. There human genes have allegedly been inserted into swine eggs, producing a herd of "hupigs."[91]

Pioneer DNA researcher Salvador Luria has criticized the Human Genome Project. He asserts that the project is run by a "small coterie of power-seeking enthusiasts" leading us into a "kinder, gentler program to 'perfect' human individuals by 'correcting' their genomes…."[92]

And one last tidbit. The Clintons chose an unusual locale for their summer '95 vacation. They stayed at the western ranch of Laurance Rockefeller. There Laurance and the president huddled for secret talks. Speculation is they discussed UFOs.[93] Or, perhaps, another of Rockefeller's favorite areas of research — *genetics.*

113

# 8

# The Left Hand
# of the Magician

*Life is a very sad piece of buffoonery, because we have…the
need to fool ourselves continuously by the… creation of [an
illusory] reality…*

—Luigi Pirandello

Have you ever seen a vanishing act? If so, you no doubt have noticed
something: the sly dexterity of the magician's hands. One hand catches
your eye, while the other stealthily palms the object that is soon to "disappear." In a sense, the one hand is truth, or that which is presented
as truth; and the other, that which is false.

Of course, as we all know, the workings of both hands are designed
to beguile us. Both hands deceive. Both lie.

But rarely do we look at both hands at once. Momentarily dazed,
we focus on the hand from which the object has vanished—the right
hand, if you will—while forgetting about the other. By the time our
suspicions are piqued, the magician has already discarded the object
from the other hand. He shows you his left hand—*see, nothing!*

Perhaps this is why the subject of UFOs refuses to die. The Right
Hand shows us that UFOs do not exist. The Left Hand, while still closed,
hints of dark secrets—crashed UFOs, bulbous-head aliens from Zeta
Reticuli, et al. But, of course when the Left Hand is inspected, we see
only an empty palm. See, the government is really telling the truth. *Or
could it be…*

You never know for sure what's in a Wizard's head. Remember
Dorothy, Lion, Scarecrow, and Tin Man? They were pretty freaked-
out—until they pulled back the curtain. Then they became downright
indignant.

The U.S. military and intelligence community can't afford to irk
the public. A lion suddenly filled with courage could be dangerous.

The left and right hands, therefore, keep the curtain tightly drawn. *Peeking is strictly prohibited.*

We've seen how "former" military intelligence personnel have come forward with far-out tales of crumpled spaceships and "little bodies," while continuing to receive fat pension checks for breaching "national security." We've seen how media types, like fat plecostomus at the bottom of an aquarium, have gulped offerings thrown down to them from above. And we've witnessed others — perhaps even ourselves — scooping up the remains.

If we'll take the time to whiff the fisherman's — i.e., *Wizard's* — left hand, we'll detect the unmistakable scent of bait. Bait designed to deceive. Bait that cannot — *should not* — be eaten.

Fish are beautiful creatures. They are agile, swift, cunning. But even so, many end up on dinner plates or as trophies on some fisherman's wall.

There have been a lot of fishy stories about stranded aliens through the years. In the 1950s, a small newspaper in Allied-occupied Germany published a photograph of a dead alien purportedly found at the site of a crashed saucer in Mexico. Two men in trench coats — resembling Gestapo agents from central casting — can be seen holding up the thing, bony and less than three feet tall, like a trophy from an African safari. It has been suggested that the "alien" is either a mannequin or a shaved monkey. Two versions of the photo have been seen: one showing the elfish being wearing boots and loincloth and another, the X-rated version, showing him — *her?* — in the nude.[1]

Numerous rumors have surfaced through the years of alien spacecraft coming to a ruinous end in Mexico and the American Southwest. Many of these accounts have come from Leonard Stringfield, a former U.S. Air Force intelligence officer, whose sources are mostly military personnel. The cases all have a familiar ring to them:

• **Tularosa, New Mexico (July 1947).** A master sergeant was reportedly ordered by the commander of Alamogordo Army Air Field to produce a special report concerning a spacecraft that crashed inside the White Sands Missile Range. The informant allegedly told Stringfield that he had personally seen photographs of the mystery disk.[2]

• **Farmington, New Mexico (Late 1940s).** A "firsthand source" assigned to an area military base claims to have seen a classified report detailing the crash of a domed, saucer-shaped object. There was little damage to the craft. Inside were two alien bodies, badly charred. The top-secret report allegedly claimed that hundreds of alien craft had flown over Farmington on the anniversary of the crash.[3]

• **Edwards Air Force Base, California (1952).** Stringfield claims that a "reliable person in a technical position" was on radar duty at Edwards Air Force Base when he spotted a rapidly descending UFO. The radar operator later learned that an alien spacecraft — more than fifty feet in diameter with a row of portholes around the center — had crashed in the desert. He heard that dead aliens, about four and a half feet tall, were found inside the craft, all of which was shipped to Wright-Patterson Air Force Base.[4]

• **Northern New Mexico (Summer 1962).** According to military sources, a crashed saucer was found embedded in a trench. Inside were two small bodies dressed in silver flight suits. The craft and bodies were secretly transported to Holloman Air Force Base near Alamogordo. Pieces of the object, sources said, were then sent to Los Alamos National Laboratory and other research facilities.[5]

In 1977, Colonel Robert Willingham, an F-94 test pilot, claimed to have witnessed the crash of an extraterrestrial craft years earlier near the Texas-Mexico border. Willingham and his copilot reportedly traveled to the crash site, whereupon they encountered armed military police. They were told to leave the area.

On their way back to base, Willingham said he saw a strange piece of metal on the ground and picked it up. The metal was honeycombed and looked like aluminum.

Willingham said he took the metal to a Marine Corps metallurgy lab in Hagerstown, Maryland, for analysis. He claimed that when he inquired about the test results, he was rebuffed.

Willingham said he was told not to discuss the incident and was forced to sign a secrecy oath. Then he did a strange thing. He talked openly about the incident with UFO investigators. He even signed an affidavit for the Center for UFO Studies.[6]

There is no subsequent report of Willingham being prosecuted for this obvious breach of security. *Why?*

An even stranger case is said to have taken place near Rio Sabinas, Mexico, on July 7, 1948. There photographs were allegedly taken of a dead alien who had crashed in the desert. The whole affair, the story goes, was hushed up by officials at Carswell Air Force Base.

Years later, photos of the alien—the so-called "Tomato Man"—were anonymously sent to UFO investigators by "an unidentified informant" obviously familiar with military protocol. The photos showed a fried "alien" inside a charred "spaceship." At least that's what our informant claimed.

Subsequent investigation revealed that the photographs were of a human accident victim, probably a pilot. The head had no hair and was swollen—*sound familiar?*—from intense heat.[7]

Consider this: the photos of our shaved monkey popped up in the fifties. This was the era of such films as *Invasion of the Saucer Men, Queen of Outer Space,* and *Attack of the 50-Foot Woman.* Special effects were in their infancy. It was a time when a giant eyeball with tentacles—or a shaved monkey—fit the bill, either to make you scream in your car at the drive-in or change your perceptions, if only a teeny bit, about aliens from "out there."

Years later, the Left Hand of the Magician threw out some juicier bait. A shaved monkey wouldn't do. *No way.* We needed something more real, more grisly. What we got was Tomato Man.

And now?

Now we get the Roswell autopsy, the film that took over where the O.J. Simpson trial left off. Unless you've just come out of a long coma, you've no doubt heard of the famous film that purportedly shows the dissection of a humanoid alien. Sort of like Tomato Man, but without the burns.

It looks damn real. And that's what Ray Santilli's banking on.

Santilli, a British rock-star archivist, says he acquired the controversial footage from an eighty-year-old retired U.S. *serviceman*—there's that word again—who claims he was ordered to film the "autopsy" following the crash at Roswell. The grainy black-and-white film shows humans in white radiation suits slicing open a humanoid creature. The "alien" itself is hairless, short, and has a noticeably large head and belly. Its eyes are large; its nose and mouth, small. Its hands and feet each have six digits. The thing appears to be female, but has no breasts.

Santilli says the military cameraman sprung the autopsy film on him after first offering up rare footage of Buddy Holly and Elvis Presley. The cameraman, whom Santilli has guaranteed anonymity, claims he took the film while on assignment with the military in New Mexico during the 1940s.[8] According to Santilli, the cameraman sold the film — a copy of the original footage he secretly retained — to help pay for "his granddaughter's wedding."[*9]

Eastman Kodak was allowed to examine a portion of the film. However, the film company received only a snippet of leader, the clear strip at the beginning of a film spool that bears no images. There was no way of knowing if this sample was from the Roswell autopsy film. It might just as well have come from a Daffy Duck cartoon.

Even coding on the edge of the film segment did little to authenticate the footage. Kodak could only say that the coding corresponded with film manufactured in 1927, 1947, and 1967. But even this finding was inconclusive. A Kodak spokesman pointed out that such coding could be copied from another piece of film.[**10]

Something indeed did crash in the desert near Roswell back in 1947. Walter Haut, public information officer for Roswell Army Air Field, informed the press that a crashed "flying saucer" had been captured by the military. Base commander Colonel William Blanchard, acting on orders from the Pentagon, had ordered Haut to release the story.[11]

In the Fox TV special *Alien Autopsy: Fact or Fiction?*, Haut was even more specific. "I was called to headquarters [and] was *given* copies of a press release which stated, in essence, that we had in our possession a flying disk," recalled Haut. "I was told to hand-deliver [these]

---

*This all has a familiar scent to it. You'll recall that military intelligence officers offered to make available copies of a film showing the landing of a UFO to filmmakers Robert Emenneger, Allan Sandler, and Linda Moulton Howe (see Foreword). The offer never materialized. In the case of the Roswell autopsy, it appears that Santilli was allowed to keep the carrot dangled before him.

**Even assuming the film is from, say, 1947, the year of the Roswell Incident, this does not preclude the possibility of *new* footage being shot on old film stock.

to the foreign news media we had in town at the time, the two [local] radio stations, and two newspapers [emphasis added]."[12]

The Roswell Army Air Field was home to the 509th Bomb Group, the elite atomic bomb unit that had only two years earlier carried out the devastating attacks on Hiroshima and Nagasaki. Nearby is Alamogordo, White Sands Missile Range, and the Trinity Site, where the first atomic bomb was exploded. This sparsely populated patch of desert was — and still is — home to numerous top-secret military projects involving rockets and high-performance jet aircraft.

Did a secret military device tumble from the skies over Roswell back in 1947?

Artist Bill Lyne thinks so. Lyne, who holds a graduate degree in fine arts from the University of Texas, asserts that stories of UFOs and aliens are part of an elaborate government conspiracy to keep secret the existence of advanced electromagnetic flying craft, based upon early designs of Nikola Tesla and first built by the Nazis in World War II.

What's more, Lynne says that rocket-sled experiments involving monkeys were the cause of the Roswell ruckus. He claims to have known the brother of a pathologist who performed tests on the monkeys who died after crashing in the desert near Roswell.[13]

Were g-force bloated, burned monkeys actually the "little bodies" that some claim to have seen in the aftermath of the Roswell crash? *Or, perhaps, human test pilots of still-secret experimental craft?*

We may never know. All the Roswell base's administrative records from March 1945 through December 1949 and all outgoing messages from October 1946 through December 1949 were destroyed, according to a 1995 General Accounting Office report requested by New Mexico Congressman Steve Schiff. "Documents that should have provided more information were destroyed," says Schiff. "The military cannot explain who destroyed them or why."[14]

The military has dealt harshly with those seeking to disseminate "unauthorized" information about the Roswell Incident — *except those peddling stories of "little bodies."* Shortly after the crash, Roswell radio station KGFL was threatened with revocation of its broadcasting license if it continued to discuss the event.[15] Frankie Rowe, daughter of a local firefighter, says she and her family were threatened by the military after she handled some of the crash debris gathered up by her father.

"You did not see anything," a military officer reportedly said while standing, with a drawn baton, over the frightened twelve-year-old. "If you can't understand this, there are things that we can do. We can take you out in the middle of the desert...this is a big desert here...no one will ever find your bodies — *ever.*"

According to Rowe, the officer then made her promise that she would never talk about the event. And she didn't, for nearly fifty years.[16]

So what gives? Does the Roswell autopsy film really show an alien from another world?

Experts who have examined the film say no.

Allen Daviau, a Hollywood cinematographer who worked on *E.T.* and other big special effects films, labels the footage "a hoax." Daviau observes that the film periodically goes out of focus. He says the cameraman — whoever he was — did this "intentionally," in order to obscure "what is not real." Furthermore, he notes that critical activities during the alleged autopsy were shot from surprisingly poor angles.[17]

Dr. Paul O'Higgins, an anatomist at London's University College, is equally skeptical. Says O'Higgins: "To judge from the film, the autopsy was carried out in a couple of hours. Yet these were alien creatures. They represented an unparalleled opportunity to science. We are expected to believe we casually cut them up in an afternoon. I would have taken weeks to do such an autopsy."

Most suspicious, O'Higgins adds, is the strikingly humanlike qualities of the alien.

"I would think the chances that an alien which evolved on another world would look so like us would be astronomically remote," O'Higgins states. "Yes, it has six fingers and a very large head, but both conditions afflict humans with chromosomal abnormalities."[18]

Cyril Wecht, a leading American forensic pathologist famous for his examination of the Zapruder assassination film, agrees that, if the body depicted in the film is indeed real, it reveals a human with a severe chromosomal disturbance. He suggests that the body might be that of a woman with Turner's Syndrome, a rare chromosomal condition that frequently claims its victims at birth. Wecht also points out the presence of a large wound visible on one of the "alien's" legs, suggestive of a radiation experiment. The body, Wecht conjectures, might be that of a woman with cancer of the cervix or uterus who received radiation treatment.[19] *Or, perhaps, the victim of government radiation exper-iments like those conducted on Alaskan natives during the 1950s?*

Says Wecht: "Somebody put together a gigantic spoof here.... They're wasting their time engaging in some small rip-off like this. They should be in Hollywood, making fantastic films with Steven Spielberg."[20]

Funny he should say that. Remember the rumor floating around Hollywood back in 1994 that a "military officer" had shown Spielberg a film purporting to be of the Roswell crash?* Maybe the rumor was only half true. Maybe some Hollywood special effects wizard cre-ated the "alien" *for the military.*

In an article entitled "Autopsy or Fraud-Topsy?" *Time* magazine notes that most special effects artists who have viewed the Roswell autopsy film consider it a product of their trade. Definitely bogus, that is. Canadian special effects specialist Gordon Smith, thought by some pros to have created the "alien," observes: "A lot of us think it came out of England, from a B-grade studio."[21]

Academy Award winner Stan Winston, the special effects master behind *Jurassic Park* and *Aliens,* concludes that a dummy is portrayed in the Santilli film footage. He characterizes the footage as "pretty unbe-lievable," adding that if his crew had created the "alien," they would be "very proud of it." Winston emphasizes that the state-of-the-art effects displayed in the film would have been *very costly* to produce.[22]

Steve Johnson, a makeup image artist, has also viewed the film. "From a special effects technician's point of view, [the cameraman] used every trick I would have asked a director to do if [he] had come to me and said [he] wanted to do an autopsy scene," says Johnson. Immodestly, he adds: "I could have done it a lot better."[23]

But Santilli stands by his man—and film.

"I've had the benefit of knowing the cameraman," says Santilli. "When you come across someone who is eighty years old, and see his army enrollment papers and discharge papers, and meet his wife and children...I know the cameraman is genuine.

"I know the film is genuine inasmuch as he shot it. What is on it is another question. Whether it is an alien creature, some kind of experiment, or a human with some chromosome disorder—the

---

*See Chapter 2.

cameraman himself does not know…. For him, it was just one more army assignment."[24]

Even many UFO researchers have labeled the film a hoax. Kevin Randle, author of several books on the Roswell Incident, believes that extraterrestrials crash-landed near Roswell back in '47, but he nevertheless calls the film "a hoax."[25] Equally skeptical is Graham Birdsall, editor of Britain's *UFO Magazine*.

"We've investigated the film," says Birdsall. "It's a fake and we intend to prove it." He feels that the "alien" may possibly be "some experiment carried out by the U.S. government," adding: "Why would it only come to light now?"[26]

Jenny Randles, a well-known British researcher, not only condemns the film as a hoax, but feels that "it is undoing all the work serious ufologists have done for 20 years." She adds: "In Roswell, above all, decent research has been done, which shows several reasons why the U.S. government may have wanted to cover up the original wreck. We now know they were testing nuclear missiles with monkeys at Roswell which, had it been discovered, would have caused outrage even then. If this film is authentic, why can't we be shown proof of its authenticity?"[27]

Curiously, just as the fuss over the Roswell autopsy film had ebbed, additional "proof" of the legendary saucer crash suddenly turned up at Roswell's UFO Museum, a locally owned shrine to the 1947 event. An Associated Press story of March 29, 1996, noted that "a mysterious piece of metal marked with intricate lines" was brought to the attention of museum operators.

"From the information we have, this is from *a man who was stationed here and was part of the crew that helped pick it up*," said museum spokesman Max Littell, referring to the hunk of metal, now framed [emphasis added]. According to AP, the specimen was given to the museum by "a local resident whose identity has not been made public." Littell added: "If some metallurgist says there is nothing in the book like this…then we are home free."[28]

But even more "proof" may be forthcoming. In a special on the Roswell Incident, aired on the Learning Channel, program producers informed the viewing audience that a "confidential source" — a Pentagon "insider" — had revealed the existence of documents detailing the recovery of "little bodies" near Roswell. The informant promised the release of these documents in the next "few months."[29] *Sound familiar?*

We now move from Roswell to windswept Wiltshire, England, a few miles from the ancient ruins of Stonehenge. Near midnight on September 26, 1994, plane spotters there picked up radio distress calls. The following morning, they converged on Boscombe Down Air Base, a secret facility known for its experimental aircraft. Several spotters were apprehended by local police at roadblocks and ordered to leave the area, according to Michael Crutch, RAF editor of *British Aviation Review.*

"People were reluctant to talk at first," he said. "They wrote down what they had seen — and we were amazed. One was a serving air force officer who saw an aircraft of unknown type disabled at the end of the runway, covered by tarpaulins. Twin inward-canted tail fins were poking out of the covering."

Officials from the Pentagon and Britain's Ministry of Defence denied any aircraft malfunction or crash had occurred. Rumors persisted, however, that two bodies — those of the flight crew killed in a cockpit fire after the forced landing — were secretly flown back to the United States aboard a Boeing 737 which, it was discovered, had a phony registration number. Earlier a USAF Galaxy transport plane was known to have flown in and out of Boscombe Down, reportedly returning the disabled secret craft to Palmdale, California, home of the Lockheed Skunk Works.

This is not the first time aviation buffs in the area have spotted mystery aircraft. An unknown type of aircraft, described as "sleek and twin-finned," has been seen zipping through the skies over Exmoor by plane spotter Jamie Hunter and others. According to Hunter, the plane is loud, sounding like a "flying train."

"The description of the twin-finned plane fits advanced U.S. aircraft under so-called 'black' programs," Christy Campbell and Nick Cook write in the *Electronic Telegraph.* "The TR-3A Black Manta, a highly secret reconnaissance aircraft first flown in 1991 and supposedly invisible to radar, is a likely candidate." The writers speculate that the craft was returning from a spy mission over Bosnia when it experienced a malfunction and crashed.[30]

Had not the Boscombe Down plane spotters arrived speedily at the scene, we might have begun to hear rumors of a "crashed saucer" and "little bodies."

# 9

# Lights! Camera! *UFOs!*

---

*Fear is the foundation of most governments.*
—John Adams

*And we are so miserably afraid of the light, all of us.*
—Henrik Ibsen

In the early morning hours of February 25, 1942, less than three months after the Japanese attack on Pearl Harbor, all hell broke loose in Los Angeles County. Air-raid sirens began to wail, rousting a million Southern Californians from their beds. Searchlights turned night into day. Dazed, people ran into the streets like crazed ants dumped from a child's ant farm.

So began the "Battle of Los Angeles." It is an incident that, in the end, would cause extensive property damage and the deaths of at least five people. But don't expect to find the "battle" in history books. It is a part of America's "forgotten" history.

Raymond Angier, a local air-raid warden, vividly recalled the opening moments of the "battle."

"When I went running outside to make sure people had doused their lights and were heading for shelters, I saw what had triggered the alarm," he reported. "A formation of six to nine luminous, white dots in triangular formation was visible in the northwest. The formation moved painfully slowly—you might call it leisurely—as if it were oblivious to the whole stampede it had created....

"You'll never know what it was like. One minute the city was bedded down for the night; the next thing you know, the streets were swarming with air raid wardens, people going in both directions and a lot of talk about the enemy overhead...."[1]

An excellent account of the incident can be found in Gordon Lore and Harold Deneault's book *Mysteries of the Skies: UFOs in Perspective* (Prentice-Hall, 1968). The authors described the "Battle of Los Angeles" this way:

> At 2:15 A.M. radar picked up "an unidentified target" 120 miles west of Los Angeles. Anti-aircraft batteries were placed on a "green" alert, ready to fire at a moment's notice. As the "target" approached the coast, a blackout was ordered at 2:21.
>
> The steady radar blip indicated that the "target" was headed directly toward Los Angeles. Minutes later, the information center was flooded with reports of "enemy planes," even though the mysterious object that had been approaching from the sea seemed to have vanished....
>
> About 3:05, as the city lay in almost total darkness, a formation of glowing objects appeared out of the northwest, thousands of feet in the air. Coming in from the sea, the triangular grouping traveled in a southeast arc over aircraft and munitions plants along the coast.
>
> Forty searchlight beams criss-crossed overhead. Bursting flares dotted the night like Fourth-of-July fireworks; tracer bullets streamed upward in a hundred directions.
>
> Anti-aircraft fire erupted around the city. Ear-shattering explosions intermingled with the whistling sounds of unexploded shells plunging down on the city streets. The streets became pockmarked under the barrage of falling shrapnel....
>
> But the formation of glowing objects sailed overhead, unperturbed by the attack.
>
> By 4:15 A.M., the firing had all but subsided, and only isolated explosions from the big guns echoed from distant parts of Los Angeles County. At dawn, Southern Californians got their first glimpse of the pockmarked streets, shattered buildings and rubble....[2]

Californians were outraged by the incident. They demanded answers from Washington.

Secretary of the Navy Frank Knox publicly proclaimed that the five-hour siege was merely a "false alarm."

"There were no planes over Los Angeles last night," Knox told reporters the following day. "At least that's our understanding." Knox laid blame for the incident squarely in the lap of the U.S. Army, whose representatives were conspicuously absent during the tense news conference.[3]

This did little to assuage the public's jittery war nerves. Said the *Long Beach Independent:* "There is a mysterious reticence about the whole affair and it appears some form of censorship is trying to halt discussion of the matter."[4]

Los Angeles County civilian defense officials urged the military to "clarify the situation." In a public statement, they revealed their suspicions about the "Battle of Los Angeles," stressing that air-raid wardens were only prepared to respond to a "real emergency."[5]

The *Washington Post* was even more critical of the military. In a February 27 editorial, the newspaper demanded that military authorities end their "stubborn silence." It urged the Army to disclose "such facts as are already known to the enemy."[6]

The Army was forced to respond. When it did, it contradicted Secretary Knox, indicating a deepening rift between the two military branches.

Army officials on the West Coast stated that "unidentified planes, other than American Army and Navy planes, were probably over Los Angeles...between 3:12 and 4:15 A.M."[7] General George C. Marshall, Army Chief of Staff, forwarded this information to Secretary of War Henry L. Stimson, who added that fifteen planes flying at altitudes of 9,000 to 18,000 feet had probably flown over the City of Angels on the night in question. During the "raid," he added, no bombs had been dropped and no U.S. Army or Navy planes had engaged "the enemy." He further stated that American forces had suffered no casualties, but failed to mention the civilians who had died during the event.[8]

The *Washington Post* didn't buy Stimson's assessment. Sarcastically, the newspaper observed that the military had explained "everything except where the planes came from, whither they were going, and why no American planes were sent in pursuit of them."[9]

The *New York Times* echoed these concerns. "If the batteries were firing on nothing at all, as Secretary Knox implies, it is a sign of expensive incompetence and jitters," the newspaper stated. "Why did no American planes go up to engage them, to pursue them, or even to identify them?... What would have happened if this had been a *real* air raid [emphasis added]?"[10]

Then there's the matter of the marksmanship of coastal gunners. According to thousands of witnesses, one large unidentified flying object remained motionless as a steady stream of antiaircraft shells blasted away at it. Shells from the heavy guns seemed to burst directly on target, causing consternation among witnesses who saw the object eventually continue on, apparently unscathed, toward the cities of Santa Monica and Long Beach.[11]

The objects sighted over Southern California were not Japanese aircraft. Following the war, Japanese navy commander Masatake Okumiya disavowed any knowledge of the Los Angeles "raid," adding that there was a severe shortage of aviation fuel and trained pilots during February 1942. Other high-level Japanese military officials, likewise, denied any Japanese involvement in the affair.[12]

Curiously, some ground observers, looking at the objects through field glasses, were surprised to discern balloons. Captain Molder of the 203rd Coast Artillery unit reported seeing a meteorological balloon, which was fired on.[13] Another observer, Paul Collins, a Douglas Aircraft Company employee, recalled sighting a series of bright red spots of light low on the horizon. The objects appeared to shoot upward, then fall with a slow zigzagging motion. Collins reported that one antiaircraft battery opened up on the lazily descending red dots.[14]

Why were American military pilots, fully prepared to engage "the enemy," ordered to stand down, despite the five-hour assault on Southern California? Why were coastal guns so ineffective? Why did the assault occur only two days after President Franklin Roosevelt publicly warned Americans that no part of the nation could consider itself safe during wartime? And what can we make of the numerous observations of balloons, as well as Collins' sighting of objects that behaved suspiciously like airborne flares?

Hollywood director Steven Spielberg loosely based his big-budget film *1941* on the "Battle of Los Angeles." The film was a spoof of war hysteria during the opening days of World War II. But the real "Battle of Los Angeles" was no laughing matter.

The events of February 25, 1942, were clearly part of an elaborate war game, planned and perpetrated — with tragic consequences — by the United States Army. Balloons, flares—possibly even a few phantom aircraft—were thrown up into the sky to create the illusion of a foreign invasion to test the preparedness of coastal defenses.

The U.S. military has a term for this sort of stuff. It's called Psychological Operations, or Psy Ops. Its purpose is to confuse and intimidate. Some have another name for it—*mind-fucking*.*

The U.S. military and intelligence community has a long history of conducting these kinds of operations. During the Vietnam War, the Pentagon's Fourth Psyop Group designed the Mitralux, a device capable of projecting startlingly real pictures on cloud banks and physical structures on the ground.[15] In the Congo, Army psy ops specialists reportedly made tapes simulating fearsome tribal gods that were intended for broadcast into the jungle to quell rebel villagers.[16] Even more sophisticated psy ops techniques for jungle warfare involved the dropping of gunfire recordings, accompanied by flashing flares, into an enemy stronghold to foster the notion that the encampment was surrounded.[17]

Then there is the Nixon White House. Ever obsessed with the presence of Fidel Castro, President Nixon considered a daring scheme to overthrow the Cuban government. The contingency plan involved the use of a submarine equipped with lasers that would project a giant image of Christ over the island republic to simulate the Second Coming. The sight of Christ floating overhead, the planners believed, would disturb the island's Catholic population and armed forces long enough for invading commandos to topple the Castro regime.[18]

---

*Psy ops techniques may not be limited to the battlefield. At a NATO-sponsored conference on stress and anxiety held in Oslo, Dr. Thomas Narut, of the U.S. Naval Hospital in Naples, gave a talk on "symbolic modeling," noting that the procedure was being used with "combat readiness units" to train people to cope with the stress of killing. Psychologists Alfred Zitani and Peter Watson, author of *War on the Mind* (Basic Books, 1978), claim that Narut later told them privately that naval men were actively being placed in foreign embassies under cover as assassins. According to the account, the assassins had undergone symbolic modeling which included violence-desensitization training, not unlike the type depicted in Stanley Kubrick's film *A Clockwork Orange*. More recently, attorney William Pepper, in his book *Orders to Kill* (Carroll & Graf, 1995), quotes confidential military sources who claim psy ops units participated in the assassination of Martin Luther King in 1968.

More recently, during the Reagan era, a psy ops *mock* invasion was carried out in Zaragoza, Spain, according to retired Colonel L. Fletcher Prouty, who served as the military's liaison officer to the CIA during the Kennedy Administration. Colonel Prouty claims that the "invasion," which involved mock executions of local villagers, is no isolated event.

"Similar events, using the same tactics, take place somewhere in the world almost daily*... The methods used in Spain are almost precisely those used by the CIA in, among other cases, the Philippines in the early 1950s and Indochina from 1945 to 1965," says Prouty, author of *JFK* (Birch Lane Press, 1992).[19]

He is convinced that Spanish troops used in the exercise were trained in the United States.

"It is important to note that tens of thousands of foreign 'paramilitary' and Special Forces troops have been trained at various U.S. military bases under CIA supervision and sponsorship," he writes. "Some of this training is highly specialized, using advanced weapons and war-related matériel. Some of it takes place at American universities and even in manufacturing plants, where advanced equipment for this type of warfare is being made.

"These special armed forces are used as agitators. It is as though the fire department were being used to start fires, the police department employed to steal and kill, and doctors ordered to make people sick, to destroy their brains, to poison them.

"In [the Spanish] case...army officers had been ordered to attack a town, with regular Spanish troops (albeit some of them disguised as natives), and to make it look and feel realistic. As undercover warriors, they were trained to do this.... Under other conditions at other times, these same trained men might have been told to hijack a civilian aircraft; they might have been told to set up a mock car-bombing; they might have been told to run a mock hostage operation. There is no difference. The only military objective of these battles, and of this type of global conflict, *is to create the appearance of war itself* [emphasis added]."[20]

_____

*Ominously, the first American troops airlifted into Bosnia as part of the UN peace-keeping force were psy ops units. Such units were used earlier during the Panama invasion, and psy ops techniques were employed unrelentingly during the Branch Davidian standoff outside Waco.

This was a psy ops mission, from start to finish, asserts Prouty: "To initiate this campaign, a psychological-warfare propaganda team arrived in town," he explains. "They put up posters, made inflammatory speeches in the village square, and showed propaganda films on the walls of buildings at night to stir up the village, warning of the existence and approach of a band of 'terrorist-trained insurgents.'"[21]

That evening, Prouty observes, as villagers watched these propaganda films, explosives were detonated on a nearby hillside. Flares and rockets lit up the sky. Helicopter gunships swooped down overhead. The "invasion" had begun.

"By the time this Special Forces PsyWar team left that town," adds Prouty, "the whole region had been alarmed by the presence of these 'insurgents.' The stage was set for the 'mock invasion of the town,' as ordered."[22]

In February 1987, a crowd of more than 35,000 in Zaragoza marched silently behind a banner reading "For Peace and Against Terrorism" in a protest called by city leaders. The marchers were protesting a local car bombing that had killed two and wounded forty-one others. The attack was blamed on Basque separatists.[23]

All of which leads us to Mock Invasions of Another Kind.

## *Invasion: Washington, D.C.*

In July 1952, Edward J. Ruppelt, head of the USAF's Project Blue Book,* had his hands full investigating sightings of strange aerial objects in the Washington, D.C., area. On July 10, the crew of a National Airlines plane spotted a light "too bright to be a lighted balloon and too slow to be a big meteor" while flying low over Quantico, Virginia, near Washington. Three days later, another commercial airline crew reported seeing an odd light sixty miles southwest of Washington. The unknown object paced the airliner, then raced off in a steep climb when the pilot turned on the plane's landing lights.[24]

---

*This "official" Air Force UFO project followed on the heels of Projects Sign and Grudge (see Chapter 3). It is now generally regarded as a crude publicity stunt—a flexing of the Right Hand of the Magician, if you will—which created the impression that UFOs were pure hokum.

The following evening, Pan American pilots William Nash and W. H. Fortenberry sighted six UFOs near Newport News, Virginia, about 130 miles south of the nation's capital. The objects seemed to be about one hundred feet in diameter, flying in a stepped-up echelon formation. Suddenly the objects executed a 150-degree turn, and were later joined by two more disks which shot up from under the airliner. As they sped off, the lights extinguished, one by one.[25]

On July 16, there was another sighting in the same area, only this time UFOs were sighted from the ground. On the beach near Langley Air Force Base, a high-level scientist and a companion sighted two amber-colored lights in the evening sky that were "much too large to be aircraft lights." The two lights executed a 180-degree turn, and were soon joined by other unidentified lights, which departed in formation from the area. The observers stated that the objects made no sound and were in view for three minutes.[26]

Only days later, Washington would be "invaded." This invasion would come in the form of the Washington National sightings.

In his book *The Report on Unidentified Flying Objects* (Ace, 1956), Ruppelt reports a strange prelude to this case. "In some aspects the Washington National Sightings could be classed as a surprise...but in other ways they weren't. A few days prior to the incident a scientist, *from an agency that I can't name,* and I were talking about the build-up of reports along the east coast of the United States. We talked for about two hours, and I was ready to leave when he said that he had one last comment to make — a prediction.... 'Within the next few days,' he told me, and I remember that he punctuated his slow, deliberate remarks by hitting the desk with his fist, 'they're going to blow up and you're going to have the granddaddy of all UFO sightings. The sighting will occur in Washington or New York,' he predicted — 'probably Washington [emphasis added].' "[27]

Ruppelt's shadowy visitor must have had a crystal ball. On July 19–20, between 11:40 P.M. and 3:00 A.M., radarscopes at Washington's National Airport and nearby Bolling and Andrews Air Force Base lit up with "bogies" — radar tracks indicating unknown airborne traffic. The objects appeared to be coasting along as slowly as 100 miles per hour, sometimes hovering, then shooting away at fantastic speeds.

"In a way the targets looked like a formation of slow airplanes, but no formations were due in the area," Ruppelt later wrote. "These were no airplanes, [the traffic controller on duty] thought, so he let out a yell for the senior controller. The senior controller took one look at the scope and called in two more [controllers].… The targets could be caused by a malfunction in the radar, they thought, so a technician was called in—the set was in perfect working order.

"The senior controller then called the control tower at National Airport; they reported that they also had unidentified targets on their scopes, so did Andrews. And both of the other radars reported the same slow speeds followed by a sudden burst of speed. One target was clocked at 7,000 miles an hour. By now the targets had moved into every sector of the scope and had flown through the prohibited flying areas over the White House and the Capitol."[28]

The mysterious objects were also seen by commercial airliners in the area. Captain "Casey" Pierman, pilot of Capital Airlines Flight 807, said the lights resembled "falling stars without tails." Another airliner, Capital Airlines Flight 610, reported being followed by an unidentified light from Herndon, Virginia, to within four miles of National Airport.[29]

In the early morning hours of the aerial assault, a controller at National Airport called control tower personnel at Andrews to tell them that he had a radar target on his scope indicating that an object was directly over the base. Andrews operators looked out and were stunned to see a "huge fiery-orange sphere" hovering in the sky.[30]

There had been a serious breach of national security. UFOs were buzzing the White House, the Capitol Building, and super-sensitive military installations. But one would hardly know it from the military's response.

National Airport controllers beseeched the Air Force to send in jet interceptors. Their request went unheeded. Then they called again—and again. Finally, near daylight, after the fracas had subsided, a lone F-94 arrived on the scene. The plane's crew searched the area for several minutes, found nothing, and quickly returned to base.*[31]

---

*Ruppelt's visitor "predicted" future sightings in Washington, possibly New York. In fact, UFOs were also observed that same evening over Staten Island and New York City's Central Park. The silvery objects, resembling "large dinner plates," glowed and emitted no sound, according to the Associated Press.

Accounts of the sightings dominated the front pages of newspapers across the country, even displacing reports on the activities of the Democratic National Convention. But headlines became even more lurid when the unidentified objects returned to Washington the following weekend.

About 10:30 P.M. on July 26, the same controllers at National Airport picked up several slow-moving targets. The strange craft were spread out in an arc around Washington, from Herndon, Virginia, to Andrews Air Force Base. Andrews, too, tracked the objects on radar.

Again, a call went out for jet interceptors. Again, there was a delay.

Finally, around midnight, two F-94s — one more than the previous weekend — were dispatched to the scene. Members of the press were ousted from the control room. But just as the jets screamed overhead, the objects disappeared from the radarscopes. Despite excellent visibility, the pilots could see nothing and returned to base.[32]

Ruppelt reported what happened next: "A few minutes after the targets left the radarscopes in Washington people in the area around Langley AFB near Newport News, Virginia, began to call Langley Tower to report that they were looking at weird bright lights that were 'rotating and giving off alternating colors.' A few minutes after the calls began to come in, the tower operators themselves saw the same or a similar light and they called for an interceptor."[33]

An F-94 arrived on the scene and was vectored toward the light by tower personnel. Spotting it, the pilot began a pursuit when, suddenly, the light went out "like somebody turning off a light bulb." The jet's radar locked on to the object, but only for a few seconds. Before departing, the F-94 got additional lock-ons, but these too were broken off within seconds.

Moments after the objects disappeared over Newport News, they again returned to Washington. Jets were summoned. This time the objects remained as two F-94s raced onto the scene.

Controllers vectored the jets toward one target after another, but each time the lights sped away, easily outdistancing the pursuit aircraft. Lieutenant William Patterson, pilot of one of the F-94s, later told the press: "I saw several bright lights. I was at my maximum speed, but even then I had no closing speed. I ceased chasing them because I saw no chance of overtaking them."[34]

In the wake of the sightings, the Air Force convened what would become the longest press conference since World War II. Air Force officials reported that the sightings had *possibly* been caused by temperature inversions, causing false radar returns. *Enter the Right Hand of the Magician.*

Ruppelt waited until he was retired to express his opinions regarding this official verdict. "The traffic controllers who operated the radar at Washington National Airport weren't just out of radar school. Every day the lives of thousands of people depended upon their interpretation of the radar targets they saw on their scopes.... Targets caused by inversions aren't rare — in the years that these men had been working with radar they had undoubtedly seen every kind of target, real or false, that radar can detect. They had told the Bolling AFB intelligence officer that the targets they saw were caused by the radar waves' bouncing off a hard, solid object. The Air Force radar operator at Andrews backed them up; so did two veteran airline pilots who saw lights right where the radar showed a UFO to be."[35]

Three years after Ruppelt's book first appeared in print, a revised edition with three additional chapters hit the newsstands. In this edition, which made no reference to revisions, Ruppelt completely reversed his previously open attitude toward UFOs, thus assuming the role of debunker which the military had etched out for him as head of Project Blue Book. Some surmised that he had given in to pressure from the military establishment.

We'll never know. In 1960, Ruppelt died unexpectedly of a heart attack.

Then there's this: just prior to the Washington National Airport sightings, Hollywood released the chilling science fiction classic, *The Day the Earth Stood Still.* The film dealt with the landing of an extraterrestrial spaceship in Washington, D.C. The timing of the film's release seems most curious.

Furthermore, there is the matter of the impotent defense of the nation's capital, despite America's paranoia over communism back in the 1950s. Why did the military not respond adequately to what possibly could have been a Soviet attack? *The military behaved as if it knew exactly what was flying about overhead.*

## *The Visitor in Rendlesham Forest*

Early on the morning of December 27, 1980, two USAF security police-man spotted strange lights outside the back gate to RAF Woodbridge, a highly secret military base which, along with nearby RAF Bentwa-ters, was then leased by the British to the American military under a NATO agreement. Thinking they had witnessed an aircraft crash, the two requested permission to proceed off base into the outlying Rendle-sham Forest. Permission was granted, and the patrolmen approached the lighted area.

There they saw a strange glowing object. It was metallic, triangu-lar in shape, and approximately seven to ten feet in diameter and seven feet high. It shone down a white light which illuminated the entire for-est. Atop the object was a pulsating red light with blue lights under-neath. The object appeared to be either hovering low over the ground or to be resting on supports. When the patrolmen moved closer, it took off through some trees and disappeared. Meanwhile, animals on a nearby farm seemed to panic.

Later that evening, an intense red light was seen through the trees. It pulsated as it moved slowly through the area. At one point, the mys-terious object threw off glowing particles and then broke into five sep-arate pieces and disappeared. Immediately, three small lights appeared further up in the sky. The objects raced about, displaying red, green, and blue lights. The last of the lights, which beamed down an inter-mittent stream of light, finally disappeared after several hours.

The next day three depressions—an inch and a half deep and seven inches wide—were found at the site of the original early-morning sight-ing. Radioactivity was detected near the center of the triangle formed by the depressions, with lower readings discernible on the side of a tree facing the depressions.[36]

What makes this case so strange is that all available information has come *directly from military personnel.* The above account, taken from a memorandum issued by Deputy Base Commander Charles I. Halt, was later released under a routine Freedom of Information request filed by American Robert Todd of the Citizens Against UFO Secrecy (CAUS). No hassles. No nasty lawsuits. No illegible photocopies or censored text.

The Air Force went to great lengths to obtain the copy for Todd. According to a letter attached to the memo, "the Air Force file copy has been properly disposed of in accordance with Air Force regulations. Fortunately, through diligent inquiry and the gracious consent of Her Majesty's Government, the British Ministry of Defence and the Royal Air Force, the US Air Force has provided a copy for you."[37]

A base security officer was even more forthcoming. According to the serviceman, he encountered small aliens—about three feet two inches tall—in the forest during the sighting. He told British UFO investigator Brenda Butler that the creatures were identical and wore silver clothing. They appeared to float in a light emanating from underneath the hovering craft.

What's more, the security officer claimed that RAF Woodbridge/Bentwaters Base Commander Colonel Gordon Williams actually communicated with the aliens. No words were spoken, just sign language and telepathy.

"Many people saw this," the serviceman asserted. "We were told to keep quiet."[38]

*Were they?*

Larry Warren, another participant in the sighting, eagerly told all who would listen that he, too, had "impressions" of seeing aliens in Rendlesham Forest. He confirmed that Commander Williams had communicated with the little ones.

"I remember feeling a presence to this day that they were there," he reported, "but...I think I couldn't comprehend seeing them and blocked it out of my mind."[39]

Security officer James Archer, another witness, told Butler and fellow British researcher Jenny Randles that, nope, he didn't exactly see aliens. He saw only "shapes" inside the UFO.

"Maybe they were like robots," he reported.[40]

Randles, one of the case's principal investigators, has uncovered some intriguing information about the Rendlesham "UFO." In her book *From Out of the Blue* (New York: Berkley Books, 1993), Randles observes that some kind of object did indeed visit the military bases back in 1980. She discovered that a military radar facility, located on the outskirts of nearby Norfolk, picked up a fast-moving object, about the size of a Boeing 737 airliner, on the radar screen. The object slowed to about

900 knots, the controllers estimated, as it approached the coast around Lowestoft. Then it swooped downward — into Rendlesham Forest, near RAF Woodbridge/Bentwaters.

A civilian controller on duty joked to his RAF companion that the object was probably a secret American aircraft. "The ones you blokes won't tell us anything about and officially 'don't exist,'" he chided. "You know the ones I mean."

They were sure of one thing. Air Force intelligence would soon be paying them a visit for the film of the radar track.[41]

They weren't disappointed. Soon thereafter, USAF intelligence officers arrived at the facility and asked for the film. Then, according to the controllers, the officers told them something really bizarre. Senior officers from Bentwaters, they stated matter-of-factly, had encountered "small alien creatures" in Rendlesham Forest.[42]

Randles grew suspicious. "From the early days I had been worried about the way the story was leaked out so casually," she wrote. "Why tell the British radar operators that the USAF needed access to their film because they might have captured a UFO that communicated with the base commander on Bentwaters? No restrictions were placed on these people not to talk.... *It was almost as if the idea that the events were a landed UFO with aliens was actively encouraged as a smokescreen to hide the real truth* [emphasis added]."[43]

In October 1986, Randles received a strange phone call from a British ex-serviceman who claimed to have extensive secret files regarding UFO crashes and *a report on an alien autopsy.* Was Randles interested in seeing the six hundred pages of material?

Randles sought a meeting with the caller. He hedged, and said he would have to call her back.

She dismissed the call as a hoax. Until he called again.

She later met the caller at a prearranged location. There she learned that the man she calls "Robert" had belonged to a special unit of the British Army but had left the previous year. Toward the end of his duty tour, his commanding officer had gradually befriended him, which seemed rather odd to him.

On occasion, he claimed, the CO would ask him and the others in his unit if they "believe in UFOs." In the weeks that followed, Robert and a couple of other servicemen were selected for "special exercises," at which time the CO again brought up the subject of UFOs.

Eventually, the CO's attentions focused on Robert, skeptical and basically uninterested in UFOs. For some reason, the CO liked Robert's attitude and soon began to share with him supposedly secret UFO information. He was shown UFO photographs and, eventually, top-secret documents, which, the CO claimed, had been acquired from an American Air Force officer assigned to Wright-Patterson Air Force Base.* The CO went on to say that the American officer had been held under house arrest and later died in a car crash.

The CO said he owed it to his friend to pass on the documents to someone who had the technical background to fully understand them. Robert seemed like that someone. The CO handed over the files, saying that he would deny that he had ever done so if questioned.

Robert agreed to pass on the files to Randles. They would meet again, in a few days, in a country park.

But Robert failed to show. Later he told Randles what had happened. According to Robert, he had been held under virtual house arrest by military authorities. His interrogators told him that he was being detained for removing "sensitive documents" from his unit and was, furthermore, told that the files were "the creation of an educated prankster and no credence should be attributed to them." They told him to say nothing about the documents. They then took back the files.[44]

This episode is eerily reminiscent of the Robert Dean revelations (see Foreword). He, too, claims to have seen top-secret military documents detailing military-alien contacts. The only question that remains is whether "Robert" — or the other Robert — are disinformation agents or the pawns of such agents. In any event, Randles — like Linda Moulton Howe, Robert Emenegger, Allan Sandler, and others before her — had some prime rabbit food dangled before her.

So what buzzed Rendlesham Forest back in December 1980?

This area of Great Britain is one steeped in supersecret military research. Radar was first deployed in the region during the early years of World War II. It remains one of the most secretive military enclaves

---

*Wright-Patterson is often mentioned in UFO lore as the site of alien "little bodies." A big carrot was being dangled here.

in all of Great Britain. It has been suggested that atomic weapons and all kinds of exotic American aircraft, unknown to the public, are housed here.

Randles points out that unusual electronic and "beam" experiments are said to have taken place in the region. She notes that a secret radar project, code-named "Cobra Mist," was set up in Orford Ness, near RAF Woodbridge/Bentwaters, by the USAF between 1971 and 1973. Officially, the project had something to do with over-the-horizon (OTH) radar, but details were scant. Curiously, the same month Colonel Halt's memo was released, all operations at the facility abruptly ceased.[45]

Later, according to Randles, the U.S. military initiated another OTH project, "Cold Witness." An unsigned document she secured referred to a NATO "warning system" that is a "highly sensitive electronic device emanating powerful electric fields with harmful effects on people in the near vicinity."[46]

Stephen Carr, another British researcher, apparently got close to breaking through the military secrecy. He claimed that OTH radar in the region was actually a breakthrough in SDI weaponry, capable of downing space hardware, including satellites. Specifically, he had concluded, based upon research, that a test of the device was carefully planned for December 1980, the time of the Rendlesham Forest UFO encounter. Unfortunately, Carr died in his early forties, before he could complete his research.*[47]

Randles notes that the region has been plagued through the years by UFO sightings causing vehicle stoppages, strange physiological effects in humans, television interference, and other odd occurrences.[48] Military jets have been lost in the area,[49] and loud, unexplained booms have been heard.**[50]

---

*This case has a sinister twist to it. Randles notes in *From Out of the Blue* that a civilian witness to the events at Rendlesham in 1980 was murdered for no apparent reason in the United States. She, herself, received a call from an eminent British scientist involved in top-secret research for the government who warned that she was "messing with something which you can end up at the bottom of the Thames."

**Randles also points out that so-called crop circles, those intricate designs that have been turning up in great profusion in Great Britain and elsewhere, began appearing in Salisbury Plain, an area of intense military activity, the same year as the Rendlesham Forest incident.

Jacques Vallee doesn't quibble when he talks of the Rendlesham Forest case. He suggests that "military groups engaged in psychological warfare have actually mastered the art of simulating close encounters and have designed exercises involving confrontations with nonlethal weapon platforms disguised as unidentified flying objects."[51] He feels these devices are most likely being "actively tested on military personnel."*[52]

Says Randles: "My personal view is that I have encountered nothing that overwhelmingly persuades me that alien craft have been engaged in some sort of long term and amazingly covert surveillance program. As such a claim is an extreme theory — particularly given that we have no clear proof that alien life theoretically exists 'out there' in the cosmos, let alone could potentially visit us on Earth should it want to — then I feel the right course of action is to treat all this with interest but caution."[53]

## *The Flying Triangle Phenomenon*

In the early days of UFO research, much was made of the physical characteristics of UFOs — most importantly, their *shape*. Lately, nobody seems to care, least of all those who have made their reputations on selling lurid stories of alien contact to the public.

*Why?*

The answer is simple. To address the truth would forever crumble the edifice upon which the extraterrestrial hypothesis rests.

Since the late 1980s, there has been a deluge of eyewitness accounts involving triangular-shaped "UFOs." These objects have been seen throughout the world. Oftentimes, they have been described as noiseless, with no discernible engine noise.

Aviation experts *know* what these silent flying triangles are. *Aviation Week & Space Technology*, considered the premier avionics magazine, has pinned the tail squarely on the donkey. In its issue of October

---

*Vallee is conceding a lot here. Despite these remarks, he still feels that most UFOs represent a still unexplained interdimensional force, a theory every bit as bizarre — and untenable — as the one positing alien visitors.

1, 1990, the magazine revealed the existence of a wide array of highly classified "black" aircraft that have been seen flitting about the skies over their home bases in the deserts of the American Southwest. *Aviation Week* notes:

> A *triangular-shaped, quiet* aircraft [has been] seen with a flight of Lockheed F-117A stealth fighters several times since the summer of 1989. This may be a demonstrator or prototype of the General Dynamics/McDonnell Douglas A-12. Navy officials recently noted that full-size test models will soon be *"exposed to public view"* during testing, suggesting that predecessors of the A-12 are *already flying* [emphasis added].[54]

This is the ugly truth that many UFO cultists have dreaded. It is the unmasking of the Wizard behind the curtain. It is *reality.*

From late 1989 throughout 1990, more than three thousand Belgians from all walks of life reported seeing huge unknown craft — silent and triangular-shaped — traversing the skies. These devices were chased by civilians on foot, by police officers in patrol cars, even by military jets.[55]

In late March 1990, air-traffic controllers at Glons and elsewhere picked up a strange object cavorting across radar screens. The object was also seen by police officers and others. Two Belgian Air Force F-16 fighters were sent aloft to take a closer look.

The jets' radar locked on to the target. The object was lazily careening across the sky, at speeds as slow as 25 miles per hour, but, as the jets approached, it descended like a rocket, dropping from an altitude of 7,500 to less than 750 feet.

Each time the jets would lock on to the elusive flying triangle, it would drop below 750 feet, just below the range of radar. Up and down. That's how it went for the duration of the sighting.[56]

These events were closely monitored by the U.S. Defense Intelligence Agency (DIA), as a recently released document suggests. The Pentagon seemed particularly interested in one disturbing incident involving a Belgian Air Force officer and his wife. According to the partially censored document, the witnesses were "alledgedly [sic] blinded by a huge bright flying object as they were driving on the autoroute. They stopped their car, but were so frightened they abandoned the vehicle and ran into the woods...."

The document went on to say that Colonel Wilfried de Brouwer, the Belgian Air Force's point man for the sightings outbreak, "addressed the possibility of the objects being USAF B-2 or F-117 stealth aircraft which would not appear on Belgian radar, but might be sighted visually if they were operating at low altitude in the Ardennes area. He made it quite clear that no USAF overflight requests had ever been received for this type mission and that the alledged [sic] observations did not correspond in any way to the observable characteristics of either U.S. aircraft."[57]

The above assessment is obfuscation at its best. The document seems to be suggesting that since the American military had not requested permission to fly over Belgian airspace, then the objects could not therefore have been of American origin. Then there is the pronouncement by de Brouwer that the objects did not "correspond in any way to the observable characteristics" of the USAF's B-2 or F-117A. *But what about the characteristics of other even more advanced "black" aircraft?*\*

Interestingly, the DIA document further notes that the Belgian Air Force had concluded that at least some sightings were attributable to "lazer [sic] beams and other forms of high intensity lighting hitting clouds."[58] *Laser beams from what?*

The Belgian Air Force, no doubt acting on behalf of the American military, has sought to push the sightings into the familiar realm of UFOs. Colonel de Brouwer told the media that movements of the devices chased by Belgian fighter pilots were "not normal behavior." He stated that the pilots had seen "something special." Shooting down speculation that the objects were secret military aircraft, de Brouwer added, "This thing hovers and doesn't make any noise."[59]

Not only did Belgian military officials pooh-pooh the idea that the devices were the result of secret American technology, it *actively supported efforts to pass off the sightings as extraterrestrial in nature.* Curiously,

---

\*Tom Walker of the *Wall Street Journal* confirmed that the military establishment squelched reports that the Belgian triangles were secret American aircraft. A French physicist, Walker was told, had worked on a secret military project dealing with *silent* supersonic aircraft. The scientist's grant was canceled, and a spokesman for the French Air Force declined to say whether the military resumed the research on its own.

the Belgian Air Force made available two Hawker Siddeley aircraft, crammed with sophisticated electronics, to assist in a Easter 1990 weekend UFO hunt organized by the Société Belge d'Etude des Phénomènes Spatiaux (SOBEPS), a Belgian UFO group known for its pro-extraterrestrial stance regarding UFOs.[60]

In addition, the Belgian military did something else unprecedented. It released "black box" tapes from pursuit F-16 aircraft showing radar contacts with the devices.[61] At the same time, Belgian Air Force officials enacted a strict gag order on the pilots of the pursuit aircraft. [62] Why? Did they get too close to the objects, discovering something they shouldn't have?

Not everyone bought the notion of extraterrestrial invasion. One witness, Belgian police officer Brigadier Heinrich Nicholl, said of a giant, silent triangle he observed hovering low in the sky: "I think it's a very sophisticated and ultra-secret military project."[63]

In any event, the nineties has witnessed sightings of triangular objects throughout the world. On July 18, 1992, an accountant was driving home from Colchester, England, when an enormous triangular-shaped device swooped down low over his car.

"There was no noise as it passed over me, or afterwards," he told Ron West of the Essex UFO Research Group. "It was about 150 feet up. It was massive — at least a span of 400 to 500 feet — a blackish color and had three pointed ends at the rear with rods sticking out…. Another car heading towards me swerved towards me, but managed to right itself in time to avoid a crash. I was shaking like a leaf [and] also felt very sick. I had to stop the car to recover…."[64]

On November 15, 1991, according to investigator Christine Lippert, a group of hunters near Marshall, Arkansas, spotted a giant boomerang-shaped craft apparently the size of three football fields, with very bright, pulsating white lights. During the sighting, three large red lights reportedly separated from the main object and moved away, much like the 1980 Rendlesham Forest case. The men grew frightened and ran away. Later, jet aircraft, an unusual sight in that part of the state, thundered onto the scene.[65]

In 1993–94, more than fifty sightings of silent, triangular-shaped craft were reported in the Canadian province of Alberta. In one case, on April 23, 1994, an Edmonton couple reported seeing an unlit triangle "the size of a large house" pass 100 feet overhead at a speed of 20 miles per hour. Later, on May 11, four other residents of Edmonton sighted a "black triangle" moving silently at high speed through the sky around midnight.[66]

In 1991–92, an intense "UFO flap" occurred in Pennsylvania. Thanks to Dr. Samuel Greco, a retired USAF major and aerospace engineer, sighting data was compiled and analyzed. Data showed that nearly eighty-five percent of the objects sighted on one particularly active day in February 1992 were triangular- or boomerang-shaped.*[67]

## Psy Ops in Puerto Rico

Through the years, bills have floated through Congress to make Puerto Rico the fifty-first state. Each time the measure has been proposed, it has been shot down. Opponents see no reason to elevate the Caribbean island to full-state status, since it is already firmly under the giant thumb of Uncle Sam.

Since the turn of the century, the United States, bolstered by military might, has sought to increase its power over vast stretches of territory. A group of celebrated historians wrote of the consequences of this early expansionistic zeal in *A People and a Nation* (Houghton Mifflin, 1982). Said the authors: "American expansionism in turn led to imperialism: the imposition of control over other peoples, denying them the freedom to make their own decisions, undermining their sovereign independence. Imperialism took a variety of forms, both formal (annexation, colonialism, or military occupation) and informal (the threat of intervention or economic manipulation). Sometimes the United States took territories; sometimes it controlled the economic life of others to such an extent that they lost their sovereignty; sometimes American troops intervened, imposed order, and stayed to govern.... The persistent American belief that other people cannot solve their own

---

*Two-thirds of the remaining sightings, when a specific shape was noted by observers, involved *saucer*-shaped craft. Dr. Greco's data, therefore, confirmed that the two most commonly reported "UFOs," at least during the Pennsylvania flap, were triangular- and saucer-shaped — the same two shapes of advanced aerodynes known to have been developed by the U.S. military.

problems and that only the American model of government will work produced what historian William Appleman Williams has called 'the tragedy of American diplomacy.' "[68]

On November 1, 1950, anti-American sentiment turned ugly when Puerto Rican nationalists unsuccessfully attempted to assassinate President Harry Truman. In the years leading up to the attack, Truman had helped form the NATO alliance; had pushed through Congress the National Security Act, establishing the National Security Council and CIA; and had furthermore plunged the country into war—the "Korean Conflict"—without the approval of Congress. Truman did much to fuel Cold War suspicions, missing few opportunities to speak publicly of the "communist menace." By the 1950s, Truman's burgeoning intelligence community had begun to seriously overreach its original mandate by engaging in covert operations aimed at overthrowing "unfriendly" governments and, as one high-ranking American official put it, stirring up economic chaos in "the camp of the enemy" through a "Department of Dirty Tricks."[69] The so-called Truman Doctrine, in effect, gave the U.S. military the power to intervene anywhere in the world, in contravention of other countries' national sovereignty, in order to "support free peoples who are resisting attempted subjugation by armed minorities or by outside pressures."*[70]

Puerto Rico has always been little more than a base of operations for the American military and intelligence community. During the 1960s, the island served as a training area for fanatical anti-Castroites backed by the CIA.[71] Earlier, in 1931, numerous Puerto Ricans were reportedly infected with cancer by the Rockefeller Institute. Thirteen test subjects eventually died.

According to authors Jonathan Vankin and John Whalen, chief pathologist Cornelius Rhoades, director of the "study," was unre-

---

*In recent years, a significant amount of revisionist history has been foisted upon the American people. For example, John Kennedy, perhaps America's most beloved president, has been relentlessly attacked in books and the media. We now know that E. Howard Hunt, the Nixon White House's CIA hatchet man, forged official documents in an all-out effort to smear Kennedy. On the other hand, Truman, the low-popularity president who brought us the NSA and CIA, is now presented to the public as an "underrated president." His bolstered image is apparently based solely upon the fact that he was fond of uttering "The buck stops here."

pentant, stating: "The Porto [sic] Ricans are the dirtiest, laziest, most degenerate and thievish race of men ever inhabiting this sphere.... I have done my best to further the process of extermination by killing off eight and transplanting cancer into several more.... All physicians take delight in the abuse and torture of the unfortunate subjects."

Rhoades was publicly dismissed as "mentally ill." But the U.S. government apparently thought otherwise. It placed Rhoades in charge of two large chemical warfare projects during the 1940s, made him a member of the Atomic Energy Commission, and even awarded him the Legion of Merit.[72]

Today Puerto Rico is awash with secret U.S. military operations. Military bases and hush-hush research facilities dot the land. A high-frequency heater, the sister transmitter of HAARP in Alaska (see Chapter Five), stands ready to perturb the earth's ionosphere.

Since 1987, a series of disturbing events, apparently military-related, have rocked the island. The incidents have all the earmarks of a massive psy ops campaign.

On November 16, 1988, Yesenia Velázquez and her family observed a huge ball of yellow light near San Germán. As they watched, two jet fighters suddenly raced onto the scene and circled the unknown object. Then, according to Velázquez, the jets seemed to *enter* the mammoth object and disappear. The sound of the jets' engines immediately stopped. Finally, the object ejected two small globes of light and shot out of sight.

The following month, a large gathering of people in the Cabo Rojo area observed a gigantic, *triangular-shaped* object in the sky. Then, suddenly, two F-14 Tomcat fighter planes appeared from behind the object. The unknown device responded to the planes' presence by turning away, reducing its speed and, eventually, stopping in midair. As in the San Germán sighting, the jets disappeared alongside the mammoth object.

Next the object descended low over Samán Lake, hovered a moment, and gave off a large flash of light. It then appeared to divide into two distinct triangular sections, which both departed rapidly.[73]

The FAA and Pentagon denied that any such cases involving military aircraft had occurred in Puerto Rico, in response to a query from a U.S. Congressman. But researcher Jorge Martín, who has investigated UFO sightings on the island for twenty years, is convinced otherwise.

According to Martín, he subsequently learned from a confidential United States Navy source that there were radar tapes of the events that were quickly classified and sent to Washington.[74]

In 1991, Puerto Rico Civil Defense director José Nolla confirmed that he was leading an effort to look into the matter. However, Martín has learned that the American military's Defense Intelligence Agency (DIA), in fact, has control of the "investigation." Nolla himself is a "former" military liaison officer with the DIA.[75]

Of course, the first question that arises is what happened to the jets seen around the giant UFOs? Were they simply gobbled up, as some witnesses believe? Or were the jets vaporized during some hideous war game? A laser display put on for the benefit of the locals, perhaps?

Curiously, these and other recent events in Puerto Rico have been virtually ignored by the media. Even UFO investigators themselves, it seems, have ignored the incidents like the plague. British author Timothy Good is one of the few individuals to afford attention to Martín's reports.[76]

Not surprisingly, Puerto Rico has been rife with "rumors" of aliens. When Good visited the island, he heard wild tales involving interaction between aliens and the U.S. government. He shrugged off such notions as an "outlandish suggestion."[77]

In Good's *Alien Update* (Avon Books, 1995), Martín writes of another frightening encounter involving Dolín Acosta, a resident of the Olivares sector of Puerto Rico. She told Martín that she was on her balcony when, suddenly, a bright beam of light shone down on her from above. Said Acosta:

> It was a very bright white light, and it came from above the balcony ceiling. There was a hole in the ceiling and I looked up. There was something like a big ball of light, and a ray of light came out of it and shone on me. When I looked at myself, I couldn't believe it—I could see my bones! It was like looking at an X-ray plate. I could see the bones in my fingers, in my arms, my body...even my toes! That object was up there and I could hear a soft sound that was coming from it, something like air being ejected at intervals, like pss...pss...pss. It then left, but for some minutes I could still see myself like that. My sister Eunice came out of her room to see what was causing the bright light and we *both* could see our bones.

When I looked at her, she had no eyes: I could clearly see her empty eye sockets, and she saw the same thing on me. After about five minutes, we were back to normal.[78]

About this same time, a loud underground explosion, like an earthquake, rocked the area. In addition, large circles—each about thirty-five feet in diameter—mysteriously appeared on the ground. The soil seemed baked, and grass stalks at the outer rim of each circle were dried up. Over the course of several days, the number of circles increased until there was a total of thirty-eight.[79]

On the evening prior to the earthquake, residents in the Maguayo region, next to the Laguna Cartagena, reported seeing a "red ball of fire" moving over the lagoon and descending in a "controlled and steady fashion." Then it slowly disappeared into the lagoon.[80]

Martín describes what happened next:

At 2:00 A.M., many residents were awakened by a strong white light coming through all the windows and openings in their houses. Curious about it, the neighbors looked out and were amazed by the sight of a huge flying saucer-type craft hovering low over the lagoon as if searching for something. According to everyone, the craft was covered by bright white light and it was circling the area very slowly. After about two minutes it left, swiftly disappearing in the sky.[81]

Following the subsequent tremor—the so-called earthquake—fissures appeared at Lajas and Cabo Rojo. Many residents reported seeing bright, blue-colored smoke arising from the ripped earth. Pedro Vargas, a teacher, reported:

I saw clearly that some cracks had appeared in the ground in my yard—and this blue smoke frightened me. Some people from the Mayagüez Agricultural and Mechanical Arts College [part of the University of Puerto Rico complex, specializing in engineering and agricultural techniques] came to check on what happened, but strangely, they refused to take samples of residue from the blue smoke and powder that remained on some of the plants. That was strange, because they were supposedly investigating what had happened. *Why then did they refuse to take the samples and analyze them? I still don't understand* [emphasis added].[82]

Soon thereafter, the area was cordoned off by soldiers in camouflaged uniforms. Others at the site were dressed in plain clothes, still others, in white contamination outfits.

Meanwhile, an unmarked military helicopter flew over the lagoon, lowering what appeared to be electronic equipment into the warm waters below. Vehicles with revolving top-mounted microwave transmitters also arrived on the scene.[83]

Zulma Ramírez de Pérez and her sister, whose family owned the land adjoining the lagoon, approached the scene.

"Several American men dressed in dark suits with a red badge approached and ordered them to leave the place at once," states Martín. "The women explained that the land was theirs, but the agents replied that they would have to leave anyway, since they were trying to find out what had happened.... The men were tall, Caucasian, blond, and dressed in fine-looking suits, but wearing what seemed to be black rubber boots. They also had metallic, silvery-looking briefcases with them, according to the two sisters." Zulma noted that her family had seen strange unidentified craft operating in the area since 1956.*[84]

A few days before the explosion, two local policemen were fishing in the lagoon when they noticed smoke escaping from the ground and people walking on a nearby hill. One of the policemen approached the hill and saw "several men dressed in silvery-looking coveralls, gloves and boots, who appeared to be checking something in the area with what looked like Geiger counters. His friend called him to follow, and as he climbed up the hill, they both noticed some other men, dressed likewise, hauling three large rolls of thick black rubber-covered electrical or communications cables, several inches wide, from big black trucks. The men then put one of the cables into the lagoon...."

Suddenly, an unmarked helicopter raced onto the scene, and someone on a loudspeaker ordered the policeman away from the hill. Two

---

*My personal physician, born in Puerto Rico, told me that he and a friend had seen two disk-shaped craft hovering low over San Juan in 1959. The objects resembled the classic "flying saucer." When he and his friend walked around a tree for a closer look, the objects were gone, apparently having sped away in an instant.

armed men in black jumpsuits disembarked from the chopper, which had landed nearby. The policemen could tell the men were federal agents.

The police officers were warned that they were in a restricted area. One of the men then approached the policemen. That's the last thing they remember.

Later the two found themselves lying face down in a dirt road outside the area. Regaining consciousness, one of the policemen heard a Spanish-speaking individual say, "Hey, they're waking up. Let's go." He saw several men scramble into a car and quickly leave. So disturbed was his companion that he later moved to New York, proclaiming he would never return to Puerto Rico.[85]

"I don't know what happened," the policeman told Martín. "Those men did something to us, because we can't remember what happened after the man with the military officer approached us...only that we woke up in the dirt road and in a dazed state.... And then, some days later, there was the explosion and earthquake. This is all very weird...."[86]

In November 1988, several hundred Puerto Ricans attending a political rally saw a luminous object hovering above the community of Betances, then the Sierra Bermeja and the Laguna Cartagena. The strange object ejected smaller shining objects which dazzled the spectators. The sighting lasted a half-hour.[87]

The following year, in August, the Laguna Cartagena was inexplicably "leased" to the United States to "preserve animal species in danger of extinction." The special agreement with the Puerto Rico government stipulated that the area would be under U.S. control for fifty years, with the option to renew the lease for an additional fifty years. Still later, U.S. officials snatched up another UFO hot spot in the Sierra Bermeja, an area closely monitored by navy vessels and planes. The area was restricted, and U.S. troops secured the area for two months.[88]

These "invasions," spanning some forty years, have much in common. They are clearly staged events — *elaborately crafted hoaxes designed to bedazzle and intimidate. These events have been perpetrated by the U.S. military.*

In Washington, we had a simple flyby of unidentified objects. In the Rendlesham Forest, years later, we had military men encountering a UFO at close range. The effects upon the soldiers were carefully monitored, and disinformation soon thereafter began to flow. Satisfied with pulling off the Rendlesham Forest caper, the hoaxers moved on to bigger things: the worldwide outbreak of flying triangles. If enlisted military personnel and officers could be fooled, then so could civilians, they reasoned. *They were right.*

Then there are the recent Puerto Rico cases. These incidents are the most troubling. They remind one of the psy ops ventures in Spain and elsewhere Colonel Prouty warned us about. They represent a dangerous new development, involving harassment of civilians and disregard of individual land rights. Many Puerto Ricans are now convinced that an alien UFO base exists on the island. Even investigator Martín now believes this.

Of course, the question remains — *Why?* Why would the U.S. military go to such lengths to convince people around the globe that UFOs are alien-controlled? Why the hoaxes? Why the smoke and mirrors?

Have the events been staged merely as a cover for military "black projects"? Or does the U.S. military have more sinister objectives in mind?

In the next chapter, we'll not only rip aside the Wizard's curtain, we'll look at the Mighty One eye to eye.

# 10

# *Keep Watching the Skies*

---

*The people never give up their liberties but under some
delusion.*                                    —Edmund Burke

The Korean War, thrust upon the American people by the Truman
Administration, was a war unlike others. It served as a blueprint for
all future wars, or "regional conflicts," as they have come to be called.
The Korean War, like Vietnam after it, was, in essence, an *illusion* of
war. *It was a war we were not supposed to win.*

During the so-called "Korean Conflict," the defense budget soared
to as high as $60 billion in a single year.[1] The total cost of the "Vietnam
Conflict" was a staggering $350 billion,[2] an expense that sent our coun-
try into an economic tailspin from which we have yet to recover.

These military engagements allowed America's vast military-industrial complex to grow fat and increasingly capricious with the public
purse strings. President Dwight D. Eisenhower, having served as
this country's highest ranking military officer in World War II, cast a
suspicious eye toward this glutinous conglomerate. Speaking in January 1961, in his farewell address to the American people, he stated:
"The conjunction of an immense military establishment and a large
arms industry is new in the American experience. The total influence—
economic, political, even spiritual—is felt in every city, every state
house, every office of the federal government. We must guard against
the acquisition of unwarranted influence, whether sought or unsought,
by the military-industrial complex. We must never let the weight of
this combination endanger our liberties or democratic processes."

Eisenhower knew firsthand of the workings of the military-industrial complex and the burgeoning intelligence community. In his second term, he sought to usher in a new era of détente with the Soviet

Union, thereby ending the arms race between the two superpowers. But this was not to be: two weeks before a Paris summit slated for May 1960, an American U-2 spy plane carrying pilot Francis Gary Powers crashed 1,200 miles inside the Soviet Union. Eisenhower had not wanted this flight to take place, fearing that any incident could scuttle the upcoming summit, but the CIA had prevailed upon the aging president for *just one more flight.* As a result of the U-2 downing, the summit failed, and Soviet Premier Nikita Krushchev rescinded an invitation for Eisenhower to visit Moscow.

In 1977, Powers told a stunned radio audience that he believed his spy craft may not have been downed by a Soviet missile, as the American public had been informed. He fueled speculation that his craft had been sabotaged.* Soon thereafter, the pilot was killed when the helicopter he was flying ran out of gas and crashed.[3]

The origins of the Cold War and the birth of the military-industrial complex can be traced back to the early days following World War II. After the surrender of Japan, a massive stockpile of weapons accumulated on Okinawa, the intended staging area for the invasion of the Japanese mainland.** But, curiously, the arms were not sent back to the United States, but were instead transported aboard ships to Korea and Indochina. Enough armaments were dispatched to these two locales to equip and support a force of 300,000.[4]

Five years later, war broke out in Korea; fifteen years after that, in Indochina — specifically, Vietnam.

General Douglas MacArthur, who was relieved of his command in Korea, had wanted to *win* the war there. Later, General Creighton

---

*Sabotage is suspected, too, in the disastrous 1980 mission by President Jimmy Carter to free American hostages held in Iran. Three helicopters, en route to rescue the captives, experienced problems; the engines of two others reportedly became clogged with desert sand. The mission was aborted, but not before another helicopter collided with a cargo plane and exploded; eight Americans died. Aircraft experts estimated that the odds of the multiple breakdowns was one in ten thousand, according to the *New York Times.* Furthermore, Sikorsky, the helicopter manufacturer, stated that filters fitted into the engines were designed to keep out sand. Had the filters been removed? One of the support crew for the operation was marine officer Oliver North, who later became active in the Reagan-Bush Administration that swept into office following the debacle.

**The dropping of atomic bombs on Hiroshima and Nagasaki made such an invasion unnecessary.

Abrams and his staff drew up a bold plan to *win* the Vietnam War but, like MacArthur before him, he was told by the Pentagon and the White House thanks but no thanks.

In the Gulf War, we witnessed a similar pattern. Just as America and its allies were about to deliver the fatal blow to Saddam Hussein and his army, we pulled back, leaving Saddam to fight another day. *Why?*

In George Orwell's frightening novel *1984*, Oceania, a futuristic country, controls its people through the constant threat and exercise of war against its enemies, Eurasia and Eastasia, and the much-hated Goldstein, an underground leader, who may or not exist. The very war itself, the reader learns, may be an *illusion* created by the State to maintain the eminence of the powerful ruling elite, and to keep the people compliant and blindly loyal.

There are striking parallels between *1984* and the world today. Much of what we see *is illusion,* whether it be wars or UFOs. We accept illusion rather than truth. We are becoming more and more like the residents of Oceania, whether we like it or not.

The Cold War has numbed us to the truth, as President Eisenhower warned. Fear, also, has played a part. After all, didn't President Kennedy try to disengage us from Vietnam shortly before he was killed? And didn't defense contractors, many of which in the early sixties were located in Dallas, grow mighty fat during that war? We have learned to fear truth and idolize *illusion,* much like the people of Oceania.

Many now regard the Cold War — promoted in many ways like a Don King boxing match — to have been an outrageous farce. How else can we explain how David Rockefeller, the consummate capitalist, was able to openly conduct banking operations in Moscow, even during the darkest days of the Cold War?[5]

Machinations of the Cold War apparently didn't sit well with James Forrestal, President Roosevelt's Secretary of the Navy and later America's first Secretary of Defense under Truman. In March 1949, he abruptly resigned his post and was almost immediately confined to Bethesda Naval Hospital, reportedly suffering from severe depression. His condition steadily improved, history has it, but despite this, on the evening of May 21, he fell from a window of his sixteenth-story hospital room. His death was ruled a suicide.

Following his death, Forrestal's extensive diaries were sealed in the White House under orders of President Truman. It would be more than a year before they would be released to the public. Walter Millis, writing in the foreword to *The Forrestal Diaries* (Viking Press, 1951), admitted that the loose-leaf diaries were examined by the White House and Department of Defense prior to their release. According to Millis, "a few passages" were not allowed to be published and, furthermore, "a rather larger portion was condensed, paraphrased or in some instances omitted entirely...." He discounted notions of any "sinister suppression."[6]

Why the mention of suppression? Did the Truman White House have reason to suspect that they might be accused of such an action?

Later, a strange story began to float through the UFO community claiming that Forrestal had personally seen one of the Roswell aliens. It had so affected him, the story goes, that he became seriously depressed, finally committing suicide.[7]

Shortly before Forrestal's diaries were published, General MacArthur met secretly with then-CIA director Walter Bedell Smith, General George Patton's old nemesis, in Tokyo.[8] Just what they discussed has never been revealed.

Then, in 1955, MacArthur met with Achille Lauro, the mayor of Naples, Italy, at the Waldorf-Astoria Hotel in New York. During the meeting, Lauro later told the *New York Times,* MacArthur made a startling prediction, particularly so given the timbre of the times. He quoted the general as saying: "The Soviets and the democracies will adopt the best characteristics of each other and, in the process of many years, there will not be a strict line of demarcation between their ideals; therefore no causes for war between them."

MacArthur then said something *very odd.*

According to Lauro, MacArthur stated that "because of the developments of science all the countries on earth will have to unite to survive and to make a common front *against attack by people from other planets* [emphasis added]." The politics of the future, Lauro said MacArthur told him, would be cosmic, or interplanetary.[9]

In 1962, MacArthur made the same comments to the graduating class of West Point. "We speak," he said, "of ultimate conflict between the united human race and the sinister forces of some other planetary galaxy." His remarks were broadcast over many radio stations.[10]

Some years later, in late 1985, President Ronald Reagan told then-Soviet leader Mikhail Gorbachev at a Geneva summit meeting that the United States and Soviets would quickly join forces and forget their differences if aliens attacked earth.

"I couldn't help but say to him, just think how easy his task and mine might be in these meetings that we held if suddenly there was a threat to this world from another species from another planet outside in the universe," Reagan said after addressing students at Fallston High School in Maryland.

"We'd forget all the little local differences that we have between our countries," he said, "and we would find out once and for all that we really are all human beings here on this Earth together."[11]

This was Reagan's first pronouncement of an impending alien invasion. Just in case anyone missed the point, he voiced the idea on still two more occasions during his presidency.

In October 1987, Reagan hosted a luncheon at the White House for visiting Soviet foreign minister Eduard Shevardnadze. It was an amiable but get-tough meeting. During the luncheon, the two laid the groundwork for reaching final accord on the INF treaty, stipulating the elimination of United States and Soviet intermediate-range nuclear missiles. In addition, Shevardnadze delivered to Reagan a proposal from Gorbachev calling for the limiting of American SDI—so-called "Star Wars"—field testing. Reagan would later tell a group of conservatives: "I'm not going to sell out SDI. I'm not going to trade it for anything."

Then, near the end of the luncheon, according to *New Republic* senior editor Fred Barnes, Reagan posed the "alien threat" question to his Soviet visitor. "Don't you think the United States and the Soviet Union would be together?" he asked. Shevardnadze said yes, adding, "we wouldn't need our defense ministers to meet."[12]

The following year, in Chicago, Reagan spoke to members of the National Strategy Forum, a foreign policy and national security group. With bold frankness, he asked the gathering what we might do if threatened by "a power from outer space, from another planet."

"Wouldn't we all of a sudden find that we didn't have any differences between us at all," he stated, "[that] we were all human beings, citizens of the world, and wouldn't we come together to fight that particular threat?"[13]

*Sound nuts?* Well, apparently not to the press or anyone else around the president. No one—not one reporter—uttered so much as a sigh of consternation. No rumblings of *Night of Camp David. Nothing.*

General MacArthur and President Reagan have not been the only ones in high places to utter such seemingly off-the-wall comments. In the early 1950s, Colonel W.C. Odell, a high-ranking Air Force intelligence officer, authored an article entitled "Planet Earth—Host to Extraterrestrial Life." His article strangely coincided with the CIA-convened Robertson Panel (see Chapter Two), which acknowledged the potential use of the UFO phenomenon in psychological warfare. In his article, Colonel Odell contended that aliens from a dying world were surveying our planet as a possible "second home," a place where they could perpetuate their kind.

Interestingly, Odell's manuscript was reportedly shown to select members of the Washington press and retired Marine Corps Major Donald Keyhoe, an early director of the National Investigations Committee on Aerial Phenomena (NICAP), a civilian UFO group that was thoroughly infiltrated by the CIA and which successfully ousted Keyhoe from his position (see Chapter Two). The manuscript had been cleared for release by Air Force Security and Review, yet there was no mention of this fact when it was dangled before Keyhoe and the press corps. (It was stipulated, however, that Odell was not to be publicly identified as a member of the armed services.) This amazing bit of candor on the part of the military came at the same time the Air Force was publicly debunking UFOs.

Keyhoe found the whole affair fishy. Apparently, so did the Washington press corps. No reports of Odell's article were ever carried by the national media. Twenty years passed before Keyhoe publicly discussed the strange incident.[14]

In the early 1960s, Brigadier General John A. McDavid, director of Communications-Electronics for the Joint Chiefs of Staff, openly stated that a meeting with alien beings would likely lead to conflict.[15] Retired USAF Colonel Joseph Bryan, the NICAP board member whom we would later learn was chief of the CIA's psychological warfare staff (see Chapter Two), stated early on that "UFOs are interplanetary devices systematically observing the Earth, either manned or remote-controlled or both. Information on UFOs has been officially withheld."[16]

Former USAF Major F. Thomas Lowrey, a graduate of Carnegie Institute of Technology and an engineer during World War II at Wright-Patterson Air Force Base, was equally candid. "I am thoroughly convinced that the 'flying saucers' come from some extraterrestrial source," he asserted. "I cannot understand the AF policy of pretending they do not exist."[17]

Why would former high-ranking military officials, under penalty of breaching national security, come forward with outlandish claims of aliens from space and impending intergalactic war? Why would Reagan make such statements, not once but at least three times during his presidency? *Why?*

The answer is obvious. *There is afoot an orchestrated psy ops campaign to convince the American public that UFOs are from outer space and that we will confront alien beings in an armed conflict.* This grand plan may have been drawn up as early as 1947, as evidenced by the Air Force's "acknowledgment" that year that a "flying saucer" had crashed in the New Mexico desert near Roswell.

Further evidence of this clandestine plan can be found in a curious study published by Dial Press, now defunct, in 1967. The study, entitled *Report from Iron Mountain on the Possibility and Desirability of Peace,* was, according to an introduction by Leonard C. Lewin, drafted by a commission "of the highest importance" convened in Washington during the early 1960s to determine the nature of problems America might confront if a condition of "permanent peace" should occur and to devise contingency proposals for that possibility. Lewin claimed that he had secretly acquired a copy of the report from a member — "John Doe" — of the so-called Special Study Group.

The study states:

> The war system [is]...indispensable to [a nation's] stable internal political structure.... The possibility of war provides the sense of external necessity without which no government can long remain in power.... The organization of a society for the possibility of war is its principal political stabilizer.... The basic authority of a modern state over its people resides in its war powers....[18]

It must be emphasized that the precedence of a society's war-making potential over its other characteristics is not the result of the "threat" presumed to exist at any one time from other societies. This is the reverse of the basic situation; "threats" against the "national interest" are usually *created* or accelerated to meet the changing needs of the war system....

Wars are not "caused" by international conflicts of interest. Proper logical sequence would make it more often accurate to say that *war-making societies require – and thus bring about – such conflicts.* The capacity of a nation to make war expresses the greatest social power it can exercise; war-making, active or contemplated, is a matter of life and death on the greatest scale subject to social control. It should therefore hardly be surprising that the military institutions in each society claim its highest priorities [emphasis added].[19]

Following this cynical appraisal of governments were specific recommendations on how the federal government might continue to exert influence over the American public in lieu of actually making war. One war "substitute," mentioned in the report, is noteworthy. The *Iron Mountain* authors gave serious consideration to the development of a fictional "threat from outer space" as a means of controlling the populace.[20] This mock invasion, the authors contended, might be pulled off if "an established and recognized extraterrestrial menace" could be presented to the public.[21]

Ominously, the Special Study Group urged "testing and evaluation" of recommended war substitutes to determine "acceptability, feasibility, and credibility."[22] It furthermore called for a "determination of minimum and optimum levels of destruction of life, property, and natural resources" required to establish "credibility of [the] external threat."[23] War games were encouraged as a means of carrying out these objectives.[24]

In 1972, Lewin told the *New York Times* that he had, in fact, written the *Iron Mountain* report as a "caricature [of] the bankruptcy of the think-tank mentality by pursuing its style of scientific thinking to its logical ends." He asserted that the importance of the underlying message contained therein justified the methods he had employed.[25]

Colonel Prouty doesn't buy Lewin's "confession." He observes that the report bears striking similarities to an assessment written by CIA superagent General Edward Lansdale and General Richard Stilwell at the behest of CIA director Allen Dulles and Army Special Warfare elements at Fort Bragg, North Carolina. Prouty says that the super-secret report, prepared for the Special Presidential Committee of President Eisenhower, established the doctrine "governing the employment of the military instrument, in peace and in war."[26]

Says Prouty of the Lewin affair: "The author, Leonard Lewin, has a perfect right to characterize his work as a 'novel.' I have spoken with Lewin at length. He is a well-informed man who was well aware of the situation in Washington as pictured in the Lansdale/Stilwell report in 1959 and its progression into the Kennedy era... The most interesting part of both 'reports' is the many ways in which they overlap and agree with each other; and, even more important, how they have survived the contrivances of the Cold War and have become thoroughly modern military doctrine."[27]

*Iron Mountain* suggests that there is likely a contingency plan—a serious proposal that *may* be put into action— *to fake an invasion from outer space, thereby establishing a need for the permanent presence of the military in the internal affairs of the United States.*

This would explain why the military continues to keep secret "black" aircraft and weapons systems which, if the Roswell incident is any indication, may have been in development since the end of World War II. Should a fake invasion from space be authorized, no doubt this unseen technology, radical in design and appearance, would be suddenly sprung upon the public in the form of "spaceships."

Of course, all this is only speculation. But then there's FEMA.

FEMA—the Federal Emergency Management Agency—was established by President Jimmy Carter to handle natural-disaster relief and civil defense planning. Since its inception, it seems to have done little to respond to its original mandate. It has been woefully ineffective in responding to hurricanes, earthquakes, and other natural disasters, giving rise to speculation that its charter is only a cover for other, more secretive activities.*

---

*FEMA was harshly criticized for its tardy response to Hurricane Andrew. Following the Los Angeles earthquake, angry crowds, comprised of displaced quake victims, stormed the local FEMA office demanding disaster aid. In an effort to spruce up its tarnished image, the agency spent more than $50,000 on billboards and $73,000 on polo shirts for staffers and solicited bids for buttons and Frisbees with FEMA's 800 number on them, according to *Newsweek.*

In October 1984, Washington syndicated columnist Jack Anderson revealed that FEMA had prepared "standby legislation" — the Defense Resources Act — that, in the event of a "national crisis," would "suspend the Constitution and the Bill of Rights, effectively eliminate private property, abolish free enterprise, and generally clamp Americans in a totalitarian vise." FEMA justified such contingency measures on the basis of "national security."[28]

During the Reagan Administration, National Guard General Louis O. Giuffrida was selected to head the agency. Giuffrida had served as a terrorism advisor to Reagan, then governor of California, and had founded the California Specialized Training Institute (CSTI), a school for police and military commandos.[29] A 1972 CSTI manual described martial law as "the legal means available to control people during a civil disorder," including "the replacement of all civil government by the military."[30] Furthermore, the manual maintained that "legitimate violence is integral to our form of government."[31] While working for Reagan in California, Giuffrida and Edwin Meese, then Governor Reagan's chief assistant, reportedly devised plans to purge the state of militants, as well as peaceful demonstrators, by initiating domestic spying operations and heavy-handed tactics to quash riots and demonstrations.[32] Earlier, as an army student, Giuffrida had drawn up a hypothetical plan for incarcerating black radicals in detention camps.[33]

According to Donald Goldberg, a researcher for the Anderson exposé, government scientists advised Giuffrida and top-level FEMA staff on mob control techniques such as "injecting terrorists with stimulants and tranquilizers to manipulate their actions in times of crisis, or *zapping them with microwaves to alter their perceptions* [emphasis added]."[34]

Oliver North, National Security Council liaison to FEMA, was asked about the Reagan Administration's "standby plans" to suspend the U.S. Constitution during the Iran-Contra hearings. Congressman Jack Brooks (D-Texas) asked North to elaborate on the plans. However, before he could respond, committee chairman Daniel Inouye cut off the interchange, referring the matter to executive session.[35] Congressman Brooks would later refer to the Reagan Administration's secret activities as a "government within a government."[36]

In 1984, FEMA, the military, and other top-level government officials met secretly to plan a "readiness exercise," code-named Rex-84.

FEMA coordinated Rex-84 with the military's Night Train 84 operations, which deployed thousands of troops near Contra supply bases in Honduras that year. FEMA's part of the exercise involved the detaining of 400,000 fictional "aliens" in military detention camps throughout the United States. According to a heavily censored FEMA memo, the exercise was described as a test of "emergency legislation, assumption of emergency powers...etc."[37]

On August 2, 1990, President George Bush declared a national emergency in response to Iraq's invasion of Kuwait. He quickly issued more than fifteen executive orders, giving his office extraordinary powers.

"Under the national emergency," Diana Reynolds wrote in the *Covert Action Information Bulletin,* "Bush was able unilaterally to break his 1991 budget agreement with Congress which had frozen defense spending, to entrench further the U.S. economy in the mire of the military-industrial complex, to override environmental protection regulations, and to make free enterprise and civil liberties conditional upon an executive determination of national security interests."

The six-month "national emergency" cost American taxpayers $1.3 billion for nonmilitary activities alone.[38] On July 6, 1989, Bush signed Executive Order 12681, decreeing that FEMA's National Preparedness Directorate would "have as a primary function intelligence, counterintelligence, investigative, or national security work."[39]

These sweeping changes in federal emergency legislation have also affected the area of communications. Beginning on December 14, 1982, secret meetings were reportedly held between high-level Reagan administration officials and executives of the nation's largest commercial communications companies, whose representatives would later staff the National Coordinating Center (NCC), part of the Pentagon's Defense Communications Agency (DCA), a supersecret facility surrounded by an imposing barbed wire fence outside Arlington, Virginia. These meetings, continuing over a three-year period, were held at the White House, the State Department, and key military command centers, SAC headquarters at Offutt Air Force Base in Nebraska and NORAD in Colorado Springs.[40]

The NCC, created in 1984, is staffed around the clock by employees of AT&T, MCI, GTE, ITT, Comsat, and other communications giants. Also at the facility are officials from the State Department, FAA, CIA, and other federal agencies. During a national emergency, declared by the President, communications company representatives are required to relinquish civil control of all satellite and telephone facilities to the federal government.*[41]

In the May 1987 issue of *Omni,* Goldberg states: "The Pentagon now has an unprecedented access to the civilian communications network: commercial databases, computer networks, electronic links, telephone lines. All it needs is the legal authority to use them. Then it could totally dominate the flow of all information in the United States. As one high-ranking White House communications official put it: 'Whoever controls communications, controls the country.' "[42]

Goldberg states that during the Reagan Administration the Pentagon increased efforts to rewrite the definition of national emergency and to provide the military with expanded powers. "The declaration of 'emergency' has always been vague," one former Reagan Administration official stated. "Different presidents have invoked it differently. This administration would declare a convenient 'emergency.' "[43]

The Clinton Administration has been no less timid in advocating increased powers for the military in the United States. In anti-terrorism legislation sent to Congress, Clinton urged more widespread wiretapping of American citizens and, if necessary, the use of military forces within the United States.[44]

Emergency preparedness, it seems, also extends to alien invasions. Just such an eventuality is examined in the new, second edition of the *Fire Officer's Guide to Disaster Control,* a manual used by FEMA in its National Fire Training Academy Open Learning Program. Specifically, the manual instructs firefighters on how to deal with transportation and communications disruptions, as well as psychological and physical effects, caused by *an alien encounter.*

---

*Is the government also flirting with ways to control the U.S. electoral process? In 1985, the NSA, under authority of NSDD 145, focused unusual attention on a computer program used to count votes in U.S. elections, according to Donald Goldberg. Representative Jack Brooks called the move "an unprecedented and ill-advised expansion of the military's influence in our society." Kansas Congressman Dan Glickman agreed. "The computer systems used by counties to collect and process votes have nothing to do with national security, and I'm really concerned about the NSA's involvement," he stated.

The manual was coauthored by the late Charles Bahme, a former Los Angeles Fire Department deputy chief. Before becoming a civilian firefighter, Bahme was security coordinator for the Chief of Naval Operations. He also claimed to have been an original eyewitness to the "Battle of Los Angeles," having seen objects on that day back in 1942 zipping through the sky "at incredible speeds."

Said Bahme: "Rumors that they were extraterrestrial craft, that one was shot down, were never confirmed. The official explanation — weather balloons — was never taken seriously."

The manual states that a firefighter should think twice about approaching anything alien. And no weapons.

"Any display of weapons could be construed as unfriendly," the manual warns.*

Coauthor William Kramer, a veteran Cincinnati firefighter, states that the manual is "intended to get fire officers thinking." Says Kramer: "Nearly everyone has told me they were impressed that a mysterious subject was taken out of the closet, and many believe we are, somehow, eventually going to make contact with other forms of intelligent life."[45]

The U.S. government clearly has the means to pull off an intergalactic invasion hoax. It can, at a moment's notice, seize control of all communications — television, radio, newspapers, computer networks, telephones, and all the rest. In *V,* the 1980s television sci-fi thriller, craft from another world suddenly appear throughout the world and, soon thereafter, the "visitors," take over the government and media, whereupon they portray themselves as benevolent beings rather than the flesh-eating intergalactic invaders they really are. Could a similar scenario, involving earth-based "invaders," actually occur one day not too far in the future? Could strange triangular- and saucer-shaped craft suddenly flood the skies? Could the media, controlled by the military

---

*Contact between earthlings and "aliens" is strictly illegal. That's the law. According to federal statute 14 CFR, Ch. V, Part 1211, such contact is punishable by up to one year in jail and a fine of $5,000. Furthermore, the law grants the National Aeronautics and Space Administration the authority to quarantine under armed guard any person, property, or animal that is "extraterrestrially exposed." Curiously, this zany law, which allows for Americans being thrown into jail without a hearing, makes no provision for quarantining "aliens" themselves. *Why?* Is the government afraid we might catch sight of a zipper?

and intelligence community, provide the images necessary to reinforce this *illusion?*

*Iron Mountain* spoke of war games being conducted to test the efficacy of war substitutes. It spoke of determining "levels of destruction of life, property, and natural resources" required to pull off a phony "external threat." Have we already witnessed some of these fun and games? What else can we make of aircraft, often in close proximity of "UFOs," developing serious electronic malfunctions or, far worse, falling from the skies? What of the plethora of "UFO attacks"? What of the widespread power grid and air-traffic control failures reported through the years? Do all these incidents have simple, logical explanations, as UFO debunkers, acting as the Right Hand of the Magician, would have us believe? Or do these cases, reported now for half a century, represent something more sinister?

Curiously, Hollywood has lately been stoking the flames of the invasion-from-space scenario.* In the fall of 1995, several big-budget films went into production, including David Twohy's *The Arrival*, starring Charlie Sheen as a scientist uncovering plans for an alien invasion, and Tim Burton's *Mars Attacks!*[46] *USA Today* reports that director James Cameron (*Terminator, The Abyss*) plans to produce yet another invasion film, *Brother Termite.*[47] *Independence Day*, the granddaddy of all alien invasion flicks, opened to packed movie houses across the country in the summer of '96.**

Television also seems to have gotten in on the act. The small screen has been inundated with programming dealing with aliens. Fox TV has given us *Space: Above and Beyond*, involving the exploits of a group of gung-ho soldiers — America's finest — staving off the ravages of alien invaders. Other programs devoted to the weird-and-alien include *The*

---

*Hollywood has often willingly served as a propaganda arm of the government. During World War II, the Hollywood "dream factory" pumped out numerous flag-waving offerings that, with a broad stretch of the imagination, might be called films. During the Cold War, we got *I Was a Communist for the FBI* and *Red Dawn*; in the midst of the Vietnam conflict, *The Green Berets* with John Wayne. Now, it seems, Hollywood has turned its attention to invasions from "out there."

**According to the *New York Times, Independence Day* took in $100 million at the box office during its first six days in release, making it the most successful movie opening ever.

*X-Files, The Other Side, Sightings,* and *Encounters.*[48] *The Invaders,* the seventies hit TV series about a lone man's struggle against alien intruders, has even received a nineties makeover.

Producers of *Star Trek* have gotten on the invasion-from-space bandwagon as well. In a recent episode of the *Star Trek* spin-off, *Deep Space Nine,* earth is threatened by an "alien invasion." The Federation, earth's intergalactic military establishment, works overtime to convince the government that it must declare martial law and allow armed Federation troops to patrol the streets. Of course, aliens who have infiltrated the Federation are behind the whole thing.

Even such mundane, down-to-earth fare as *Baywatch* has promoted an alien message. In a recent episode of the waves-and-babes epic, the show's star, David Hasselhoff, strikes an ominous note just before a UFO-guru scientist is snatched up by a brightly glowing object. The scientist's followers believe in friendly aliens, while Hasselhoff will have none of it. Says Hasselhoff grimly to the comely scientist just before her abduction: "What if they [the aliens] don't give a damn about us and they're just out for themselves?" *Could a real alien invasion be far off?*

A lot of these invasion themes hit us below the belt, so to speak, at the subconscious level. Aren't things really bad today? Wouldn't it be great if something "out there" could come and save us, even if it means being conquered? Aren't we, at some level, waiting for the celestial cavalry to appear?

It could be that the invasion scenarists envision "peaceful" contact with another species, thereby ushering in a "New Age."* Perhaps the UFO gurus, keen on the "teachings of the Space Brothers," might become earth's new spiritual masters. As Patrick Henry said before being strung up by *British* invaders: "It is natural for man to indulge in the illusions of hope. We are apt to shut our eyes against a painful truth, and listen to the song of that siren till she transforms us into beasts."[49]

---

*It is interesting to note that President Clinton recently issued an executive order decreeing that government documents, fifty years or older, can no longer be withheld for any reason from public scrutiny. According to Ann Devroy of the *Washington Post,* " 'hundreds of millions of pages of information' classified in the past 50 years will be automatically declassified and released." It has been a half-century since the Roswell "flying saucer" crash. Is an astounding announcement in the offing?

In the March-April 1996 issue of *Utne Reader,* under the heading "What the World Needs Now," "visionary" Jenny Holzer — whose *Truisms* include "A strong sense of duty imprisons you," "Confusing yourself is a way to stay honest," and "Children are the most cruel of all" — writes: "I really think we need something like a Martian invasion that will make us look to one another for help. It might take the form of an environmental crisis, or another five or six epidemics, if the current couple won't do. I hate to sound cynical, but I think it will take something on that scale before people cease operating on greed...."[50]

It's curious Ms. Holzer refers to Mars. Recently, scientists have been coming out of the woodwork proclaiming that Mars may not be as dead as we once thought. *San Francisco Chronicle* science writer Charles Petit observes:

> New evidence even suggests that primitive life could have moved from Mars to Earth, or Earth to Mars, hitchhiking on bits of rock blasted into space by giant meteor crashes. Such a hypothesis might be confirmed if Martian life were found and discovered to have qualities in common with Earth life, implying cross-fertilization long ago. A class of meteors found on Earth recently has been identified as being pieces of Mars. *Although there is no sign of life in them,* analysis suggests that some kinds of bacteria or viruses would have survived the trip if they had been encased inside the stones [emphasis added].[51]

The United States plans to launch survey probes to the Red Planet in the future. Will it "discover" evidence of life there? Could such a find serve to prepare the public for a full-fledged "alien encounter"? Is it only coincidence that a spokesperson for the SETI listening post in New South Wales, just before its mission was to end, announced that microwave signals, possibly sent by intelligent life forms on distant planets, had been detected?[52]

Then there are the curious photographs former NASA consultant Richard Hoagland has been bandying about lately. The photos, supposedly taken of the Martian surface by the Viking Orbiter back in 1976, show what appears to be a Sphinx-like head, surrounded by other odd structures, staring up into the heavens. Hoagland states that the photos prove that intelligent life once populated Mars.[53] Strangely,

Hoagland never mentions the possibility that the photos are fake, the result of sophisticated photographic chicanery. Perhaps the photos were placed in the NASA archives for someone like Hoagland to find. Or perhaps Hoagland is not who he claims to be. *Who knows?* After all, we live in a nation of smoke and mirrors, a place where the Wizard, undetected, beguiles and misdirects.

Some years ago, in a textbook entitled *Introductory Space Science: Volume II* (Department of Physics, USAF), cadets at the Air Force Academy in Colorado Springs were provided with a lengthy introduction to the subject of UFOs. The text categorically denied that UFOs were advanced secret weapon systems. Instead, it regaled the cadets with ancient accounts of earthlings being visited by "little people" from the stars. One such account, taken from India's *Book of Dzyan*, told of an alien race which waged war with earth. The text suggested that the account might be evidence of "an extraterrestrial colonization," validating myths of "Gods" visiting earth.

"While they [the aliens] were many leagues from the city of their enemies," the Air Force text stated, recounting the *Dzyan* legend, "they launched a great shining lance that rode on a beam of light. It burst apart in the city of their enemies with a great ball of flame that shot up to the heavens, almost to the stars. All those who were in the city were horribly burned and even those who were not in the city — but nearby — were burned also. Those who looked upon the lance and the ball of fire were blinded forever afterward. Those who entered the city on foot became ill and died...."

If this hadn't been taken from an ancient manuscript, it might well have served as a primer on the effects of EMP weaponry (see Chapter Five). *A beam of light, burn victims, people permanently blinded, radiation effects.* Was the military coyly preparing its cadets for the use of EMP weaponry in actual combat conditions?

The Air Force text concluded: "The most stimulating theory for us is that UFOs are material objects which are either 'Manned' or remote-controlled by beings who are alien to this planet.... [The data suggests] the existence of at least three and maybe four different groups of aliens (possibly at different states of development).... It implies the existence of intelligent life on a majority of the planets in our solar system, or a surprisingly strong interest in Earth by members of other solar systems...."

*Blah. Blah. Blah.*

Machiavelli once said: "The great majority of mankind is satisfied with appearances, as though they were realities."

Let's hope not.

In any event, now that you've seen the Wizard, you might care to recall the 1951 sci-fi thriller, *The Thing.* Just having staved off an alien invasion, an actor portraying a reporter in the film grasps a microphone and sputters the following for all to hear: *"Keep watching the skies.... keep watching the skies...."*

That was then. This is now.

In light of what you now know, you might also care to watch your back.

# Notes

FOREWORD

1. "RAAF Captures Flying Saucer on Ranch in Roswell Region," *Roswell Daily Record,* July 8, 1947.
2. Kevin D. Randle and Donald R. Schmitt, *UFO Crash at Roswell* (New York: Avon, 1991), p. 57.
3. "Gen. Ramey Empties Roswell Saucer," *Roswell Daily Record,* July 9, 1947.
4. A.J.S. Rayl, "Inside the Military UFO Underground," *Omni,* April 1994, pp. 50, 53–4.
5. Linda Moulton Howe, *An Alien Harvest* (Huntingdon Valley, Pa.: Linda Moulton Howe Productions, 1989), pp. 137–42.
6. Ibid., pp. 153, 156.

Chapter One: WHERE ARE THEY?

1. "Sagan vs. Butt-Head," *Maclean's,* May 9, 1994, p. 11.
2. Joseph A. Angelo, Jr., *The Extraterrestrial Encyclopedia* (New York: Facts on File Publications, 1985), pp. 61–2.
3. Michael Arvey, *UFOs* (St. Paul: Greenhaven Press, 1989), pp. 21–2.
4. Richard Michael Rasmussen, *Extraterrestrial Life* (San Diego: Lucent Books, 1991), pp. 66–7.
5. Robert T. Rood and James S. Trefil, *Are We Alone?* (New York: Charles Scribner's Sons, 1981), pp. 103–5.
6. Ibid., p. 246.
7. Ibid., p. 249.
8. Angelo, *Extraterrestrial Encyclopedia,* pp. 27–8.
9. Rood and Trefil, *Are We Alone?,* p. 247.
10. Ibid., pp. 250–1.
11. "NASA Urged to Seek Out Intelligent Life," *Observer* (Manchester, England), February 26, 1995.
12. Arvey, *UFOs,* p. 19.
13. Rood and Trefil, *Are We Alone?,* p. 251.
14. C. G. Jung, *Flying Saucers: A Modern Myth of Things Seen in the Skies* (New York: Harcourt, Brace, 1959), p. 162.
15. Anthony Mansueto, "Visions of Cosmopolis," *Omni,* October 1994, p. 66.

16. Jacques Vallee, *Revelations: Alien Contact and Human Deception* (New York: Ballantine Books, 1991), pp. 261–2.
17. Ibid., pp. 264–5.
18. Ibid., pp. 265–8.
19. Ibid., pp. 270–1.
20. Ibid., pp. 271–3.

**Chapter Two: "IGNORE THAT MAN BEHIND THE CURTAIN"**

1. Michael Arvey, *UFOs* (St. Paul: Greenhaven Press, 1989), pp. 48–50.
2. Associated Press, "Air Force General Says Army Not Doing Experiments," *Roswell Daily Record,* July 8, 1947.
3. Report from Lieutenant General Nathan F. Twining, Commander, Air Materiel Command, to Brigadier General George Schulgen, Army Air Forces, Washington, D.C., September 23, 1947.
4. Jack Anderson, "UFO Report Takes Flight," *Press-Journal* (Vero Beach, Fla.), June 2, 1995.
5. "Report of Air Force Research Regarding the 'Roswell Incident,'" Department of the Air Force, July 1994, p. 5.
6. Ibid., p. 21.
7. Ibid.
8. Anderson, "UFO Report Takes Flight."
9. Patrick Huyghe, "Project X," *Omni,* November 1994, p. 86.
10. Philip Mantle, "Dear UFO Disbeliever," *Independent* (London), March 29, 1995.
11. Ibid.
12. Kevin D. Randle and Donald R. Schmitt, *The Truth About the UFO Crash at Roswell* (New York: Avon Books, 1994), pp. 18–28.
13. Edoardo Russo, "Roswell Autopsy Showing in Italy," Internet, May 24, 1995.
14. Timothy Good, *Above Top Secret: The Worldwide UFO Cover-Up* (New York: William Morrow, 1988), pp. 545–51.
15. Ibid., p. 123.
16. Jacques Vallee, *Revelations: Alien Contact and Human Deception* (New York: Ballantine Books, 1991), p. 41.
17. KRILL UFO Revelation: A Situation Report on our Acquisition of Advanced Technology and Interaction With Alien Cultures, Internet, August 8, 1991.
18. Margaret Sachs, *The UFO Encyclopedia* (New York: Perigee Books, 1980), p. 191.
19. Timothy Green Beckley, *The UFO Silencers* (New Brunswick, N.J.: Inner Light Publications, 1990), p. 11.
20. Sachs, *UFO Encyclopedia.*

21. Report of Meetings of the Scientific Advisory Panel on Unidentified Flying Objects, February 16, 1953.

22. David Michael Jacobs, *The UFO Controversy in America* (Bloomington: Indiana University Press, 1975), p. 97.

23. Good, *Above Top Secret*, p. 357.

24. Ibid., pp. 352-3.

25. Lawrence Fawcett and Barry J. Greenwood, *The UFO Cover-Up* (New York: Fireside, 1992), pp. 206-7.

26. Bo Poertner, "Disney Encounter Lifts UFO Believers," *Orlando Sentinel*, May 3, 1995.

27. Vallee, *Revelations*, p. 90.

28. Good, *Above Top Secret*, pp. 262-3.

29. Ibid., pp. 273-7.

30. Ibid., p. 277.

31. Edward U. Condon, *Scientific Study of Unidentified Flying Objects* (New York: E.P. Dutton, 1969), p. 509.

32. Ibid., p. 26.

33. Ibid., pp. 522-3.

**Chapter Three: LET'S GET REAL**

1. "Flying Saucers—The Real Story: U.S. Built First One in 1942," *U.S. News & World Report*, April 7, 1950, p. 14.

2. Ibid., p. 13.

3. Ibid., p. 15.

4. Ibid.

5. Abe Dane, "Flying Saucers: The Real Story," *Popular Mechanics*, January 1995, p. 53.

6. Ibid.

7. Ibid.

8. Directive from Major General L. C. Craigie to Commanding General, Air Materiel Command, Wright Field, Dayton, Ohio, December 30, 1947.

9. Edward U. Condon, *Scientific Study of Unidentified Flying Objects* (New York: E.P. Dutton, 1969), p. 506.

10. Ibid.

11. Ibid., p. 509.

12. David Michael Jacobs, *The UFO Controversy in America* (Bloomington: Indiana University Press, 1975), p. 46.

13. Margaret Sachs, *The UFO Encyclopedia* (New York: Perigee Books, 1980), pp. 242-7.

14. Dane, "Flying Saucers: The Real Story," p. 121.

15. Ibid.

16. Associated Press, "Pentagon Unveils Pilotless Aircraft," *Courier-Journal* (Louisville, Ky.), June 12, 1995.

17. Michael A. Dornheim, "DarkStar Destroyed on Second Flight," *Aviation Week & Space Technology,* April 29, 1996, p. 24.
18. Ibid.
19. Michael A. Dornheim, "DarkStar Makes 'Solo' First Flight," *Aviation Week & Space Technology,* April 8, 1996, p. 23.
20. Jonathan Vankin and John Whalen, *50 Greatest Conspiracies of All Time* (New York: Citadel Press, 1995), p. 88.
21. Ibid., p. 85.
22. Associated Press, "Balls of Fire Stalk U.S. Fighters in Night Assaults Over Germany," *New York Times,* January 2, 1945.
23. Renato Vesco and David Hatcher Childress, *Man-Made UFOs, 1944–1994: 50 Years of Suppression* (Stelle, Ill.: Adventures Unlimited Press, 1994), Introduction.
24. Ibid., illustrated insert.
25. Timothy Good, *Above Top Secret: The Worldwide UFO Cover-Up* (New York: William Morrow, 1988), pp. 225–6.
26. L. Fletcher Prouty, *JFK: The CIA, Vietnam and the Plot to Assassinate John F. Kennedy* (New York: Birch Lane Press, 1992), pp. 10–11.
27. Vankin and Whalen, *50 Greatest Conspiracies,* pp. 303–9.
28. Vesco and Childress, *Man-Made UFOs,* p. 162.
29. "Swarm of Mysterious Rockets Is Seen Over Capital of Sweden," *New York Times,* August 12, 1946.
30. "Swedes Use Radar in Fight on Missiles," *New York Times,* August 13, 1946.
31. Ibid.; "Swarm of Mysterious Rockets Is Seen Over Capital of Sweden."
32. "Swedes Use Radar in Fight on Missiles."
33. "Swarm of Mysterious Rockets Is Seen Over Capital of Sweden."
34. United Press, "One Falls Near Stockholm," *New York Times,* August 13, 1946.
35. Ibid.
36. Jacobs, *UFO Controversy in America,* p. 36.
37. Vesco and Childress, *Man-Made UFOs,* p. 64.
38. Ibid., p. 10.
39. "Secret Advanced Vehicles Demonstrate Technologies for Future Military Use," *Aviation Week & Space Technology,* October 1, 1990, p. 22.
40. Ibid., p. 20.
41. Ibid.
42. Ibid., p. 22.
43. Timothy Good, *Alien Contact: Top-Secret UFO Files Revealed* (New York: William Morrow, 1993), pp. 138–9.
44. "Wide Area With View of Base Shut," *Las Vegas Review-Journal*, April 11, 1995.
45. Good, *Alien Contact,* pp. 149–50.

46. Jacques Vallee, *Revelations: Alien Contact and Human Deception* (New York: Ballantine Books, 1991), p. 83.

47. Ibid., p. 54.

48. Lawrence Fawcett and Barry J. Greenwood, *The UFO Cover-Up* (New York: Fireside, 1984), pp. 195–201.

49. Ibid., pp. 82–4.

50. Good, *Above Top Secret*, p. 243.

51. Ibid., p. 218.

52. Timothy Good, ed., *Alien Update* (New York: Avon Books, 1993), pp. 169–73.

53. Graham Birdsall, "Welcome to the Real World," *UFO Magazine* (Quest Publications), May-June 1995, p. 27.

54. Ibid., p. 28.

55. Ibid.

56. Ibid.

57. Andrew Cockburn, "Clinton Spree Fills Coffers of Defense Contractors," *Anchorage Daily News*, October 8, 1995.

58. CBS Evening News, December 15, 1995.

59. William M. Welch and Jack Kelley, "Terrain, Rain, Darkness Hampered Rescuers," *USA Today*, April 4, 1996.

**Chapter Four: WARNING: IT HAS BEEN DETERMINED THAT UFOS MAY BE HAZARDOUS TO YOUR HEALTH**

1. Ion Hobana and Julien Weverbergh, *UFO's From Behind the Iron Curtain* (New York: Bantam Books, 1975), pp. 10–30.

2. "Tesla, at 78, Bares New 'Death-Beam,'" *New York Times,* July 11, 1934.

3. Nick Begich and Jeane Manning, *Angels Don't Play This HAARP* (Anchorage: Earthpulse Press, 1995), p. 1.

4. "Tesla's New Device Like Bolts of Thor," *New York Times,* December 8, 1915.

5. "'Death Ray' for Planes," *New York Times,* September 22, 1940.

6. "Tesla's Death Ray," *Sightings,* January 14, 1996.

7. Ibid.

8. Timothy Good, *Above Top Secret: The Worldwide UFO Cover-Up* (New York: William Morrow, 1988), pp. 221–3.

9. Ibid., p. 224.

10. Ibid., pp. 217–8.

11. *Literature Gazette* (Moscow), November 9, 1990.

12. *Just Cause,* December 1993.

13. Gordon Creighton, "Naughty Henry Gris Says It Again! Soviet Space Center Knocked Out by UFOs," *Flying Saucer Review* 28, No. 6 (1983), pp. 27–8.

14. Jenny Randles, *The UFO Conspiracy* (New York: Barnes & Noble, 1993), pp. 144–6.

15. Steve Newman, Chronicle Features, "Earthwatch: A Diary of Our Planet," *Los Angeles Times,* August 17, 1995; "Argentinian Plane Buzzed by a Spaceship, Says Pilot," *The Age* (Melbourne, Australia), August 3, 1995.
16. "33 Persons Feared Dead in Braniff Plane Crash," *Dallas Morning News,* September 30, 1959.
17. Civil Aeronautics Board Aircraft Accident Report, SA-346 (File No. 1–0060), May 5, 1961.
18. Donald E. Keyhoe, *Aliens From Space: The Real Story of Unidentified Flying Objects* (New York: Signet, 1974), p. 160.
19. Civil Aeronautics Board Aircraft Accident Report, May 5, 1961.
20. Interview with principal witness, July 1982.
21. USAF Accident/Incident Report, March 13, 1968.
22. Associated Press, "Missing B52 Search Stops," *San Antonio Express,* March 15, 1968.
23. Associated Press, "Aircraft Debris Found," *New York Times,* March 10, 1968.
24. USAF Accident/Incident Report, March 13, 1968.
25. "Missing B52 Search Stops."
26. "The Longest Night," *Newsweek,* November 22, 1965, pp. 27–33.
27. John Fuller, *Incident at Exeter* (New York: G.P. Putnam's Sons, 1966), pp. 232–3.
28. Ibid., p. 235.
29. Ibid.
30. Ibid., pp. 235–6.
31. Ibid., p. 236.
32. Ibid., p. 237.
33. Wendelle C. Stevens and Paul Dong, *UFOs Over Modern China* (Tucson: UFO Photo Archives, 1983), p. 132.
34. Mark Rodeghier, *UFO Reports Involving Vehicle Interference* (Evanston, Ill.: Center for UFO Studies, 1981).
35. Ibid., pp. 88–9.
36. Ibid.
37. Ibid., p. 77.
38. Ibid., pp. 83–4.
39. Ibid., p. 112.
40. J. Allen Hynek, *The UFO Experience: A Scientific Inquiry* (Chicago: Henry Regnery, 1972), pp. 123–4.
41. Ibid., p. 124.
42. Ibid., p. 125.
43. Ibid., pp. 125–6.
44. Air Intelligence Information Report (USAF), No. 141957, November 2–8, 1957.
45. Gordon Creighton, "The Spanish Government Opens Its Files," *Flying Saucer Review* 23, No. 3 (1977), p. 3.

46. Rodeghier, *UFO Reports Involving Vehicle Interference*, p. 71.
47. Ibid., p. 75.
48. The K Files, "Buzzed by Flying Pyramid," *Burton Daily Mail* (Staffs, England), March 3, 1995.
49. Edward U. Condon, *Scientific Study of Unidentified Flying Objects* (New York: E.P. Dutton, 1969), pp. 316–8; "UFO Case 'of Greatest Scientific Interest,'" *Winnipeg Free Press*, May 24, 1967.
50. Chris Rutkowski, "The Falcon Lake Incident," *Flying Saucer Review* 27, Nos. 1, 2, and 3 (1981); Derik Hodgson, "Burns Back, Says Michalak," *Winnipeg Free Press*, January 16, 1968.
51. Jim and Coral Lorenzen, *UFOs Over the Americas* (New York: Signet Books, 1968), p. 41.
52. John F. Schuessler, "Victims of a Close Encounter," *Fate*, May 1984, pp. 32–6; Cindy Horswell, "State, Private Agencies Probing Claim of UFO Encounter," *Houston Chronicle*, September 25, 1981.
53. William Barrett, "UFO Report," *Dallas Times Herald*, September 21, 1981.
54. Jacques Vallee, *Confrontations: A Scientist's Search for Alien Contact* (New York: Ballantine Books, 1990), p. 124.

**Chapter Five: DEATH FROM ABOVE**
1. David A. Fulghum, "Russian Power Design to Drive U.S. Weapons," *Aviation Week & Space Technology*, April 10, 1995, pp. 54–5.
2. Jim Keith, *Casebook on Alternative 3* (Lilburn, Ga.: IllumiNet Press, 1993), p. 49.
3. Albert Speer, *Inside the Third Reich* (New York: Macmillan, 1970), p. 464.
4. Eugene Davidson, *The Trial of the Germans* (New York: Macmillan, 1969), p. 7.
5. H. Keith Florig, "The Future Battlefield: A Blast of Gigawatts?" *Spectrum*, March 1988, p. 50.
6. "UFOs Over Russia," *Flying Saucers*, May 1966, pp. 6–10.
7. L. M. Gindilis, D. A. Menkov, and I. G. Petrovskaya, "Observations of Anomalous Atmospheric Phenomena in the USSR: Statistical Analysis," USSR Academy of Sciences Institute of Space Research, Report No. PR 473, 1979.
8. Raymond Fowler, *Casebook of a UFO Investigator* (New Jersey: Prentice-Hall, 1981), pp. 182–3.
9. Linda Moulton Howe, *An Alien Harvest* (Huntington Valley, Pa.: Linda Moulton Howe Productions, 1989), pp. 23–4.
10. Lawrence Fawcett and Barry J. Greenwood, *The UFO Cover-Up* (New York: Fireside, 1984), pp. 29–30.
11. Ibid., p. 31.
12. Margaret Sachs, *The UFO Encyclopedia* (New York: Perigee Books, 1980), p. 8.

13. Gary Hodder, "U.S. Military Base Interested in Bell Island Lightning Ball," *Evening Telegram* (St. John's, Newfoundland), April 12, 1978.
14. Steve Newman, Chronicle Features, "Earthweek: A Diary of Our Planet," *Anchorage Daily News,* February 4, 1996.
15. United Press International, "Investigators Probing Mysterious Radio Signals," *Houston Chronicle,* November 21, 1977.
16. United Press International, "Satellite Starts Talking to Earth After Nine Years," *Arkansas Gazette* (Little Rock), August 4, 1977.
17. George C. Wilson, "Pentagon to Curtail Electromagnetic Tests," *Washington Post,* May 15, 1988.
18. Vincent J. Schodolski, "Workers Blow Whistle on Air Force's Secret Nevada Base," *San Francisco Examiner,* May 28, 1995.
19. Warren Bates, "Judge Asked to Toss Out Groom Lake Suit," *Las Vegas Review-Journal,* May 24, 1995.
20. Warren Bates, "Groom Lake Chemicals Can Be Secret," *Las Vegas Review-Journal,* October 3, 1995.
21. "Taos Hum," *Sightings,* August 16, 1995.
22. Donald E. Keyhoe, *Aliens From Space: The Real Story of Unidentified Flying Objects* (New York: Signet, 1974), p. 89.
23. Jim and Coral Lorenzen, "Burned by UFOs," *Fate,* October 1968, pp. 39–40.
24. Gordon H. Evans, "Do UFOs Use a Paralysis Ray?" *Fate,* December 1966, pp. 102–3.
25. Florig, "The Future Battlefield: A Blast of Gigawatts?" p. 53.
26. Ibid., p. 54.
27. Brad Steiger and Joan Whritenour, *Flying Saucers Are Hostile* (New York: Award Books, 1967), pp. 23–4, 36–7.
28. "UFO Heads Toward Lawmen," *Brazosport Facts* (Clute, Tex.), September 6, 1965; "Ellington Probes UFO Seen by Local Deputies," *Brazosport Facts,* September 9, 1965.
29. Rhonda Moran, "The Night of the UFO," *Brazosport Facts,* September 13, 1995.

**Chapter Six: TERROR IN THE ARCTIC**

1. "The Top 10 Censored Stories," *Utne Reader,* May-June 1995, p. 36.
2. "High-Frequency Active Auroral Research Program," *Arctic Research 8,* Fall 1994, p. 54.
3. John Mintz, "Pentagon Fights Secret Scenario Speculation Over Alaska Antennas," *Washington Post,* April 17, 1995.
4. Ibid.
5. Ibid.
6. Mark Farmer, "Mystery in Alaska," *Popular Science,* September 1995, p. 81.
7. Mintz, "Pentagon Fights Secret Scenario Speculation Over Alaska Antennas."

8. "NSB Sues Feds Over Radiation Exposure," *North Slope Sentinel* (North Pole, Alaska), May 12, 1995.

9. Nancy Tarnai, "Borough Targets Funds to Investigate Govt. Iodine Testing of Alaska Natives," *North Slope Sentinel,* December 22, 1995.

10. Dimitra Lavrakas, "Project Chariot — 30 Years of Secrecy," *Arctic Sounder* (Kotzebue, Alaska), October 13, 1995.

11. Ibid.

12. Nick Begich and Jeane Manning, *Angels Don't Play This HAARP* (Anchorage: Earthpulse Press, 1995), p. 4.

13. Ibid., pp. 5–7.

14. Ibid., p. 7.

15. Ibid, p. 6.

16. Farmer, "Mystery in Alaska," p. 93.

17. Ibid., p. 94.

18. Begich and Manning, *Angels Don't Play This HAARP,* p. 63.

19. Ibid., pp. 62–3.

20. "Policy of Non-Lethal Weapons," Department of Defense Directive, Office of the Assistant Secretary of Defense, July 21, 1994.

21. Begich and Manning, *Angels Don't Play This HAARP,* p. 173.

22. Ibid.

23. Ibid., pp. 180–1.

24. Lt. Colonel David J. Dean (ed.), *Low Intensity Conflict and Modern Technology,* Air University Press, Center for Aerospace Doctrine, Research, and Education, Maxwell AFB, Ala., June 1986, pp. 249–51.

25. Begich and Manning, *Angels Don't Play This HAARP,* p. 170.

26. R. Jacobsen and H. Wachtel, Proceedings of the 6th Annual Meeting of the Bioelectromagnetic Society, Atlanta, July 15–19, 1984.

27. "Expert Meeting on Certain Systems and on Implementation Mechanisms in International Law," International Committee of the Red Cross, Geneva, Switzerland, July 1994.

28. Begich and Manning, *Angels Don't Play This HAARP,* p. 199.

29. Ibid., p. 200.

30. Ibid., p. 180.

31. Ibid., p. 174.

32. Jim Paulin, "Military Brings More Medical Care to Villages," *Arctic Sounder,* April 13, 1995.

33. Anna M. Pickett, "Guard Bias Widespread, Board Calls for Change," *Tundra Times* (Anchorage), May 24, 1995.

34. Eric Schmitt, "Pentagon to Seek Scaled-Back List of Base Closings," *New York Times,* February 25, 1995.

35. Claire Zickuhr and Gar Smith, "Project HAARP: The Military's Plan to Alter the Ionosphere," *Earth Island Journal,* Fall 1994.

36. Mintz, "Pentagon Fights Secret Scenario Speculation Over Alaska Antennas."

37. Maureen Clark, Associated Press, "FAA Increases Efforts to Prevent Accidents," *Anchorage Daily News,* August 26, 1995.
38. Jim Paulin, "Fuel Plane Crashes at Kivalina," *Arctic Sounder,* April 20, 1995.
39. "Pilots Spotting for Fish Die in Midair Collision," *Anchorage Daily News,* July 16, 1995.
40. Associated Press, "Fairbanks Pilot Makes Safe Emergency Landing on River," *Anchorage Daily News,* July 16, 1995.
41. "Two Die in Plane Crash in Brooks Range," *North Slope Sentinel,* September 1, 1995.
42. Stan Jones, "Investigators Begin Crash Work," *Anchorage Daily News,* September 24, 1995.
43. Stan Jones, "AWACS Report Names No Names," *Anchorage Daily News,* February 25, 1996.
44. Mike Doogan, "Colonel Disputes AWACS Crash Fault, But Takes the Hit," *Anchorage Daily News,* April 14, 1996.
45. "Eilson A-10 Pilot Rescued After Crash," *Fairbanks Daily News-Miner,* October 11, 1995.
46. "Caribou Quirks Worry Village That Needs Them," *Anchorage Daily News,* August 6, 1995.
47. "Caribou Deaths Studied," *North Slope Sentinel,* June 23, 1995.
48. The Impact Team, *The Weather Conspiracy: The Coming of the New Ice Age* (New York: Ballantine Books, 1977), p. 167.
49. Ibid., pp. 178, 181.
50. Ibid., p. 191.
51. Ibid., p. 192.
52. Ibid., pp. 200–1.
53. "Weather Modification," *Saturday Review,* February 5, 1977, p. 4.
54. Impact Team, *Weather Conspiracy,* p. 75.
55. Ibid.
56. Ibid.
57. Charlene L. Fu, Associated Press, "Water Rises in 10 China Provinces," *Anchorage Daily News,* July 9, 1995.
58. Susana Hayward, Associated Press, "Worst Drought in Decades Bedevils Mexican Ranchers," *Anchorage Daily News,* July 9, 1995.
59. Steve Newman, Chronicle Features, "Earthweek: A Diary of Our Planet," *Anchorage Daily News,* June 4, 1995.
60. Steve Newman, Chronicle Features, "Earthweek: A Diary of Our Planet," *Anchorage Daily News,* September 10, 17, and 24, 1995; October 1, 8, 15, and 22, 1995.
61. "Alaska Earthquakes Reveal Earth's Wandering Ways," *North Slope Sentinel,* October 20, 1995.
62. Begich and Manning, *Angels Don't Play This HAARP,* p. 194.
63. Newman, Chronicle Features, *Anchorage Daily News,* January 14, 1996.

64. Associated Press, "Poker Flat Launches Space Seeding Project," *Anchorage Daily News,* February 5, 1995.

65. Michael Drew, "Aurora, Rocket on Schedule," *Fairbanks Daily News-Miner,* March 28, 1995.

66. Draft, NSA/AAO [North Slope of Alaska & Adjacent Arctic Ocean] ARM (Atmospheric Radiation Measurement [Program]) Science Education and Training (ASET) Plan, April 1995.

67. Charles Petit, "Video Captures Flashes at Edge of Space," *San Francisco Chronicle,* December 7, 1994.

68. Earl Finkler, "Possible UFO's Observed in Barrow Skies?" *North Slope Sentinel,* January 6, 1995.

69. Dimitra Lavrakas, "Barrow Not Only Village to See Lights," *Arctic Sounder,* January 12, 1995.

70. Finkler, "Possible UFO's Observed in Barrow Skies?"

## Chapter Seven: ABDUCTIONS OF THE MIND

1. Ludwig Mayer, *Die Technik der Hypnose* (Munich: J. F. Lehmanns Verlag, 1953), p. 225.

2. Martin Cannon, *The Controllers: A New Hypothesis of Alien Abductions* (privately published), n.d., p. 58.

3. Ibid., pp. 103–4.

4. John Marks, *The Search for the Manchurian Candidate* (New York: W. W. Norton, 1979), pp. 24–31; Alan W. Scheflin and Edward M. Opton, Jr., *The Mind Manipulators* (New York: Paddington Press, 1978), pp. 103, 112–9.

5. Marks, *Manchurian Candidate,* pp. 31–6; Scheflin and Opton, *Mind Manipulators,* pp. 103, 120–31.

6. Marks, *Manchurian Candidate,* pp. 61, 112; Scheflin and Opton, *Mind Manipulators,* pp. 157–8.

7. Marks, *Manchurian Candidate,* pp. 211–5; Scheflin and Opton, *Mind Manipulators,* pp. 154–5.

8. Marks, *Manchurian Candidate,* pp. 61–6, 72–7; Scheflin and Opton, *Mind Manipulators,* pp. 127, 131–59.

9. Marks, *Manchurian Candidate,* pp. 38–42, 46–7.

10. Marks, *Manchurian Candidate,* p. 67; Scheflin and Opton, *Mind Manipulators,* pp. 167–8, 183–91.

11. Scheflin and Opton, *Mind Manipulators,* pp. 168, 183, 191–2.

12. Marks, *Manchurian Candidate,* p. 11.

13. Memorandum from CIA director Allen Dulles to FBI director J. Edgar Hoover, OA 53–37, April 25, 1956.

14. Memorandum from Richard Helms, CIA Deputy Director for Plans, to J. Lee Rankin, general counsel, President's Commission on the Assassination of President Kennedy, Commission No. 1131, June 19, 1964.

15. Jonathan Vankin and John Whalen, *50 Greatest Conspiracies of All Time* (New York: Citadel Press, 1995), pp. 35–9.

16. Cannon, *Controllers*, p. 28.

17. John Lilly, *The Scientist* (Berkeley: Ronin Publishing, 1988), p. 91.

18. Marks, *Manchurian Candidate*, pp. 151–3.

19. Cannon, *Controllers*, pp. 17–18; Lincoln Lawrence (pseud.), *Were We Controlled?* (New York: University Books, 1967), p. 36.

20. J. M. R. Delgado, "Intracerebral Radio Stimulation and Recording in Completely Free Patients," *Psychotechnology* (New York: Holt, Rinehart and Winston, 1973), p. 195.

21. José M. R. Delgado, *Physical Control of the Mind: Toward a Psychocivilized Society* (New York: Harper and Row, 1971), p. 179.

22. Ibid., pp. 252–3.

23. Scheflin and Opton, *Mind Manipulators*, pp. 334–7.

24. Gordon Thomas, *Journey into Madness* (New York: Bantam Books, 1989), p. 276.

25. Scheflin and Opton, *Mind Manipulators*, p. 337.

26. Joseph A. Meyer, "Crime Deterrent Transponder System," *Transactions on Aerospace and Electronic Systems*, IEEE, January 1971, p. 2.

27. Ibid., p. 11.

28. Ibid.

29. Lawrence, *Were We Controlled?*, p. 52.

30. Cannon, *Controllers*, pp. 35–6; *Project MK-ULTRA, the CIA's Program of Research in Behavioral Modification*, Joint Hearing before the Select Committee on Health and Scientific Research of the Committee on Human Resources, United States Senate (Washington: Government Printing Office, 1977).

31. Cannon, *Controllers*, p. 29.

32. Ibid.

33. Lawrence, *Were We Controlled?*

34. Memorandum from CIA director John McCone to Secret Service chief James Rowley, National Archives, March 3, 1964; Dick Russell, *The Man Who Knew Too Much* (New York: Carroll & Graf, 1992), p. 675.

35. Russell, *Man Who Knew Too Much*, p. 677.

36. Edward Jay Epstein, *Legend* (New York: Reader's Digest Press/McGraw-Hill, 1978), pp. 157–8, 310.

37. Cannon, *Controllers*, p. 33.

38. Russell, *Man Who Knew Too Much*.

39. "Damon Runyon Jr. Is Killed in Plunge," *New York Times*, April 15, 1968.

40. Walter Bowart, *Operation Mind Control* (New York: Dell, 1978), pp. 261–4.

41. Cannon, *Controllers*, p. 7.

42. R.J. MacGregor, *A Brief Survey of Literature Relating to Influence of Low Intensity Microwaves on Nervous Function* (Santa Monica: RAND Corporation, 1970).

43. Margaret Cheney, *Tesla: Man Out of Time* (New York: Dell, 1981), pp. 101–4.

44. Lawrence, *Were We Controlled?*, p. 29.

45. Robert O. Becker, M.D., and Gary Selden, *The Body Electric: Electromagnetism and the Foundation of Life* (New York: William Morrow, 1985), pp. 318–9.

46. Alex Constantine, *Psychic Dictatorship in the U.S.A.* (Portland: Feral House, 1995), p. 46.

47. Kathy Cordova, "The Truth is Out There," *Taos News*, March 16, 1995.

48. Ibid.

49. "President's Committee on Radiation Hears Mind Control Survivor's Testimony," *Free Thinking*, March 1995.

50. Edward U. Condon, *Scientific Study of Unidentified Flying Objects* (New York: E.P. Dutton, 1969), p. 44.

51. Thomas Hargrove and Guido H. Stempel III, Scripps Howard News Service, "Flying Saucers? More Than Half of Us Think They're Real," *Alexandria Journal* (Alexandria, Va.), August 2, 1995.

52. Ibid.

53. Zack Van Eyck, "Abducted by Aliens — AND by Secret Military?" *Deseret News* (Salt Lake City), December 1, 1995.

54. Clay Evans, "Encounters Too Far Out for Skeptics," *Daily Camera* (Boulder, Colo.), August 28, 1995.

55. A. J. S. Rayl, "Anatomy of an Abduction," *Omni*, February 1995, p. 60.

56. Ibid.

57. Cannon, *Controllers*, p. 111.

58. Ibid., pp. 111–2.

59. Ibid., pp. 112–3.

60. Ibid., p. 113.

61. Scheflin and Opton, *Mind Manipulators*, pp. 149–50.

62. Ibid., pp. 318–20.

63. Cannon, *Controllers*, p. 94.

64. Russell, *Man Who Knew Too Much*, p. 141; Otto Tolischus, *Tokyo Record* (New York: Reynal and Hitchcock, 1943), pp. 429–49.

65. Tolischus, *Tokyo Record*, pp. 399–400.

66. Cannon, *Controllers*, pp. 124–5.

67. Ibid., pp. 113–4.

68. Ibid., p. 114.

69. Ibid.

70. Ibid., pp. 115–6.

71. Jacques Vallee, *Dimensions: A Casebook of Alien Contact* (New York: Ballantine Books, 1989), pp. 223, 225.

72. Leonard Stringfield, *Inside Saucer Post...3-0 Blue* (Cincinnati: CRIFO, 1957), pp. 41-2.
73. Cannon, *Controllers,* p. 116.
74. Ibid., pp. 116-7.
75. Ibid., p. 117.
76. James Gleick, "The Doctor's Plot," *New Republic,* May 30, 1994, pp. 31-2.
77. Ibid., pp. 32-3.
78. Cannon, *Controllers,* pp. 64-5.
79. John E. Mack, *Abduction: Human Encounters With Aliens* (New York: Ballantine Books, 1994), p. 39.
80. Ibid., pp. 143-4.
81. Ibid., p. 235.
82. Ibid., p. 420.
83. Alex Beam, "Harvard's Mack Talks Back," *Boston Globe,* May 12, 1995.
84. "Psychologist Loses His License," *Sacramento Bee,* August 11, 1995.
85. Gleick, "The Doctor's Plot," p. 32.
86. Sean Piccoli, "UFO Buffs Meet," *Washington Times,* May 30, 1995.
87. "White House Alien Policy," *Common Cause,* Fall 1995.
88. "The Hybrids Are Coming," *UFO Magazine* (Quest Publications), November-December 1995, p. 8.
89. Jim Keith, *Casebook on Alternative 3* (Lilburn, Ga.: IllumniNet Press, 1994), pp. 130-1.
90. Vankin and Whalen, *50 Greatest Conspiracies of All Time,* pp. 21-4.
91. Keith, *Casebook on Alternative 3,* p. 137.
92. Ibid., p. 131.
93. George Rush and Joanna Molloy, "Prez' Hunt for Campaign Cash May Turn Up Some UFOs First," *New York Daily News,* August 24, 1995.

**Chapter Eight: THE LEFT HAND OF THE MAGICIAN**

1. Margaret Sachs, *The UFO Encyclopedia* (New York: Perigee Books, 1980), p. 75.
2. Kevin D. Randle, *A History of UFO Crashes* (New York: Avon Books, 1995), p. 183.
3. Ibid., p. 190.
4. Ibid., p. 196.
5. Ibid., p. 200.
6. Ibid., pp. 192-3.
7. Ibid., p. 188.
8. Julian Champkin, "A Real Alien...or an Earthly Hoax?" *Daily Mail* (London), August 24, 1995.
9. Vicky Ward, "Hot Property from Outer Space," *Independent* (London), July 6, 1995.

10. William Patalon III, "E.T. or Hoax? Kodak Can't Tell," *Democrat and Chronicle* (Rochester, N.Y.), August 26, 1995.
11. Kevin D. Randle and Donald R. Schmitt, *UFO Crash at Roswell* (New York: Avon Books, 1991), p. 57.
12. "Alien Autopsy: Fact or Fiction?" Fox TV, August 1995.
13. Renato Vesco and David Hatcher Childress, *Man-Made UFOs, 1944–1994: 50 Years of Suppression* (Stelle, Ill.: Adventures Unlimited Press, 1994), back section.
14. Associated Press, July 29, 1995.
15. "The Roswell Incident," Learning Channel, January 26, 1996.
16. "Alien Autopsy: Fact or Fiction?"; Kevin D. Randle and Donald R. Schmitt, *The Truth About the UFO Crash at Roswell* (New York: Avon Books, 1994), pp. 88–9.
17. "Alien Autopsy: Fact or Fiction?"
18. Robin McKie, London Observer Service, "Film of Supposed Alien Autopsy Puzzles Scientists," *Thousand Oaks Star* (Thousand Oaks, Calif.), July 26, 1995.
19. "Alien Autopsy: Fact or Fiction?"
20. Ibid.
21. Richard Corliss, "Autopsy or Fraud-Topsy," *Time,* November 27, 1995, p. 105.
22. "Alien Autopsy: Fact or Fiction."
23. "The Roswell Autopsy," *Sightings,* August 16, 1995.
24. Champkin, "A Real Alien…or an Earthly Hoax?"
25. Corliss, "Autopsy or Fraud-Topsy."
26. *Sunday Sun* (Tyne & Wear, England), July 28, 1995.
27. Ward, "Hot Property from Outer Space."
28. Associated Press, "UFO Museum to Check Out Metal," *Tucson Citizen,* March 29, 1996.
29. "The Roswell Incident."
30. Christy Campbell and Nick Cook, "Secret US Spy Plane 'Crashed at Stonehenge,'" *Electronic Telegraph,* Internet, December 19, 1994.

**Chapter Nine: LIGHTS! CAMERA! *UFOS!***

1. Gordon I. R. Lore, Jr., and Harold H. Deneault, Jr., *Mysteries of the Skies: UFOs in Perspective* (New York: Prentice-Hall, 1968), pp. 74–5.
2. Ibid., pp. 76–7.
3. "Knox Indicates Raid Just 'Jittery Nerves,'" *Los Angeles Times,* February 26, 1942.
4. Timothy Good, *Above Top Secret: The Worldwide UFO Cover-Up* (New York: William Morrow, 1988), p. 16.
5. "Knox Indicates Raid Just 'Jittery Nerves.'"
6. "Recipe for Jitters," *Washington Post,* February 27, 1942.

7. "Pacific Coast's Alert Was Real, Army Reports," *Washington Post*, February 27, 1942.

8. Ibid.

9. "Recipe for Jitters."

10. "The Los Angeles Mystery," *New York Times*, February 28, 1942.

11. Good, *Above Top Secret*, p. 15.

12. Lore and Deneault, *Mysteries of the Skies*, pp. 85–6.

13. Ibid., p. 82.

14. Good, *Above Top Secret*, pp. 15–16.

15. Peter Watson, *War on the Mind* (New York: Basic Books, 1978), p. 413.

16. Ibid., p. 410.

17. Ibid., p. 411.

18. Jacques Vallee, *Dimensions: A Casebook of Alien Contact* (New York: Ballantine Books, 1989), p. 224.

19. L. Fletcher Prouty, *JFK: The CIA, Vietnam and the Plot to Assassinate John F. Kennedy* (New York: Birch Lane Press, 1992), p. 30.

20. Ibid., pp. 30–1.

21. Ibid., p. 32.

22. Ibid.

23. Associated Press, "Spaniards Protest Terrorism," *New York Times*, February 2, 1987.

24. Edward J. Ruppelt, *The Report on Unidentified Flying Objects* (New York: Ace, 1956), pp. 208–9.

25. Coral E. Lorenzen, *Flying Saucers: The Startling Evidence of the Invasion from Outer Space* (New York: Signet, 1962), p. 37.

26. Ruppelt, *Report on Unidentified Flying Objects*, pp. 208–9.

27. Ibid., pp. 207–8.

28. Ibid., pp. 210–11.

29. Associated Press, "Flying Objects Near Washington Spotted by Both Pilots and Radar," *New York Times*, July 22, 1952.

30. Ruppelt, *Report on Unidentified Flying Objects*, p. 212.

31. Ibid.

32. Ibid., p. 217.

33. Ibid., p. 218.

34. Ibid., pp. 218–9.

35. Ibid., p. 213.

36. Report issued by Deputy Base Commander Lt. Colonel Charles I. Halt, USAF, to British Ministry of Defence, January 31, 1981.

37. Letter sent to Robert Todd by Colonel Peter W. Bent, Commander, Headquarters, 513th Combat Support Group, USAF, New York, June 14, 1983.

38. Jenny Randles, *From Out of the Blue* (New York: Berkley Books, 1993), pp. 62–3.

39. Ibid., p. 63.
40. Ibid., p. 64.
41. Ibid., pp. 5–9.
42. Ibid., p. 62.
43. Ibid., p. 201.
44. Ibid., pp. 102–11.
45. Ibid., p. 213.
46. Ibid.
47. Ibid., pp. 214–5.
48. Ibid., p. 213.
49. Ibid., p. 123.
50. Ibid., pp. 134–5.
51. Jacques Vallee, *Revelations: Alien Contact and Human Deception* (New York: Ballantine Books, 1991), p. 97.
52. Ibid., p. 171.
53. Randles, *From Out of the Blue,* pp. 224–5.
54. "Secret Advanced Vehicles Demonstrate Technologies for Future Military Use," *Aviation Week & Space Technology,* October 1, 1990, p. 20.
55. Tom Walker, "Belgian Scientists Seriously Pursue a Triangular UFO," *Wall Street Journal,* October 10, 1990.
56. Marie-Thérèse de Brosses, "A UFO on the F-16's Radar," *Paris Match,* July 5, 1990.
57. Timothy Good, *Alien Contact: Top-Secret UFO Files Revealed* (New York: William Morrow, 1993), p. 267.
58. Ibid.
59. Walker, "Belgian Scientists Seriously Pursue a Triangular UFO."
60. "Flying Triangle Has Belgians Going Round in Circles," *Financial Times* (London), April 18, 1990.
61. De Brosses, "A UFO on the F-16's Radar," pp. 48–9.
62. Walker, "Belgian Scientists Seriously Pursue a Triangular UFO."
63. Ibid.
64. Timothy Good (ed.), *Alien Update* (New York: Avon Books, 1995), pp. 274–5.
65. Ibid., p. 240.
66. "Black Triangles in the Sky," *Alberta Report,* June 13, 1994.
67. Good, *Alien Update,* p. 138.
68. Mary Beth Norton, et al., *A People and a Nation* (Boston: Houghton Mifflin, 1982), pp. 609–10.
69. Ibid., p. 799.
70. Ibid., p. 798.
71. Dick Russell, *The Man Who Knew Too Much* (New York: Carroll & Graf, 1992), p. 294.
72. Jonathan Vankin and John Whalen, *50 Greatest Conspiracies of All Time* (New York: Citadel Press, 1995), pp. 297–8.

73. Good, *Alien Contact,* pp. 25–6.

74. Ibid., pp. 26–7.

75. Ibid., p. 27.

76. Ibid., pp. 25–8; Good, *Alien Update,* pp. 6–35.

77. Ibid., p. 28.

78. Good, *Alien Update,* p. 12.

79. Ibid., pp. 12–13.

80. Ibid., p. 13.

81. Ibid., pp. 13–14.

82. Ibid., p. 14.

83. Ibid., pp. 14–15.

84. Ibid., pp. 15–16.

85. Ibid., pp. 17–19.

86. Ibid., p. 19.

87. Ibid., p. 20.

88. Ibid.

**Chapter Ten:** *KEEP WATCHING THE SKIES*

1. Mary Beth Norton, et al., *A People and a Nation* (Boston: Houghton Mifflin, 1982), p. 808.

2. Ibid., p. 910.

3. Jim Marrs, *Crossfire: The Plot That Killed Kennedy* (New York: Carroll & Graf, 1989), p. 115.

4. L. Fletcher Prouty, *JFK: The CIA, Vietnam and the Plot to Kill John F. Kennedy* (New York: Birch Lane Press, 1992), pp. 17–18.

5. Ibid., p. 344.

6. Walter Millis (ed.), *The Forrestal Diaries* (New York: Viking Press, 1951), pp. x, xiv.

7. Jacques Vallee, *Revelations: Alien Contact and Human Deception* (New York: Ballantine Books, 1991), p. 58.

8. Dick Russell, *The Man Who Knew Too Much* (New York: Carroll & Graf, 1992), p. 134.

9. "M'Arthur Greets Mayor of Naples," *New York Times,* October 8, 1955.

10. Donald E. Keyhoe, *Aliens From Space: The Real Story of Unidentified Flying Objects* (New York: Signet, 1974), pp. 50–1.

11. Reuters, "Reagan Imagines Star Wars," *International Herald Tribune* (Paris), December 5, 1985.

12. Fred Barnes, "Reagan Reaps Arms-Control Harvest," *New Republic.* Reprint in *Plain Dealer* (Cleveland), October 11, 1987.

13. Associated Press, "Reagan Muses on Space Threat," *Rocky Mountain News* (Denver), May 5, 1988.

14. Keyhoe, *Aliens From Space,* pp. 131–2, 247.

15. Ibid., p. 58.

16. Ibid., pp. 258–9.
17. Ibid., p. 259.
18. Anonymous, *Report From Iron Mountain on the Possibility and Desirability of Peace* (New York: Dial Press, 1967), p. 39.
19. Ibid., p. 30.
20. Ibid., p. 86.
21. Ibid., p. 84.
22. Ibid., p. 97.
23. Ibid., p. 99.
24. Ibid., p. 100.
25. Victor Navasky, "Anatomy of a Hoax," *Nation*, June 12, 1995, pp. 816–7.
26. Prouty, *JFK*, p. 182.
27. Ibid., p. 187.
28. Jonathan Vankin and John Whalen, *50 Greatest Conspiracies of All Time* (New York: Citadel Press, 1995), p. 27.
29. Ben Bradlee, Jr., *Guts and Glory: The Rise and Fall of Oliver North* (New York: Donald I. Fine, 1988), p. 135.
30. Vankin and Whalen, *50 Greatest Conspiracies*, p. 31.
31. Ibid., p. 28.
32. Bradlee, *Guts and Glory.*
33. Ibid.; Alfonso Chardy, "Reagan Advisers Ran 'Secret' Government," *Miami Herald,* July 5, 1987.
34. Vankin and Whalen, *50 Greatest Conspiracies*, p. 29.
35. Bradlee, *Guts and Glory*, p. 560.
36. Theodore Draper, *A Very Thin Line* (New York: Hill and Wang, 1991), p. 578.
37. Bradlee, *Guts and Glory*, pp. 133–4; Vankin and Whalen, *50 Greatest Conspiracies*, pp. 30–1.
38. Diana Reynolds, "Domestic Consequences of the Gulf War," *Covert Action Information Bulletin,* Summer 1991.
39. *Guardian* (New York), January 16, 1991.
40. Donald Goldberg, "The National Guards," *Omni*, May 1987, p. 132.
41. Ibid., p. 50.
42. Ibid., p. 132.
43. Ibid., p. 50.
44. Michael Ross, "Clinton Decries Congress' Stand on Terrorism," *Los Angeles Times,* May 28, 1995.
45. A.J.S. Rayl, "UFO Update: In Their New Instruction Manual, Firefighters Are Briefed on the Art and Science of UFOs," *Omni*, January 1995, p. 79.
46. "Coming Soon: An Alien Invasion," *Newsweek*, July 17, 1995, p. 8.
47. "Big Screen Aliens," *USA Today*, April 2, 1996.
48. Leon Jaroff, "Weird Science," *Time*, May 15, 1995, pp. 75–6.

49. Patrick Henry, speech before Virginia Convention, Richmond, March 23, 1775.
50. "What the World Needs Now," *Utne Reader*, March-April 1996, p. 70.
51. Charles Petit, "Search for Life on Mars," *San Francisco Chronicle*, December 13, 1995.
52. Eleanor Sprawson, "Time Runs Out in Search for Aliens," *Melbourne Herald Sun*, June 26, 1995.
53. Wayne Laugesen, "The Face of Mars," *Boulder Weekly* (Boulder, Colo.), January 4, 1996.

# Index

research and development
spending by, 38
*People and a Nation, A* (Norton, et
al.), 145
Pepper, William, 129n
Peru, earthquake in, 88
Peterson, Col., 18
Philippines, reported psy ops in, 130
*See also* Psychological Opera-
tions (Psy Ops)
Phillips Laboratories, weapons
research of, 62, 67, 75
Pierman, Capt. "Casey," 133
Place With No Name, 31–3
"Planet Earth—Host to Extraterres-
trial Life" (Odell), 158
Plowshares Program (AEC), 77
Point Hope, Alaska, dead caribou
found near, 85
Point Loma Naval Electronics Lab-
oratory, Calif., 109
Poker Flat Research Range, 88, 90
*Popular Mechanics,* 25
Port Isabel, Tex., 51
Powers, Gary Francis, 154
President's Advisory Committee on
Climate Control, 87
President's Committee on Radia-
tion, 102
Price, Nathan C., 24
Program for Extraordinary Experi-
ence Research, 111
Project Blue Book, 131, 131n, 135
Project Censored (Sonoma State
University), 73, 104
Project Chariot, 77
Project Cobra Mist, 140
Project Cold Witness, 140
Project Grudge, 23, 45n, 131n
Project HAARP, 73–6, 74n, 77–80,
81, 83, 85, 87, 89, 90, 147
Project Mogul, 10-11, 11n
Project Sign, 22–3, 131n

Prophet, Elizabeth Clare, 109–10
Prouty, Col. L. Fletcher, 130–1, 152,
160–1
psychoelectronics, 94–5, 98
Psychological Operations (Psy
Ops), 15, 45n, 129–31, 129n,
130n, 141, 147, 152, 158, 159
Psychological warfare. *See* Psychological Operations (Psy Ops)
Puerto Rico:
CIA and U.S. military base of
operations in, 146, 147
earthquake in, 149–50, 151
harassment of villagers in, 150–1
high-frequency heater in, 79,
147
human experimentation in,
146–7
possible psy ops in, 147, 152
*See also* Psychological Operations (Psy Ops)
rumors of alien base in, 152
UFOs sighted in, 147–52
Putt, Col. D. L., 28

Quantico, Va., UFO sighted from
aircraft over, 131
Quarles, Doris, 68
*Queen of Outer Space,* 118

Radio-Physics Institute, USSR, 46
RAF Bentwaters, 136, 137, 138, 140
*See also* Rendlesham Forest,
England
RAF Woodbridge, 136, 137, 138, 140
*See also* Rendlesham Forest,
England
RAND Corporation, and assess-
ment of microwave effects, 100
Randle, Kevin, 123
Randles, Jenny, 46, 123, 137–41,
140n
Rankin, J. Lee, 93

To order books, please send full amount
plus $4.00 for postage and handling.

Send orders to:

**GALDE PRESS, INC.**
**PO Box 460**
**Lakeville, Minnesota 55044**

**Credit card orders call 1–800–777–3454**

*Write for free catalog!*